E G L I

B C L

734

840651

DATE DUE

DEC 2 1 1984			

THE CULT OF POWER

DICTATORS IN THE TWENTIETH CENTURY

EDITED BY
JOSEPH HELD

EAST EUROPEAN MONOGRAPHS, BOULDER
DISTRIBUTED BY COLUMBIA UNIVERSITY PRESS, NEW YORK

1983

EAST EUROPEAN MONOGRAPHS, NO. CXL

THIS BOOK IS DEDICATED TO THE STUDENTS OF
RUTGERS UNIVERSITY, CAMDEN,
UNIVERSITY COLLEGE, CLASS 1981,
WITH RESPECT AND ADMIRATION

ACKNOWLEDGEMENTS

This book could not have come about without the kind and often enthusiastic cooperation of many persons within and outside Rutgers University. Appreciation should go, first of all, to the Rutgers University Research Council whose financial help enabled me to organize and complete the experimental course on which the book is based. I must also thank Provost Walter K. Gordon, whose support for the entire program proved invaluable. My dear friends, Associate Dean Sidney Katz and Ivan Volgyes provided help and encouragement for the completion of the project. All the participants in the symposium who had kindly submitted the results of their research to the editor must be thanked. The students who participated in the program had done a marvelous job in stimulating our thinking. The staff of the University College, Camden, Rutgers University, provided much needed help. I must thank Mrs. Elizabeth A. Skyta for her invaluable help in correcting the many errors in the manuscript, and Mrs. Roberta Diamondstein who typed the final version. Finally, Patricia Wiles had done a magnificent job of putting the manuscript on the computer that facilitated early publication.

Rutgers University,
Camden, September, 1982

TABLE OF CONTENTS

FOREWORD

STEPHEN FISCHER-GALATI

"L'État c'est moi!" pronounced by Louis XIV was a source of pride for the French citizenry of the seventeenth century. It is, however, a source of dismay for descendants of that citizenry as expressed by Ayatollah Khomeini three centuries later. But for the people of Iran the Ayatollah's motto is revered in the same spirit as that of the French worshippers of the "Roi Soleil."

This is to say the the French saying *plus ça change plus c'est la même chose* is probably closer to the truth than the presumptions of contemporary historians, sociologists, political scientists and other believers in—or at least exponents of—the idea of progress. Authoritarian, absolutist, dictatorial rulers and regimes have been the rule rather than the exception throughout the course of recorded—and even unrecorded—history despite their temporary eclipse by the beliefs and hopes generated by the democratic revolutions of the eighteenth century.

Regrettably, the philosophers and translators of the ideas and ideals of the Enlightenment into political practice had a mistaken concept of the nature of man, history, and politics and addressed the wrong issues. They attacked the legitimacy bestowed upon ruling monarchs and elites by established religions, removed God from politics, all in the belief that reason would prevail and insure the happiness of mankind. But government by the people, for the people, of the people was both unrealistic and unworkable from its very inception and new leaders emerged who had to adapt their political and social goals to the realities of historical traditions. With the notable, and temporary, exception of the traditionless United States of America, the ideals and ideas of the Age of Democratic Revolution went into at least partial oblivion by the end of the eighteenth century as new forms of authoritarian governance took shape. And whereas we may regard Napoleon's dictatorship as less oppressive than that of Robespierre and his associates, they both were in fact dictatorships and both were illegitimate in terms of historic experience and tradition.

Napoleon's authoritarianism was feared because it used the masses for the adulation of "anti-Christ;" the radicals' because they used the masses for the destruction of all accepted values and traditions. Thus, the containment of "enlightened" dictators and of the revolutionary mob became the goal of all legitimate rulers who had opposed the French Revolution, be they those of Parliamentary England or of the divinely-ordained Romanov or Habsburg empires. The "Holy Alliance" may have been—in Metternich's own words—a "Lauttön-endes Nichts" but it represented an unequivocal, and acceptable, formulation of the doctrine that political legitimacy can only be bestowed by God to ruling monarchs committed to carrying out the wishes of the Almighty.

It mattered little whether God's presence was direct, as in the case of his "emissary" Alexander I of Russia, or whether His presence was merely symbolic as in "God save the King" or "in God we trust," as long as legitimate rulers—bearing God's seal of approval—opposed political illegitimacy.

The enemies of legitimacy, however, those who had learned the lessons of the French Revolution and of the Napoleonic era, were ready to adapt their tactics and strategies accordingly. They had, in one form or another, to seek, if not necessarily gain, the allegiance of the masses for the execution of their own political goals. The people, its genius, its will, its spirit—the "Volkgeist," the "People's Will," Vox populi, vox Dei"—became essential ingredients of all nationalist, revolutionary, or other panaceas devised and advocated by anti-establishment intellectuals, students, youths, opportunists, agitators and others in their search for alternative roads to power to those preempted by legitimate, traditional, and mass-accepted authority. Few, if any, such would-be leaders, however, sought emulation of the fundamental premises and principles enunciated by the exponents of "bourgeois democracy" of the Age of Democratic Revolution.

To "the people," so essential an ingredient for the attainment of power, were invariably attributed special assets and qualifications which, however, had to be moulded by those who understood the people's needs, goals and mission. The masses had to be led and educated, "civilized," to accept new ideologies and ways of life which would eventually lead to happinesss, which would insure the greatest good for the greatest number. They were to be instruments for the attainment of power sought by those who could not gain power or were excluded from power by the traditional, historically or divinely-sanctioned, elites.

This search for legitimacy through fulfillment of the masses' alleged historic rights and muted aspirations did, per se, fail to alter the masses' basic acceptance of prevailing legitimate orders until factors beyond the making of power-hungry "educators," "civilizers," "secularizers," determined the course of events. The "Volkgeist" was no substitute for "Blood and Iron," the "Southern Slav" movement did not undermine the "Kaisertreue" enjoyed by the successors of the Holy Roman emperors, the Russian peasants' ostensibly intuitive socialism or natural revolutionary qualities did not destroy "Mother Russia" or the "Little Romanov Fathers." Nor did the "civilizing of the natives" undo their traditional allegiances and mores. For indeed, the traditional establishments, divinely ordained and/or traditionally if not hereditarily in power, were far more resilient than the newcomers, the revolutionaries, the reformers, and all others who sought to challenge their legitimacy had ever anticipated.

What caused the conditions for change were factors generic to non-manmade revolutions. The industrial, scientific and technological revolutions of the nineteenth and twentieth centuries caused such massive social, economic, and political dislocations and created the potential for massive destruction through military power that in the span of less than a century the historic traditions of hundreds of years were undermined if not altogether destroyed. And it was because of the destruction of the first and the second world wars that confused, illiterate, and disarrayed masses could be manipulated by ruthless, unscrupulous, power-seekers who promised everything as self-appointed saviours of their own people if not of the entire world.

It is in this context that the dictators of the twentieth century can be understood historically. Lenin, Stalin, Hitler, Mussolini, Ceauşescu, Ayatollah Khomeini are but a few of the many power hungry, historically-illegitimate rulers who exploited the "objective conditions" created by factors beyond the control of ruling establishments by offering panaceas to fearful, ignorant, and gullible masses. All dictators of the twentieth century, however, had to provide ideological justifications for the legitimacy and all, sooner or later, as the failure of the new orders and ideologies became evident to all, had to seek identification with the historic traditions of their people. Marxism, Leninism, Hitlerism, Maoism, Nasserism all had to be reconciled with traditional, primarily religious, ideologies and even Ayatollah Khomeini's interpretations of the Koran had to be adapted to more traditional views of the nature of Islam. The dictators of the twentieth century have reclaimed historic legacies and have proclaimed themselves as executors of the historic aspirations of their people. They have restored the pomp and ceremony of their legitimate predecessors but, unlike their presumed predecessors, the dictators of the twentieth century have lacked any of the "noblesse oblige" that was derived from hereditary political legitimacy and traditional religious sanction. Instead, they have been relying on the ultimate sources of support for vulgar power—fear, prejudice, violence, and armed might. And it is only by such means that they have retained power and that they may eventually lose it. Mussolini was indeed right in his analysis of totalitarian systems when he stated that such systems can only be destroyed by force of arms. And Chairman Mao complemented this view in fewer but equally accurate words.

Inasmuch as the forces which made possible the rise and maintenance of dictatorships of the twentieth century are, if anything, more pervasive in 1984 than at any time in the last fifty years, the teachings of Chairman Mao, of Hitler and Mussolini, of Ayatollah Khomeini, of Qadhdhafi, Lenin, Castro, and perhaps even of Arafat are likely to be more effective in the foreseeable future than those of Locke, Gandhi, and John Paul II, and the systems based on those teachings more lasting and self-perpetuating than those envisaged by earlier prophets and exponents (not to mention opponents) of modern totalitarianism and dictatorship.

CHAPTER I

AUTHORITARIAN LEADERSHIP:
A COGNITIVE-INTERACTIONIST VIEW

PETER SUEDFELD

I intend to propose an alternative to traditional psychological analyses of authoritarian leadership. The use of the term "alternative" should be taken as a broadening of perspectives, rather than the proposed replacement of one point of view with another. The position that I am going to contrast with the currently popular techniques is one that I call cognitive interactionism, referring to cognitive processes as being modified by and in turn modifying environmental factors. This approach can be criticized as one restricted to "cold cognition": that is, the emphasis is on intellectual processes. This is not meant to imply that the emotional fervor often involved in situations of authoritarian leadership is not important, nor that the impact of such leadership on human values is unimportant; but the theory takes the information provessing, decision-making, and problem-solving bases of political behavior as its primary focus.

The focus is derived from the hypothesis that authoritarian behavior, just like other kinds of behavior, is a problem-solving attempt to deal with the demands and pressures of circumstances. This interpretation applies not only to the behavior of individual leaders, but also to that of decision-making or advisory groups, as well as to the ordinary individual who in the aggregate enables leaders to exist by providing followers. This approach differs from more traditional psychological viewpoints in a number of ways. As I shall show, some of these are conceptual and theoretical, while others are methodological.

Conceptual Bases

Although in the comparisons that follow, the traditional view is represented by the two major approaches that have been used to study authoritarian leaders and followers (personality scales and psychobiography, both based on psychodynamic principles), the

general criticisms apply also to theoretical approaches whose foundation is ego psychology, neo-Freudianism, power orientation, political
style or any other personality system.

In their approach to the study of authoritarian leaders and followers, psychologists have traditionally tended to concentrate on the concept of the authoritarian personality.[1] This is not unreasonable; after
all, it is the focus on the individual that sets psychology apart from
other social sciences. Furthermore, not only psychologists but people
in general have always explained actions on the basis of the actor's personality characteristics. In fact, the tendency to use this type of ex-
planatory construct is so pervasive and so often incorrect as to be
called "the fundamental attribution error" by social psychologists.[2]

The classic work of Adorno et al.[3] identified a set of traits which
supposedly co-vary and which together make up the authoritarian
personality. These include egocentrism, adherence to conventional
standards, rejection of ambiguity, extrapunitiveness, distrust and suspicion of others, a hierarchical view of relationships, a dislike of in-
trospection, a dependence on a power greater than oneself, etc.

This work has been criticized on the basis of its conceptual narrow-
ness. Critics argued that the so-called authoritarian personality was in-
appropriately restricted to right-wing authoritarianism, and that at
traction to authoritarian leaders and structures should be approached
from a more content-free point of view.[4]

Adorno himself[5] indicated such a view in regard to what he called
"rigid" low scorers on the F-Scale measure of authoritarianism. These
individuals were characterized by strong superego tendencies and
compulsivity, just as were high scorers; but in the case of low scorers
"paternal authority and its social substitutes. . . are frequently replaced by the image of some collectivity, possibly moulded after the
archaic image of what Freud calls the brother horde. Their main
taboo is directed against violations of actual or supposed brother
love".[6] Another group, the protesting low scorers, are also seen as
having much in common with authoritarian high scorers.

Rokeach's[7] definition of dogmatism provided a concept of authoritarianism that embraced both the left and the right ends of the
political spectrum. This theory was an attempt to define both of
these extremes in common terms, which in effect concentrated on
cognitive variables such as openness to counterattitudinal information.
The D-Scale, Rokeach's answer to the Adorno et al. F-Scale, was supposed to be content-free in this sense. A related approach, Tomkins's[8]
Polarity Scale measure of humanistic-normative judgment, seems

more widely applicable but has not yet been used much by researchers in this area. Empirical results with the D-Scale, as well as with other measures that purport to tap authoritarianism uncontaminated by specific political affiliation, have been rather mixed. In some cases, leftist extremists have been found to be as high on measures of authoritarianism as one would expect rightists to be.[9] On the other hand, enough negative results have been reported that a recent review[10] argues for discarding the concept of left-wing authoritarianism.

As usual, it is probably the case that the optimal course lies somewhere between the two poles of either completely accepting or completely rejecting the hypothesis: for example, more sophisticated research has shown that scores on the importance of some values (e.g., equality) can discriminate between left- and right-wing political adherents while scores on other values (e.g., freedom) discriminate between extremists and centrists;[11] that one can also distinguish between centrists and potential extremists;[12] and that specific national and other contexts must be taken into account when measuring authoritarianism.[13]

Four possible explanations for the inconsistency of results spring to mind: that the D-Scale and other measures, like the F-Scale, are inadequate to measure the construct of authoritarianism; that the construct itself is too general and vague to be either useful or measurable; that there are indeed actual, not merely artifactual, content-related differences within the construct; and that the whole literature suffers from insufficient attention to a great number of variables, both intrapersonal and other, that strongly influence both the test scores and the political affiliation of subjects. I would guess that almost everyone interested in this area would agree with at least two of these propositions, a reasonable basis for suggesting that some other research perspective might be more fruitful.

Moving from the use of personality scales to other personality-centered theories of authoritarian leadership and followership, we find attempts to analyze the behavior of large groups of individuals on psychodynamic grounds. Perhaps the best known attempt in this vein was Reich's[14] analysis of the attractions of Fascism, including identification with the leader, anti-Semitism, and extrapunitiveness, all on the basis of biological repression and inadequacy. These negative aspects of modern society have led to the development of the mechanistic-mystical conception of life. Foreshadowing the later debate over right-wing and left-wing authoritarianism, Reich eventually came to argue that Communist practice in the Soviet Union suppressed the individual in the same way, and otherwise was similar to, German Nazism. His own position was in favor of restructuring social conditions to emphasize local community power, sexual freedom, and "genuine" liberation.

Another, more orthodox, writer[15] looked at the followers of great leaders. He argued that the willingness to become such a follower may be explained on the basis of projection to the degree that the leader's qualities are experienced as extraordinary or even supernatural. Group "case" studies on the Jewish Prophets of the 7th and 8th centuries, B.C., the disciples of Jesus, and followers of Hitler are presented to support this hypothesis.

The study of actual political leaders has been influenced by both practical and theoretical considerations. High-level authoritarian leaders have not subjected themselves to the personality scale technique. Among the closest approximations has been the use of personality tests with a sample of parliamentary deputies in Italy.[16] DiRenzo found that the deputies were more dogmatic than the norm and, more supportive of interactionist hypotheses, that dogmatism was reliably correlated with threats to the existence of the deputy's party (continuing loss of voting strength and in one case being constitutionally banned). Another example was the systematic use of depth interviews as well as projective tests to study to group of top Nazi leaders on trial at Nuremberg.[17]

The majority of studies again concentrates on personality factors. Explanations of why and how some individuals obtain and exercise untrammeled power over entire nations have consistently focused on their childhood experiences, motivations, education, successes and failures in other spheres of life and so on.[18] Leaders have been studied primarily through the use of case study methods analyzing their lives, verbal productions, and political actions. Secondarily, demographic and similar measures have been taken. Again, the assumption is that the characteristics which develop as a function of these events influence all of the person's attitudes and behaviors in his leadership role, and that the difference between such leaders and others can be understood if we can only explain these traits.

The cognitive interactionist view considers these assumptions to be highly questionable, and their empirical results to be inadequate. To begin with, proponents of this approach view authoritarianism as one way to process information, and separate it from political, religious, social or any other kind of content. This, at least as a goal, is not completely unprecedented: intolerance of ambiguity is one component of the F-Scale, while closed-mindedness is central to Rokeach's concept of dogmatism and a single judgmental criterion to Tomkins's "normative" outlook.

Cognitively-oriented researchers can pay attention to a wide range of available ideologies. For example, there are many movements and ideologies that, while political in implication, do not fit into any of the standard models. Environmentalist movements, religious cults, terrorist groups, human potential programs, and the like can attract people whose normative political positions differ widely and cannot be subsumed under the traditional theoretical constructs. The alternative is for a view of political attitudes and behavior (and their religious, social, economic, and other counterparts) as reflecting the way in which people cope with the problems posed by their environment. The competing position, attribution to personality traits as relatively unchanging, unresponsive to the situation, and underlying a wide range of political positions, has been unverified and in some aspects empirically disconfirmed.[19]

This is not to deny that life experiences may make some people particularly susceptible to either becoming or attaching themselves to authoritarian leaders, nor that some leaders of this kind may have been the power-hungry psychopaths of popular depiction. It is also quite likely (although comparatively seldom considered) that genetic and constitutional factors, which certainly affect brain functioning, have an influence on political behavior. On a broader scale, cultural and societal factors, social structures in both primary and secondary groups, and so on, are important in facilitating or hindering authoritarian political relationships. The difference in focus is that while all of these variables are accepted by the cognitive interactionist as contributing to levels of authoritarian predisposition or susceptibility, we are primarily concerned with the conditions that are likely to affect the actual emergence of authoritarian behavior, and with the characteristics of that behavior as it is manifested in leadership (and followership) activities.

The cognitive view of authoritarianism looks at those aspects of the informational environment that influence problem-solving approaches. These do include personality variables; but beyond these, and frequently more important, are the factors that together may define the level of stress experienced by the individual. Stress is perceived as leading to cognitive simplification, which in turn can lead to authoritarian behavior.

Versions of this approach are seen in the work of Erich Fromm[20] and, more recently, Irving Janis:[21] both show how, under high levels of stress, cognitive processes become simplified, rigid, narrow, and dependent on only a few highly salient sources and types of information. Given the importance of consensual validation[22] and such aspects of influence as perceived expertise, power, and attractiveness[23] in attitude change, it is not surprising that this highly salient source of information should frequently be a dramatic leader, movement, or philosophy.

Psychologists do not have a monopoly on the recognition that stress—personal, political, societal or other—affects cognitive processes. Most relevant to our approach has been the work of such political scientists as O. R. Holsti and others whose content analytic techniques have focused on the effects of crisis situations on decision-making.[24] This research has looked at such historical events as the outbreak of World War I, the Cuban missile crisis, and the Korean and Vietnam Wars. The studies of Janis,[25] examining American foreign policy decisions (including some of the same ones), and individual analyses such as those of the Israeli bombing of Egypt in 1970,[26] have all shown consistent patterns of cognitive simplification. The cognitive interactionist approach encompasses these studies, but uses a different and more flexible technique to measure aspects of a much wider variety of situations and problems. It is this flexibility that enables the cognitive interactionist to focus on the interactions among leaders, followers, and environmental pressures with a view to explicating the development and functioning of authoritarian structures.

The emphasis on the interaction between the environment and the cognitive processes of the individual casts authoritarianism in a new light. The cognitive interactionist approach would maintain that cognitive simplification and subsequent "authoritarianism" increase or decrease predictably and lawfully with such environmental parameters as information load, time available to process the information, perceived payoffs, diversity of informational sources and interpretations, the nature of the decision-making structure, the ability to deal with information load by cognitive chunking or by division of labor, the established rules for maintaining or modifying flexibility, the perceived need for simple and/or rapid decisions, and so on. Thus, authoritarianism does not exist in an environmental vacuum.

Our theory would hold that authoritarian structures develop as a function of low complexity in decision-making and information processing. Certainly such structures meet the criteria for low complexity, which are mentioned elsewhere in this paper. Why such low levels may be preferred in a particular situation must be examined on a case-by-case basis. In general, there is agreement that integrative complexity is diminished when the situation is one of impending or actual crisis: under conditions of serious threat, time pressure, information underload or overload, and high uncertainty. These factors can be exacerbated by intrapersonal characteristics such as personality predispositions, fatigue, illness, age, or adverse life events; and probably by cultural factors such as the usual norms of decision-making and leadership in a specific society. The latter factors have not yet been studied in this particular context.

At any rate, let us stipulate that authoritarian leadership relations are most likely to arise when societal experience is predisposed toward dependence on a single source of information and decisions, and when this predisposition is further activated by a stressful environment. Why then, the deification of the dictator? After all, it is possible to rely on a leader to solve a particular set of problems without making him into a god. We need only look at such individuals as Cincinnatus or an institutional role such as that of North American Indian war chiefs, to see examples of autocratic leaders replacing the normal multi-faceted government of a group during periods of crisis, only to step back when the emergency is over.

It seems to me that deification serves the needs of both the authoritarian leader and his followers, and in very similar ways. First, it strongly reinforces the usual bases of power[27] that authoritarian leaders exercise: that is, reward and coercive power, charisma (or from the point of view of the follower, identification) and expertise (at least as the leader is perceived to be competent to solve the immediate problem). In cases where the legitimacy of the authoritarian leader is doubtful or controversial, which are probably predominant in 20th century dictatorships, deification also helps to settle the matter since godlike individuals are legitimate leaders by definition.

The mystique that surrounds such a leader makes both him and his followers feel more secure that he is in fact able to reward and punish justly. Since compliance depends on whether the leader is perceived as being both powerful and knowing,[28] the ever-watchful and all-powerful leader (and his invisible but observant and powerful instruments, such as secret police) can be invoked in the same way as an unobservable but omniscient God—but very differently from the more mundane and circumscribed judges and policemen we see around us. Similarly, the pomp and ceremony surrounding such an individual make him more admirable and less like the common herd, increasing both his self-confidence and the confidence of his subjects. The phenomenon is found not only with individual leaders, but with entire movements. Hoffer,[29] among others, has described how the apparent strength of mass movements, communicated through parades, uniforms, banners, martial music and the like, permits powerless individuals to gain self-respect through identification with the group.

I should point out that in cases of emergency, it is not sufficient that the masses trust the wisdom and the ability of the leader; he must ttust them himself, since a vacillating dictator is like a vacillating drill sergeant, not much use to himself or anybody else. Again, the trappings of apotheosis serve to distance the leader and endow him with superhuman abilities, adding to his aptitude for making the swift and clear decisions that the circumstances seem to require. The same pattern is sometimes found with democratic leaders in crisis situations (e.g., Franklin D. Roosevelt, DeGaulle), although here the opposition to deification tends to be more vocal than that dared by the dissenting subjects of authoritarian demi-gods.

Naturally, there are other sources of the pressure for deification which may be relevant to particular cases. These may include the gratification of the leader's ego and those of his subordinates, the establishment of links with historical traditional leadership in particular societies, the mobilization of the spirit of self-sacrifice on the part of the populace, the instilling of fear in the hearts of opponents, both domestic and foreign, and so on. Once again, the hypotheses of cognitive interaction offer a different (and perhaps more testable) way of looking at the phenomenon, not necessarily a replacement for other interpretations.

This point of view does not deal with authoritarianism as a trans-temporally or trans-situationally stable personality variable. Individuals who behave with high levels of integrative complexity at one time or in one kind of situation may act as "classical" authoritarians when the circumstances change (although, again, we do recognize that because of chronic differences in information processing style people may be predisposed toward different levels of authoritarian thinking). Particular environmental demands may make it more likely that individuals of the "appropriate" level of complexity rise to leadership positions, and that individuals aspiring to or holding such positions modify their functioning in the "appropriate" way.

The cognitive interactionist system looks at what is probably the most important aspect of the leader: not his childhood traumas, not the books he read while growing up, but rather the way in which he exercises his power and responds to the people and circumstances in which his leadership is relevant. It is a contemporary view, not a biographical one, although it is of course quite possible to trace changes in information processing complexity biographically or even historically.

Evaluative Bias

From the beginning, authoritarian followers and leaders have frequently been perceived as mentally unbalanced, or at least as maladjusted. Adorno et al., while being clear that some low scorers also show psychological and psychiatric symptoms, generally argued that the strong superego and weak ego of the authoritarian individual represented a neurotic pattern that interfered with adequate adjustment to the world.[30] Once again, the original work of the Adorno group was considerably more complex than the version transmitted by secondary sources and popularizers. Both the data and the theory lost much of their richness in transmission, with the result that many current presentations attribute to the original researchers the view that authoritarians are necessarily neurotic if not worse. These obviously pejorative implications and interpretations of the F-Scale have been so exaggerated that fervent attempts have been made to exonerate the high scorer from the perceived accusation.[31] Similar implications as to the weaknesses of the dogmatic and normative individual can be found in the work of Rokeach[32] and Tomkins.[33]

The cognitive interactionist does not condemn "authoritarianism" as inherently evil, sick, or even undesirable. It is, rather, one possible way of dealing with an environmental problem, and it may or may not be an adaptive, adequate, or satisfying way depending upon specific circumstances. A simple command and obedience sequence may be perceived as authoritarian; assuming that the leader is competent, such a sequence may be optimal in some circumstances. In others, reflection, discussion, compromise, information search and participatory decision-making may be better. In addition, circumstances may change while the actors do not, so that an authoritarian relationship developed as being adaptive in a particular environment may become maladaptive when a new environment is encountered. In such cases, flexibility appears to be the crucial test of survival.

For example, the first study using archival data scored for integrative complexity[34] examined the behavior of revolutionary leaders. The results showed that a pattern of low complexity (our analogue of authoritarian behavior) during the armed struggle, followed by a shift toward higher levels after the revolution took over the government, was most likely to be associated with the continued success of the leader. Individuals who were either too complex during the struggle, or too simple afterwards, tended to lose their positions and frequently their lives. The data, collected from the writings of 19 revolutionary leaders in five revolutions spanning three centuries, were consistent for more than 80% of the individual leaders in the sample. Looking at specific men, we found that those leaders who were relatively complex during the revolution (e.g., Alexander Hamilton) tended not to reach the highest levels of power afterward, possibly because their complexity may have been interpreted as lukewarmness or insufficient fervor by their colleagues. Originally simple leaders who stayed at that level too long (e.g., Bukharin) were pushed out of their positions by more adaptable rivals.

A corollary of the cognitive approach is that it is feasible to modify authoritarian information processing patterns. Unlike those social scientists who feel that the authoritarian individual can only be "cured" through psychotherapy or some similar basic personality change, the cognitive interactionist can conceive of training procedures to help maintain relatively complex, flexible, information-oriented, and independent decision-making styles.

Research Methodology

One of the glaring disadvantages of the traditional approach is that it has used completely different methodologies to look at the aspects of leadership and followership in the political context.

The work of Adorno et al. set a pattern for the traditional approach in its use of interviews, projective tests, and above all of psychometric techniques. The F-Scale, which eventually became by far the most frequently used measure of authoritarianism, has been widely criticized on methodological grounds such as its susceptibility to response-set artifacts.[35] Regardless of the validity of these attacks, the same general path has been followed by researchers accepting the personality framework for political psychology. Students of dogmatism, motivational hierarchies, values, needs, and so on, all tend to draw from the same general set of techniques.[36]

The reliance on interviews and personality scales has been a major weakness of the research. There is no guarantee that those individuals who agree to answer questions about their values and ways of thinking are either representative of the group from which they are sampled or have enough insight, detachment, and dedication to the progress of social science to give the answer that truly reflects their underlying orientations.

Another problem in relying upon intrusive measures such as questionnaires, projective tests, or clinical interviews, becomes obvious when we look at psychological studies of authoritarian personality. The subject samples are overwhelmingly comprised of students and voters, with only a very few investigators gaining access to even middle-level politicians, and none to the kind of authoritarian leader who attracts the attention of the world. Such leaders typically are not eager to spend their time accommodating social scientists. As a result, the technique used to deal with these individuals is most frequently psychobiographical.

Typically, studies of leaders reflect some version of psychodynamic theorizing. The searcher through archives concentrates on early life patterns such as parental relationships, the resolution of the Oedipal conflict, sibling rivalries, or sexual experiences[37] or on contemporary expressions that are thought to reflect such experiences—for example, figures of speech that might reflect relevant personality traits such as oral-sadistic personality, anal retentiveness, etc.[38]

Needless to say, there are serious difficulties with this procedure as well.[39] In an overwhelming number of cases, very little reliable information is available about the childhood and adolescence of the individual, and in every case the selection and interpretation of material is open to bias and distortion. It should suffice to mention a few infamous examples. Among these are the obviously biased attacks on Whittaker Chambers[40] and Woodrow Wilson;[41] the analysis of Leonardo da Vinci's personality, much of which was based on a mistranslated word;[42] and a whole host of papers and books extrapolating with unjustified assurance from minimal or even no data.[43]

It is, of course, clear that the psychobiographical approach can lead to interesting hypotheses, as well as to some entertaining reading; but to treat it as an hypothesis-testing procedure seems inappropriate. Some psychohistorians have obviously taken too far the claim of one of their most eminent colleagues that because of their training they may be able to "recognize major trends even where the facts are not all available."[44]

Intermediate levels between case studies and direct objective measurement would be content analytic and expert consensus indices of personality. Among these may be the work of Luck[45] in seeking preferred figures of speech used by such authoritarian leaders as

Lenin, Stalin, Hitler, Mao, and Liu Shao-Ch'i. Luck concluded that destructive oral imagery characterized Hitler's productions and violent anal imagery those of Stalin, with inferences as to the personalities of these leaders being drawn from the data.[46] Another approach is to use a group of observers who rate historical figures on a number of personality variables, obtaining consensus on presumably valid and reliable indices of individual differences among political leaders,[47] and a somewhat similar procedure has been used to ascribe personality characteristics to protagonists in the American Revolution.[48]

Because personal access to and cooperation of subjects is not an issue, our alternative viewpoint does not require different methods for leaders and followers; and it should not. The cognitive simplification interpretation holds equally for the charismatic dictator who follows an all-embracing religious or political doctrine and for the followers who obey the doctrine as he personifies and promulgates it.

The complexity approach uses the same basic construct and the same or highly similar measurement criteria for all three components in the situation: the leader, the follower, and the environment. The behavior of both leaders and followers is scored from archival documents, using a generally applicable scoring manual. The informational complexity of the environment is also susceptible to analysis on the basis of the amount and types of information available, their interconnections, rate of change, and outcome potentials.[49]

Rather than personality-focused measures, we use structural analyses of materials spoken or written in the normal course of events. One approach uses an analysis of such factors as rejection of uncertainty or conflict, search for information, amalgamation of several positions or ideas into a synthesized unit, and the recognition of functional relationships to arrive at integrative complexity scores on a paragraph-by-paragraph basis.[50] Another[51] uses a lexicon of words implying simple or complex positions (e.g., inclusivity and certainty in such words as "never" or "unquestionably," opposed to flexible and graded perceptions implied by the use of such words as "relatively," "sometimes," "possibly"). Obviously, word counts are technically much easier to perform, since they can be computerized; on the other hand, they require massive amounts of material to obtain reliable results and these quantities are not always available for a particular source or leader. In addition, there are some theoretical objections to using a simple measure of complexity, since it can be argued that such indices are highly susceptible to stylistic and other extraneous variables.

Another technique is to look at popular adherence to simple vs. complex problem solutions. This approach was exemplified in two stimulating papers demonstrating the relationship between cognitive functioning and societal stress during the Great Depression of the 1930s. Fundamentalist, but not other church membership went up drastically; other measures of search for certainty, rejection of deviants, and support for authority showed the same pattern. The implication is clear: under environmental stress, the information processing of the population moved toward lower levels of complexity, which resulted in increased adherence to simple dogma.[52] The attractiveness of authoritarian movements during difficult times has also been noted by Hoffer[53] and Rokeach,[54] among others.

Archival analysis is obviously a non-obtrusive technique, so that the problems of response set, evaluation apprehension and other experimental artifacts are avoided. Data collection is not restricted by the willingness of potential subjects to cooperate. In fact, it is not even restricted by the fact that some of the subjects whom we might want to study are dead. Complexity scoring can measure integrative level even when the source is unknown, as in anonymous or group-produced government documents, a source that is completely unusable for psychobiographical analysts. The scoring techniques seem to work quite well for material in translation, or can be applied in the original language, so that the thorny cross-cultural problem of translating a personality test or figure of speech without distortion does not arise.

Paragraph scoring is based on an adaptation of the scoring manual for the Paragraph Completion Test.[55] That test presents the subject with a number of sentence beginnings, and requires the completion of the sentence plus additional thoughts on the same topic. The stems are selected to tap attitudes toward a number of important social and personal issues such as authority, rejection and uncertainty. The scoring is done on a 1-7 scale, with lower scores indicating simple information processing patterns. These are identifiable through signs of categorical acceptance or rejection of arguments and people, rigid rules, the use of only one judgmental criterion, and a search for rapid and reliable closure. As one ascends through the scale, there is first the recognition that more than one position on an issue can exist; then an acceptance that several contradictory or at least inconsistent positions may each have some legitimacy; later, a combinatorial use of elements from various schemata; and at last, a complex synthesis of such elements in the service of a flexible, mutually beneficial, and articulated functional goal. Along with this progression, there is increasing tolerance of uncertainty and ambiguity, a wider search for information before making decisions, and a higher level of tentativeness and flexibility.

It is not difficult to adapt this scheme to the scoring of archival material; the criteria are the same, and the technique is easily transferable from the structured sentences to speeches and writings. There are some general rules that have had to be added, such as the elimination as unscorable of certain kinds of material (e.g., sarcasm, pure description), and the reparagraphing of materials; but on the whole, new scorers can reach reliability levels of .80 or better with an expert after 5 to 10 days of training.[56]

Word scoring is even easier, once the lexicon has been devised. This, however, is not such a simple matter, since a random look through any dictionary will show a large number of words that can be categorized within relevant dimensions such as inclusiveness, rigidity, and so on. Ertel's lexicon is based on six relevant categories: frequency and duration (e.g., always versus frequently); quantity (all, several); degree and measure (completely, relatively); certainty (unquestionably, apparently); exclusion-inclusion (only, also); and necessity-possibility (must, may). Unfortunately, the lexicon of terms under each of these categories has been developed only in German so far, although my research team is working on a translation.

Another approach uses specific terms that are likely to appear in the material being scored. For example, Kirk,[57] in her study of Politburo members, categorized such terms as "imperialism" and "socialist struggle" as opposed to "international cooperation," to indicate black-and-white vs. cooperative images, and distinguished both of these from neutral terms such as "the Soviet economy" or "France." Again, interscorer reliabilities of .75 to .85 were obtained. This procedure makes the technique perhaps more specifically applicable; at the same time, one must be careful not to allow evaluative or content biases to contaminate the assignment of terms to categories.

Cognitive Interactionist Research on Authoritarian Leadership

The amount of research using cognitive analysis techniques in this context is relatively small. Studies correlating measures of complexity with those more traditionally used in the field have found negative correlations of -.25 to -.55 between F-Scale responses and conceptual complexity as measured by the Paragraph Completion Test,[58] and less consistent relationships between Paragraph Completion and the D-Scale (as one might expect if the D-Scale is a more general cognitive measure than the F-Scale). It should be pointed out here that the Paragraph Completion Test is based on a theoretical foundation somewhat different from ours: the authors who developed this test[59] regarded conceptual complexity as being in fact a stable personality trait whose expression could be modified by environmental conditions. This is in contrast to our current view, whose emphasis is on the interplay between the environment and behavior, without measuring the mediating variable of cognitive predisposition.

Another study, using the Interpersonal Topical Inventory measure of conceptual complexity,[60] found that it did not significantly correlate with age, sex, birth order, religious denomination, political party preference or grade point average among a sample of Canadian university students.[61] Among those factors with which complexity did correlate, two relevant ones were that there were lower complexity scores for subjects who reported a religous affiliation as opposed to those who reported none, and for those subjects who claimed that in an election they voted for the party rather than the individual candidate.[62] The latter finding may be an example of the importance of specific contexts, since the implications of this voting style are different in the Canadian Parliamentary system from what they might be in the American Presidential system.

Another correlational study[63] found the lowest levels of cognitive complexity among subjects who were high on repression; high complexity was exhibited by non-dogmatic sensitizers. Other dogmatism/sensitization combinations were moderate in cognitive differentiation, which was measured by Kelly's Rep Test.[64] Suedfeld and Epstein[65] obtained higher complexity scores among individuals protesting against the war in Vietnam than among Army Reserve officers and an unselected control group. These differences, however, were probably contaminated by educational factors. Sidanius and Ekehammar[66] reported that there was higher cognitive differentiation (related to complexity although not either theoretically or empiricialy identical) among Swedish radicals than among either liberals or conservatives. It is difficult to judge this finding in relation to the other correlations between complexity and relevant personality characteristics because of the differences of measurement techniques as well as in the subjects who participated; perhaps the most important conclusion to be drawn is that it is both easy and dangerous to overgeneralize from limited data.

Still another study[67] used a number of archival measures of complexity (verbal diversification, sentence length, complex vs. simple words). Complexity was negatively correlated with need for affiliation and positively with need for power; its correlation with need for achievement was U-shaped. This was the first attempt to measure the relationship between complexity and motive imagery in the archival productions of political leaders, the subjects having been Democratic and Republican presidential nominees in the United States.

The paragraph-based scoring technique has been used in several archival studies related to the occurrence and resolution of personal and international crises.[68] The technique has been used primarily for the study of governmental and other decision-making in times of international crisis.

Studies of politicians have included the work on revolutionary leaders,[69] which was the first such archival research using integrative complexity. A later paper[70] found that isolationists in the U. S. Senate showed lower complexity than internationalists. Kronheim[71] analyzed changes in the political positions of three prominent French socialist leaders during the period 1893 to 1905. All three showed a relatively low degree of complexity during a period of socialist solidarity (1893-1895), with predicted changes as a function of modified political position and historical events.

Word count measures have been used to validate a more general content analytic procedure for the tracking of decision-making,[72] to evaluate foreign policy positions of American leaders,[73] and to analyze the productions of authors, artists, politicians, and philosophers.[74] Ertel found that complexity level was lowest in the speeches of Communist and Nazi parliamentary deputies in Weimar Germany. In an impressive demonstration of environmental effects, Hitler's speeches showed very low complexity before his accession to power, followed by an increase to approximately the level of present-day parliamentary deputies immediately after he took office. This in turn was followed by a gradual decrease in complexity from 1937 to 1945. The same author also reports that speakers in the German parliament around 1970 tended to be interrupted by applause after particularly low-complexity sentences, a datum that has clear implications for would-be authoritarian leaders (or even non-authoritarian ones); and that authors using a dialectical paradigm (e.g., Marx, Marcuse) showed significantly lower complexity than non-dialectical theorists (e.g., Popper, Weber). This last finding was replicated in three other studies.

Finally, Kirk[75] analyzed the speeches and articles of members of the Soviet Politburo between 1974 and 1979. Politburo members who had frequent contact with Western leaders showed higher levels of complexity than those who did not. Individuals who showed complex information processing on the issue of East-West relations were more in favor of cooperating with the West, while leaders whose view of these relationships were simple were opposed to detente. The last two of these hypotheses were tested by comparing the level of complexity as scored in speeches or writings about East-West relationships with ratings by a group of specialists on Soviet affairs.

The cognitive interactionist approach does not need to stand alone, although so far no researcher has combined it with a more traditional (e.g., psychobiographical) technique. One can easily postulate relationships between early life experience and cognitive behavior; in fact, some of the information processing theories are quite explicit about such relationships.[76] In this case, the explanations are themselves related to cognitive structure, but similar connections can be drawn between psychodynamic interpretations and intellectual factors.

The leaders discussed in this volume, as well as their successors, allies, opponents, and followers, have produced a great deal of material that could be looked at from a cognitive interactionist viewpoint; and it may be that the new techniques could provide much more predictive power than anything currently available if we analyzed the material for its implications about information processing. For example, we could study such issues as the degree to which a leader and his subordinates adjust their information processing style as environmental needs change; the differences in integrative complexity among leaders, subordinates, and rank-and-file followers; what happens when two opponents show disparate levels of information processing complexity; whether an abrupt change in complexity can be used as a predictor of significant changes in policy; the degree to which the complexity level of a new leader relates to changes in legal and governmental structures under his administration; and differences in leaders who come to power under conditions that vary in legality and stressfulness. These and many other questions may be answerable by the cognitive interactionist approach, and if so answered, may greatly increase not only our understanding of political leadership, but also our ability to improve political decisions in the real world.

1. Adorno, T.W., Frenkel-Brunswick, E., Levinson, D.J. & Sanford, R.N., *The Authoritarian Personality*. New York: Harper & Row, 1950.

2. Ross, L. E. "The Intuitive Psychologist and His Shortcomings: Distortions in the Atttibution Process." In L. Berkowitz (ed.), *Advances in Experimental Social Psychology*, Vol. 10. New York: Academic Press, 1977.

3. Adorno et al., 1950.

4. Shils, E. A., "Authoritarianism: 'Right' and 'Left'." In Christie & Jahoda, 1954.

5. Adorno, T. W., "Types and Syndromes," in Adorno et al., 1950.

6. Adorno et al., 1950, p. 771.

7. Rokeach, M. *The Open and Closed Mind*. New York: Basic Books, 1960.

8. Tomkins, S. S. "Left and Right: A Basic Dimension of Ideology and Personality." In R. W. White (ed.), *The Study of Lives*. New York: Atherton, 1963.

9. Eysenck, H. J. & Coulter, T. T. "The Personality and Attitudes of Working Class British Communists and Fascists." *Journal of Social Psychology*, 1972, 87, 59-73; Ray, J.J. (ed.), *Conservatism as Heresy: An Australian Reader*. Sydney: Australian and New Zealand Book Company, 1974; Smithers, A. G. & Lobley, D. N. "The Relationship Between Dogmatism and Radicalism/Conservatism." In H. J. Eysenk & G. D. Wilson (eds.), *The Psychological Basis of Ideology*. Lancaster: MTP Press, 1978.

10. Stone, W. F. "The Myth of Left-Wing Authoritarianism." *Political Psychology*, 1980, 2 (3/4), 3-19.

11. Cochrane, R., Billig, M., & Hogg, M., "Politics and Values in Britain: A Test of Rokeach's Two-Value Model." *British Journal of Social and Clinical Psychology*, 1979, 18, 159-167.

12. Billig, M. & Cochrane, R., "Values of British Political Extremists and Potential Extremists: A Discriminant Analysis." *European Journal of Social Psychology*, 1979, 9, 205-222.

13. Miller, J., Slomczynski, K. M., & Schoenberg, R. J., "Assessing Comparability of Measurement in Cross-National Research: Authoritarian-Conservatism in Different Sociocultural Settings," *Social Psychology Quarterly*, 1981, 44, 178-191.

14. Reich, W., *The Mass Psychology of Fascism*. New York: Farrar, Straus, 1970 (First English Publication, 1946).

15. Hummel, R.P., "Psychology of Charismatic Followers." *Psychological Reports*, 1975, 37, 759-770.

* The author's research and the preparation of this paper were supported by grants from the Social Sciences and Humanities Research Council of Canada.

16. DiRenzo, G. J., *Personality, Power and Politics: A Social Psychological Analysis of the Italian Deputy and His Parliamentary System*. Notre Dame, Indiana: University of Notre Dame, 1967.

17. Gilbert, G. M. *The Psychology of Dictatorship*. New York: Ronald, 1950.

18. Bychowski, G. *Dictators and Disciples: From Caesar to Stalin*. New York: International Universities Press, 1948; Lasswell, H. D., *Power and Personality*. New York: Norton, 1948; Liu, A. P. L., "The Ideology and Personality of the Radical Left in the People's Republic of China," *Political Psychology*, 2 (2), 3-21; Rejai, M. with Phillips, K., *Leaders of Revolution*. Beverly Hills: Sage, 1979.

19. Endler, N. S. "The Case for Person-Situation Interaction." *Canadian Psychological Review*, 1975, 16, 12-21; Fishbein, M. & Ajzen, I., *Belief, Attitude, Intention, and Behavior: An Introduction to Theory and Research*. Reading, Mass.: Addison Wesley, 1975; Mischel, W. "Toward a Cognitive Social Learning Reconceptualization of Personality." *Psychological Review*, 1973, 80, 252-283.

20. Fromm, E. *Escape from Freedom*. New York: Holt, 1941.

21. Janis, I. L. *Victims of Groupthink*. Boston: Houghton Mifflin, 1972.

22. Burnstein, E. & Sentis, K. "Attitude Polarization in Groups." In R. E. Petty, T. M. Ostrom & T. C. Brock (eds.), *Cognitive Responses in Persuasion*. Hillsdale, N. J.: Erlbaum, 1981.

23. Raven, B. H. "Social Influence and Power." In I. D. Steiner & M. Fishbein (eds.), *Current Studies in Social Psychology*. New York: Holt, Rinehart & Winston, 1965.

24. Hermann, M. G. "Indicators of Stress in Policy Makers During Foreign Policy Crises." *Political Psychology*, 1979, 1, 27-46.

25. Janis, 1972.

26. Shlaim, A. & Tanter, R. "Decision-Process, Choice, and Consequences: Israel's Deep Penetration Bombing in Egypt, 1979." *World Politics*, 1978, 30, 483-560.

27. Raven, 1965.

28. Kelman, H.C. "Compliance, Identification, and Internalization: Three Processes of Attitude Change." *Journal of Conflict Resolution*: 1958, 2, 51-60.

29. Hoffer, P. C. "Psychohistory and Empirical Group Affiliation: Extraction of Personality Traits from Historical Manuscripts." *Journal of Interdisciplinary History*, 1978, 9, 131-145.

30. Adorno, et al., 1950; Levinson, M. H. "Psychological Ill Health in Relation to Potential Fascism: A Study of Psychiatric Clinic Patients." In Adorno et al., 1950.

31. Ray, 1974.

32. Rokeach, 1960.

33. Tomkins, 1963.

34. Suedfeld, P. & Rank, A. D. "Revolutionarv Leaders: Long-Term Success as a Function of Changes in Conceptual Complexity." *Journal of Personality and Social Psychology*, 1976, 34, 169-178.

35. Christie, R. & Jahoda, M. (eds.), *Studies in the Scope and the Method of "The Authoritarian Personality"*. Glencoe, Ill.: Free Press, 1954.

36. Knutson, J. N. (Gen. Ed.), *Handbook of Political Psychology*. San Francisco: Jossey-Bass, 1973.

37. deMause, L. "The Independence of Psychohistory." *History of Childhood Quarterly*, 1975, 3, 163-183.

38. Luck, D. "A Psycholinguistic Approach to Leader Personality: Hitler, Stalin, Mao, and Liu Shao-Ch'i." *Studies in Comparative Communism*, 1974, 7, 426-453.

39. Barzun, J. *Clio and the Doctors: Psychohistory, Quanto-History, and History*. Chicago: University of Chicago Press, 1974; Crosby, F. & Crosby, T. "Psychobiography and Psychohistory." In S. Long (ed.), *Handbook of Political Behavior*, in press.

40. Zeligs, M., *Friendship and Fratricide: An Analysis of Whittaker Chambers and Alger Hiss*. New York: Viking, 1966.

41. Freud, S., & Bullitt, W. C., *Thomas Woodrow Wilson: A Psychological Study*. Boston: Houghton Mifflin, 1967.

42. Freud, S. *Leonardo Da Vinci: A Study in Psychosexuality*. New York: Random House, 1947 (Orig. publ. 1910).

43. Anderson, T. H. "Becoming Sane with Psychohistory," *The Historian*, 1978, 41, 1-20; Crosby & Crosby, in press; Glad, B., "Contributions of Psychobiography," in Knutson, 1973.

44. Erikson, E. H., *Young Man Luther: A Study in Psychoanalysis and History*. New York: Norton, 1958, p. 51.

45. Luck, 1974.

46. Luck, D. "A Psycholinguistic Approach to Leader Personality: Imagery of Aggression, Sex, and Death in Lenin and Stalin." *Soviet Studies*, 1978, 30, 491-515.

47. Historical Figures Assessment Collaborative. "Assessing historical figures: The use of observer-based personality descriptions." *Historical Methods Newsletter*, 1977, 10, 66-76.

48. Hoffer, 1978.

49. Schroder, H. M., Driver, M. J., & Streufert, S., *Human Information Processing: Individuals and Groups Functioning in Complex Social Situations*. New York: Holt, Rinehart & Winston, 1967.

50. Schroder et al., 1967; Suedfeld, P. "Die Messung Integrativer Komplexität in Archivmaterialen." In H. Mandl and G. L. Huber (eds.), *Kognitive Komplexität*. Göttingen: Hogrefe, 1978.

51. Ertel, S. *Between Fiction and Fact: Exploiting Word Count Information*. Paper read at the European Conference on Social Psychology, Literature and Deviance, Paris, 1975; Hermann, M. G., "Leader Personality and Foreign Policy Behavior." In J. N. Rosenau (ed.), *Comparing Foreign Policies: Theories, Findings, and Methods*. New York: Sage, Holsted, 1974.

52. Sales, S. M. "Economic Threat as a Determinant of Conversion Rates in Authoritarian and Nonauthoritarian Churches." *Journal of Personality and Social Psychology*, 1972, 23, 420-428; Sales, S. M. "Threat as a Factor in Authoritarianism: An Analysis of Archival Data." *Journal of Personality and Social Psychology*, 1973, 28, 44-57.

53. Hoffer, E., *The True Believer*. New York: Harper, 1951.

54. Rokeach, 1960.

55. Schroder et al., 1967.

56. Suedfeld, 1978.

57. Kirk, E. J., *Cognitive Complexity in the Language of Politburo Members: Reflections of Soviet Attitudes Toward Detente With the West*. Paper presented at the meeting of the International Society of Political Psychology, Boston, June, 1980.

58. Schroder et al., 1967.

59. Harvey, O. J., Hunt, D. E., & Schroder, H. M., *Conceptual Systems and Personality Organization*. New York: Wiley, 1961; Schroder et al., 1967.

60. Tuckman, B. W. "Integrative Complexity: Its Measurement and Relation to Creativity." *Educational and Psychological Measurement*, 1966, 26, 369-383.

61. Russell, G. W. & Sandilands, M. L. "Some Correlates of Conceptual Complexity." *Psychological Reports*, 1973, 33, 587-593.

62. Russell, & Sandilands, 1973.

63. Starbird, D. H. & Biller, H. B. "An Exploratory Study of the Interaction of Cognitive Complexity, Dogmatism and Repression-Sensitization Among College Students." *Journal of Genetic Psychology*, 1976, 128, 227-232.

64. Kelly, G. A., *The Psychology of Personal Constructs*. New York: Norton, 1955.

65. Suedfeld, P. & Epstein, Y. M. "Attitudes, Values, and Ascription of Responsibility: The Calley Case." *Journal of Social Issues*, 1973, 29, 63-71.

66. Sidanius, J. & Ekehammar, B. "Cognitive Differentiation and Socio-Political Ideology: An Exploratory Study." *Psychological Reports*, 1977, 41, 203-211.

67. Case, L. L., "Content Complexity and n Ach, n Pow, and n Aff, in Archival Materials." Unpublished manuscript, Macalaster College, 1979.

68. Levi, A. & Tetlock, P. E. "A Cognitive Analysis of Japan's 1941 Decision for War." *Journal of Conflict Resolution*, 1980, 24, 195-211; Porter, C. A. & Suedfeld, P. "Integrative Complexity in the Correspondence of Literary Figures: Effects of Personal and Societal Stress." *Journal of Personality and Social Psychology*, 1981, 40, 321-330; Raphael, T. D., *The Cognitive Complexity of Foreign Policy Elites and Conflict Behavior: Forecasting International Crises—The Berlin Conflict, 1946-1962*. Unpublished Ph.D. dissertation, The American University, 1980; Suedfeld, P. & Tetlock, P. E. "Integrative Complexity of Communications in International Crises." *Journal of Conflict Resolution*, 1977, 21, 169-184; Suedfeld, P., Tetlock, P. E., & Ramirez, C., "War, Peace, and Integrative Complexity." *Journal of Conflict Resolution*, 1977, 21, 427-442; Tetlock, P. E. "Identifying Victims of Groupthink from Public Statements of Decision Makers." *Journal of Personality and Social Psychology*, 1979, 37, 1314-1324.

69. Suedfeld & Rank, 1976.

70. Tetlock, P. E. "Personality and Isolationism: Content Analysis of Senatorial Speeches." *Journal of Personality and Social Psychology*, 1981, 41, 737-743.

71. Kronheim, S. P., *Conservative Drift in French Socialism, 1893-1905*. Unpublished M. A. Thesis, University of Maine, 1977.

72. Saris-Gallhofer, I. N., Saris, W. E. & Morton, E. L. "A Validation Study of Holsti's Content Analysis Procedure." *Quality and Quantity*, 1978, 12, 131-145.

73. Hermann, 1974; Hermann, M. G. "Explaining Foreign Policy Behavior Using the Personality Characteristics of Political Leaders." *International Studies Quarterly*, 1980, 24, 7-46.

74. Ertel, 1975.

75. Kirk, 1980.

76. Harvey et al., 1961.

CHAPTER II

PERSONALITY STRUCTURE AND CHANGE IN COMMUNIST SYSTEMS: DICTATORSHIP AND SOCIETY IN EASTERN EUROPE

IVAN VOLGYES

Introduction

It seems to be tautological to say that the twentieth century is "unique;" after all, every century, every event in the history of mankind is *sui generis*. Patterns—such as can be discerned—are discerned only after the events have taken place and always by those who are "observers" of history; interpreting events as fitting into a particular pattern is easier, after all, than *acting* as if they *had* to fit into it. But one unique aspect of the twentieth century has been the clearly observable phenomenon of "civilizing" dictatorial behavior—using the term in a rather unusual context. By this I mean that dictatorial behavior is different in the twentieth century in the sense that a "modern" dictator attempts to draw the masses into a coat-tail of following his orders, whims or unspoken desires, forcing them to hail the chief as a "god" to be celebrated and praised above all else. A Genghis Khan or Attila the Hun—these well-known liberals of Asiatic persuasion—Lorenzo the Magnificent, or the various other dictators either masquerading in royal robes *deus ex machina*, or rising from gentle poverty coveting the same garbs, have rarely given a hoot as to what the *feelings* of the population were toward them: provided that they obeyed the dictator, paid their taxes and acted like proper "subjects," they were left alone.

The twentieth century culminated the process of civil libertarian movements in the implementation of the theory of a "civil" society, where participant "citizens" had real input into decision making, in the selection of laws, and decisionmakers even encouraged them to make decisions concerning laws they felt to be just or unjust and choose to or not to obey. But the twentieth century had also become

known as the century of unbridled dictatorships, a century that
spawned Hitler and Stalin, Khomeini and Idi Amin. What was common to all dictatorships of this century, however, unlike those of
previous centuries, was that the dictators demanded not merely
obedience and passive acceptance, but attempted to bring the masses
through "symbolic participation" into the political arena. It was no
longer enough to obey the chief: one had to hail *him*, praise *him* at
all times, give *him* *k'vod*, march on the streets hysterically shouting
his name, trembling at *his* sight (or that of his double), and paying
homage to *his* embalmed body, *his* mausoleum, *his* grave or to a
camera which once may have taken *his* picture.

Communist dictators—it would seem to anyone steeped in Marxist
dogma—should be immune to the "cult of the dictator," for after all
it is supposedly the great social forces and not the individual that
make history. But classical Marxist dogma had quickly been transformed by the primitive Asiatic Communism practiced by Stalin and
his successors. The cult of personality is *not* an accident of history as
communist historians would try to assert; rather it is an integral and,
unfortunately, all important part of the value system of the unbridled
leader, the omniscient First Secretary and the omnipotent dictator.
Very few communist leaders have failed to succumb to this temptation once they have reached the exalted heights of absolute power
from which the road only leads to ignominy and death for the formerly omniscient and omnipotent tyrant. Almost everyone is vulnerable to listening to his own exalted praise, but few descend to the level
of Stalin who had written of himself: "Stalin is the deserving follower
of Lenin's work, or as they say it in the party: Stalin is the Lenin
of today."[1]

It is to this aspect of the Communist systems, the value transformation it intends to accomplish among the subjects, that this paper is
devoted. In short, it addresses the question of personality changes
that take place in communist systems, where the pseudo-participant
must constantly mold his behavior in accordance with a set of values
imposed on him from the outside, values he must internalize and exhibit throughout his daily life.[2] Our interest is not how compulsion
renders individuals to debase themselves in holding to "a stark, naked,
physical need to survive, however hopeless, and to gain some sense
of identity and worth, however contemptible;"[3] we are concerned
with the "schematic map," the perception of objective reality of individuals living in communist societies that are dictatorial in nature
and how the influences that exist in these societies affect the personality of the members of the society.[4]

This paper, thus, is restricted somewhat to the following considerations:

1. The goals of communist systems regarding personality development;

2. The systemic inputs into personality formations;

3. The successes and failures of the system in reaching its stated
goals;

The specific locus of the paper is Eastern Europe and the USSR;
since the author knows little about Asiatic, African, or Cuban affairs,
no reference will be made to these systems, regardless of their claimed
level of development. The time-frame of the paper refers to the end
of the 1970s and the beginning of the 1980s; the author's last visit
to Eastern Europe was in 1982. Long-range historical development,
whenever possible, must however be neglected because of space limitations.

One more *caveat* should still be entered: the breadth of the topic
is so immense that no culture-specific statement is intended. The
author is fully aware of the complexity of the cultural area and the
modest generalizations made in this paper are merely the beginning
of a series of investigations into the specific phenomena.

Personality Formation and Systemic Goals

Personality in the psychological literature "refers to the actions,
thoughts, and feelings characteristic of an individual" as well as to
"regularities of behavior" that a people evidence.[5] In this sense, it is
the repository of "past experiences, images, symbols, concepts, beliefs, attached emotions, ideologies, plans, commitments, resolutions,
and expectations."[6] We are most concerned here with conscious, interpersonal, and intra-systemic processes of serial action, with assumed
social commitments and roles, attitudes, interests, and values, *both
as expressed in behavior and as internalized concepts.*[7]

It is clear, moreover, that the "influence of cultural patterns upon
individuals has certain characteristic differences" and are not easily
applicable from one society to another.[8] The process of acculturation
of these differences is referred to as "socialization."[9] The process of
socialization, in turn, attempts to define systemic personality characteristics demanded of individuals, and group members are expected
to play certain roles in society and act in accordance with certain expectations in given situations.

The formation of personality depends, therefore, on (a) individual traits; (b) national character; and (c) socializers. The individual traits, the formation of various psychological processes, the development of the id, the ego, or the superego, should not be neglected;[10] for the purposes of this study, the author feels, however, that he knows far too little about the topic to include it in the paper. Perhaps, in the future, trained psychologists will venture into this field with greater alacrity than exhbited by them lately. The second concept, national character, cannot be neglected in its entirety. Although in bloom during the 1950s, its flowers have been picked by a rapid on-slaught of "scientism" both in psychology and sociology; today, no-thing but a neglected and withering stem remains.[11] Yet, for those studying Eastern Europe, the study of national character remains ever important, for under the similarity of a superstructure, the diametri-cally opposite reactions of people in the region can only be traced to differences in the culture-specific characteristics of the various nation-alities. The limits imposed on "systemic formations" are those which are defined by the national character of the people, and, therefore, the concept will be treated *in extenso* throughout this paper.

The socializers are those organs and agents that attempt to instill desired values into the population as a whole, and, as such, they are the most important for the purposes of our study.[12] The agents of political socialization are primary or secondary in character: the cri-terion here is whether or not they involve interpersonal face-to-face conduct.[13] The primary agents are: the family, peer-groups, and, to some extent, the churches; the secondary—ranging in hierarchical im-portance—are the schools, the churches, the youth groups, the mili-tary, and the party. The aim of the primary agencies is to create a successful, "happy" individual whose "personal" and "societal" suc-cess can be assured in the system. The aim of all of these secondary agencies is the creation of a specific, "Communist man," whose goal in life is concomitant with the desired purposes of the party.[14]

What are the attributes of a Communist man? Though there have been many attempts at defining it, so far no single individual has suc-ceeded, either in the USSR or elsewhere, in tackling the task success-fully and comprehensively.[15] In its simplest form, it is the application of an *idealized* historical hindsight to behavioral presence; a sort of socialist realism in personality formation.[16] It is basically the appli-cation of an idealized personality structure of Lenin—at times with the inclusion of the present-day leadership from Stalin to Brezhnev, from Mao to Jarulzelski, and from Kadar to Zhivkov—to the personalities of the millions of subjects.[17] In its latest formulation, the concept includes the incorporation of a Communist *Weltanschauung*, conscious positive attitudes toward study and socially useful labor of all kinds, a Communist moral outlook beneficial toward the building of Communism, and a positive attitude toward the type of æsthetic and physical culture desired by the regime.[18]

For the regimes of Eastern Europe, such an authoritative list has not been prepared; each state has had to be content with preparing its own lists. Moreover, because of the political exigencies, the shifting domestic and exogenous priority shifts, the major themes of political message aimed at creating a Communist personality have been constantly shifting. Generally, however, eight major themes have commingled with each other. These themes are: the building of socialism, anti-imperialism, socialist morality, patriotism, anti-individualism, the benefit of a socialist commonwealth, anti-nationalism, and socialist "democracy," at times utilized as a pseudonym for anti-Stalinism.[19] These were the *desired* goals of the regimes, but, in trying to gain these objectives, the regimes have constantly run into major obstacles. These obstacles were: (a) historical heritage mitigating against the creation of a Communist man; (b) historical exigencies forcing a change of theories in midstream under the power of alterations in the domestic and foreign setting; (c) contrary socialization pressures from family, peer groups, church, and external sources; and (d) national character inputs rendering efforts by the party minimal or inoperative.

Authoritarian Systemic Inputs into Personality Formation

Theoretically, the systems in existence in Eastern Europe and the USSR are classified as developed socialist; they are, in reality, authoritarian democracies. As such, the democracy of the system applies to the formal participatory levels (input), and the authoritarian elements apply to the systemic-operational levels (output). In this respect, as well, the very term "democratic centralism," which defines "authoritarian democracy," tends to create the type of "institutional paranoia" exhibited by most Soviet refugees in the Harvard Research Project in the late 1950s.[20] The major contribution of the system is to create the duality of modal behavior and the systemic effect of this duality on personality formation is important to consider.

One may argue as to whether the system as a whole is "authoritarian." Indeed, such studies on the authoritarian personality were conducted in the 1950s; most of these focused on Nazi Germany and

Stalinist USSR and Eastern Europe. The field of authoritarian personality study has been somewhat in disrepute, and the latest volume concerning this topic was published in 1967.[21] Although there were such
efforts as Sale's study, for example, focussing on the creation of authoritarian personality under crisis and applying the theories of authoritarian personality formation to democratic polities—namely the U.S.—
under stress, there were very few attempts at theory-building.[22]

When one does consider that Communist societies are in constant
stress—wheteher it is the nature of the system that inevitably creates
stress or extrasystemic factors that are responsible for the existence
of stress is open to debate—the inescapable conclusion must be drawn
that these regimes have tended to foster the creation of "authoritarian"
personalities. What, then, are the traditional elements of authoritarian
personalities? From the first studies published in 1936, through the
studies of Gerth, Edwards, Katz and Cantril, Fromm, Maslow, and
Adorno's immense volume, the following characteristics have
emerged:[23]

1. the tendency to hierarchy;
2. the generalization of superiority-inferiority;
3. the drive for power;
4. hostility, hatred, prejudice;
5. judging by externals;
6. single scale of values;
7. identification of kindness with weakness;
8. the tendency to use people;
9. the sadistic-masochistic tendency;
10. incapability of being ultimately satisfied;
11. strong guilt feelings and conflicts.[24]

When we add to these: (1) the built-in paranoia caused by the nature
of the system; and (2) the cognitive dissonance resulting from the
changing ideological character of the system, the "check-list" involved
offers us an impressive list of personality traits which can be at least
"pulled over" the *corpus delicti* of Communist systems in their "developed" state.

One could, of course, and should question whether in the "reality-
check" authoritarianism has ever completely operated in Eastern
Europe.[25] After all, the creation of such a personality is mollified by
the "contrary-socializers" mentioned above, on the one hand, and
by the very existence of the eastern European *Schlamperei* that so
consistently characterizes the system, on the other. When the Soviet
ideologists decry the "survival of capitalism in the minds of the people," it is precisely this type of *Schlamperei* they are referring to:

the system cannot, in short, create the desired Communist man, the authoritarian *par excellence*, because the non-Communist influences remain far too strong. Nonetheless, the goals remain stated, and the socializing perspectives remain well-clarified.

Let us not deal at this point directly with the "authoritarian personality" (outlined above), the characteristics of which have been delineated in the totalitarian studies of the 1950s: instead of concentra-- ting on these facets, we should try to examine some system-specific characteristics. Though, I am certain, an entire catalogue of such characteristics could be found by each researcher studying the field, I would like to concentrate here on three characteristics that I consider the most significant from the perspectives of the demands of the system. They are: (1) extremist behavior; (2) internal institutionalized paranoia; and (3) cognitive dissonance.

Communist authoritarian systems, both in the USSR and in Eastern Europe, require extreme manifestations of behavior, especially in the controlled feedback loop.[26] There is rarely to be a "mild" response manifestation; it is always a maximalist response that the system requires. One is required either to "love" the Communist Tito or to "hate the chained dog of imperialism." One is required to "love" socialist labor and "hate the loafers," to exhibit maximum enthusiasm at May Day parades, or to "raise one's stormy voice of protest" against the "Zionist fascists."

The requirements of such manifestations have found fertile soil in the national character of the people of Eastern Europe in general. For the historical and social character exhibited in the region has always been conducive to extremist emotions; especially with the Magyars and the Poles, but with the possible exception of the Czechs, practically everywhere in the region this has been the modal behavior. Consequently, the systemic demands have reinforced basic behavior and personality patterns and have created manifestations that are— however dangerous to the regime—of its own desire and creation.

The institutionalized internal paranoia is a source of never-ending conflicts for the system, as well as for the participants; nonetheless, it is also a systemic factor in especially the most rigid systems of the region.[27] Existing in a system that offers little or no continuity—for indeed, Communist systems are characterized by a frequency of changes in ideology and in the *modus operandi* that is rarely witnessed in the West, by a *modus operandi*, moreover, that rarely penetrates the cognitive factors of the citizen's store of knowledge—the spontaneous protective device of the individual is to exhibit paranoia. In accepting this facet, however, the individual begins to treat abnormal events as normal, at least in their outward manifestations. For example, though one knew that the marshals of the Soviet Union at the Tukhachevskii trial were not traitors, soon one had to treat them as if they had been traitors. Put differently, as Spinoza stated, institutional paranoia appears as "Many people are seized by one and the same effect with great consistency. All his senses are so affected by one object that he believes this project to be present even if it is not."[28] The sudden enthusiasm that had to be generated to support the Nazi-Soviet Pact in the USSR or the condemnation of the "national traitors" in Eastern Europe is a case in point and this institutional paranoia—coupled with the continuous presence of fear that one cannot acknowledge in personality behavior—leads one to deal with the topic through the adoption of cognitive dissonance in behavioral and personality patterns.

That the human mind craves consonance has been well-known from the psychological literature over many decades.[29] How human personalities have reacted to dissonance is also well-known from the consonance-dissonance theories of social psychologists. Attempts to reduce dissonance may take place in three ways: "The person may try to change one or more of the beliefs, opinions, or behaviors involved in the dissonance; to acquire new information or beliefs that will increase the existing consonance and thus cause the total dissonance to be reduced; or to forget or reduce the importance of those cognitions that are in a dissonant relationship."[30]

Specifically, in Eastern Europe and to some extent even in the USSR, today one may witness the existence of a curious phenomenon: after a considerable period of desiring to create true believers, most of the systems have become content to create citizens *who do not try* to reduce the cognitive dissonance. Strange as it may seem, for the regimes of the region, it is better to try to have a citizenry composed of cynics than of true believers; the latter—upon finding out that the stated goals, knowledge-bases, and facts are incorrect—may be a danger to and may revolt against the system. The Soviet and Communist leaderships have learned the lessons of 1956 in Hungary and Czechoslovakia well: Communist revolutionaries with contending and possibly dangerous "Communist" ideas are more dangerous to the systems than accepting cynics. The Hungarian attitude of "That's what there is, that's what you have to love"—in other words the *acceptance* of rule and not a *belief* in it—is far more preferable than idealistic notions of "socialism with a human face."

The dissonance and the cynicism with which it is resolved are especially strong between attitudinal preferences of belief-systems as outlined in the ideology, on the one hand, and behavior in reality, on the other. This dissonance, which appears to be intolerable to people living in societies where "official" *Weltanschauungs* do not force people to proclaim views on any and all subjects at the drop of a hat, is somewhat ameliorated by a function which ideology does serve and serves well, namely, ideology as a vocabulary. Since the population is used to accepting the presence of cognitive dissonance, they accept the official ideological resolution of that dissonance and incorporate "the revision" in their vocabulary. I repeat, they incorporate it not in their acceptance of the discordant facts, but in the official explanation for the discordant fact. To give an absurd example, a Hungarian party instructor explained at a middle-level party seminar in 1978 that, in reality, the capitalist economy is rapidly dying. The party-members enrolled in this seminar accepted this idiotic explanation in their written themes for the party seminar, but the students added the old Hungarian adage as a sidelight among themselves: "But what a way to go!"[31]

To summarize then: The Communist systems in Eastern Europe desire the kind of personality characterized by (a) extremist manifestations at the party's bidding; (b) an institutional paranoia that allows the party to rule relatively unhampered by competition; and (c) cognitive dissonance that characterizes attitude-systems and puts a premium on pragmatic behavior in the handling of pragmatic questions. Let us now turn to see how these personality structures are translated into day-to-day operations.

The Operational Code of Personality Modes:
Behavior in the Eastern European Communist States

In examining the personality modes and the behavior translated from these modes, one can come up with a typology of three forms of behavior that can be called modal in Eastern Europe and the USSR today. The three main divisions refer to different modes of behavior among: (a) the elites; (b) the middle-level officials; and (c) the population in general. Let me repeat that individual distinctions do exist and there are those which "stick out" of every category; however, here we are concerned with total behavioral patterns only.

The elites are generally characterized by an attitude that can best be termed managerial cynicism. They are called upon to manage a world whose parameters are outlined for them and are not likely to want to change them. At best, they can hope for minimal changes and the attacks levied at the system—with rare exception—can only come from the "left." Consequently, such relatively moderate leaders as Rakowski or Nyers, cannot mount successful challenges to the leadership and, therefore, they themselves feel that the parameters force them into competition on the basis of *policy preferences*, e.g., "My policies work!" and not "My policies are more ideologically correct."

The managerial cynics, as a group, can be divided into three main groups; upward, status quo, and declining in power. In studying the personality characteristics of these elites, in their behavior manifestations we can typologize them according to styles developed by Gerald Bell. According to Bell, the three styles that most clearly characterize their behavior are those of the "attackers," the "performers," and the "pleasers."[32]

The attackers can operate only in societies where there are avenues for upward mobility within the leadership. They are generally in the forefront of states where—following the death of a leader—an open power struggle is taking place or in systems where the leadership is rapidly aging and is in search of "young" talent. The attacker is aggressive, using Marxist vocabulary, he attacks known and not very important ills, flogs them to death, and even tries to get maximum exposure. He is not very concerned with a single issue or with performance *qua* performance; rather, his approach is that of an up-and-coming U. S. corporate executive. What is important here is that the cognitive dissonance manifest between his attacking position and his own daily operational activities is masked by what organizational theorists call "posturing" toward the different clientele. The attacker is a careerist at close to the top of the pile, an insatiable work-horse who, by the cumulation of office, functions, and tasks, attempts to make himself a logical choice for ever-higher rungs of the ladder.

The performer organizational personality characterizes all the contemporary top elites of the various Eastern European countries and the top elites of the USSR. By and large, with the possible exceptions of Ceauşescu and Tito, they are unflamboyant, solid, prodding pragmatists. They use ideology to proclaim to the population that they are the solid performers and to suggest that, if only external and internal forces did not try to slow them down, they would work even harder for the benefit of the citizenry. In short, the performers are all their own very best enemies, creating either a real or a theoretical opposition to themselves and then holding that opposition up to the general public as a threat against the practiced, moderate policies in existence. They are cynics, but their cynicism is couched in the belief that their policies are the best—not the best possible, but the best practical ones under the given circumstances. In short, a *selten kommt etwas besser nach er* approach is practiced, and this approach is the most successful for keeping the present leadership in power.[33]

The most interesting personality and leadership style is that of the elites who have been unable to maintain power and are on their way down into lower and lower positions of responsibility. Here, the personality structure assumed the style of Bell's avoider, avoiding conflict—and decision-making—as well. In a sense, they are sinking into bureaucratic models of behavior and the lower they sink the more they become comfortable with clear-cut divisions of "integrated activities which are regarded as duties inherent in the office."[34] They are on their way down, and there is never a return from the abyss under the current form of authoritarian setting for—in contrast to earlier forms of Stalinist authoritarianism—their current positions enjoy as little popular support as their earlier positions did.

These individuals fall into two basic categories: the hail-fellow-well-met and the stern taskmaster. Neither of these, however, are really interested in performance, but in their ability to hang on to their jobs until a better one comes along, or until retirement. Better than anyone else, they themselves know that they are through, and the personality they exhibit depends entirely on their individual traits; the crooked *tolkachy* are contrasted with the honest, but inept, former workers struck down in the process of development by the Comrade Petrovich principle.

Avoidance also characterizes the personality structure of the middle-level officials, the backbone of the entire administrative and productive system of the Communist states of Eastern Europe. If ever the bureaucratic principle in personality formation can be observed in behavior, it can be observed in them. Weber's formulation of the bureaucratic authoritarianism is always coupled with the classic American formulation of the "CYA" principle so clearly practiced in U. S. bureaucratic organization. Their tenure in their jobs is generally longlasting, almost always life-long; the practitioners of the art are always separated from the public by desks, counters, and *power* to do or *not* to do certain things. Even if such power in reality is translated into avoidance of decision-making, the symbols of power are important for the holding of the title.

Compounding the troubles with the relatively high weight assigned to nomenclatures that normally would be minimal, in Communist societies, even in the service sector, middle-range officials assume that they are representatives of the *State*; a manager of a state store assumes that he *is* the state and therefore assumes power and personality factors that go with the holding of power, such as yelling at or being rude to the general public. And since Communist states are in a permanent state of scarcity and the productive activities are geared to the constant recreation of security, the power of the middle-level functionary becomes an overwhelming personality trait. Favors are given by them—meat for a few customers, Western facial creams for the favored ladies, etc.—and the reciprocation of these favors is expected in daily activities by those given them. Regardless of the terminology, whether we call this behavior, as Veblen did, a "trained incapacity," a "professional deformation" as Warnotte viewed it, or as an "occupational psychosis" to use Dewey's phraseology, the assumption and the exhibition of the bureaucratic personality is a direct result of the political system that fostered it.

But the bureaucratic personality and behavior problem exhibited toward the subordinates is merely a part of the commonly described "*radfahrer*"-syndrome. If ever there was a "class" that is characterized by the upward motion of bending, coupled with the downward motion of kicking, it is the bureaucratic middle-level official group dominant over such a large portion of the system. Dependence on superiors has never been so great; after all, superiors are placed in their position by the party. Even if the power-holder above is to be schemed against, the outward manifestation of behavior is totally submissive. There are always ways to get rid of the "inferior" individuals, and submissiveness, even to incompetent leadership, is preferred to being sent "back to work."

If there is anything that ameliorates the situation, it stems from two aspects of the system: scarcity and social struggle—aspects that are clearly linked to each other. The first aspect involves the fact, mentioned above, that scarcity dominates and will continue to dominate all areas of activity. Precisely because of that scarcity, a patron-client relationship has evolved, a never-ending system of *protekcio*, or *protekcija*, of favors taken and given. This mutual dependence cuts across all areas of activity and humanizes the impersonal bureaucratic personality at least toward *some* of the subjects.

The second aspect that ameliorates the complete dominance of bureaucratic personality and the assumption of superior conduct-

activity also stems from the nature of scarcity that characterizes the system. In such systems the population wages a *bellum omnium contra omnis* for the maximization of daily rewards translated in existential benefits. Except for a very few individuals, in such systems everyone is a subject and is forced into the battle-lines with near equality. Thus, the manager, who has the all-pervasive power over the powerless workers in his factory, has to stand in line at the food store for meat or oranges, the man in charge of allocation of apartments in a district is forced to battle his way for car-allocation at the other end of the consumer-manager spectrum. This dependence *cum* power does sometimes tend to humanize conduct, but the cases in which such tendencies are exhibited can be considered to be far from modal for the operation of officialdom on the middle level in general.

Finally, let us now turn to the third category of people, those without power, those exploited by the system and subject to it. If the authoritarian system has succeeded in instilling any desired attitudes in the general population, its success would have to be manifested on this level specifically. Similarly, the failures of the system would be most manifest on this level, as well. In examining the personality of the general public, it seems quite clear to me that the regime has succeeded in creating a population that meets at least one of its standards of demand: it is a submissive population.

Submissiveness, however, is not a trait that exists alone. In the personality development of groups in accordance with the desired norms, as Honigmann maintains, such development is always coupled with negative trends; hence, submissiveness leads to rebelliousness just as certainly as the superiority and inferiority traits are coupled with each other in the development of an authoritarian personality. The submissiveness exists on all levels, but it is mostly characteristic of the attitudes of individuals at the bottom of the hierarchical totem pole, those of the subjects in general. They are submissive to officials, to official demands, to official goals; they are, in short, behaving like subjects and not like participants.

That submissiveness, however, is only an *official* and public manifestation of a desired behavior, and it is largely this, of course, that the regimes desire. As soon as compulsion is not forced, the subject, as has been amply demonstrated, looks for ways of "getting around" the demands of the system. This "back-door approach to existence" is not merely an avoidance; I submit that it is an active exhibition of getting around the systemic demands, perhaps even sabotaging them. And when that possibility narrows, when the backdoor is being closed, when the efficiency of repression allows no room for the submissive subject to maneuver his way out of the corner, the other side of his personality comes out—that of rebellious behavior. Reinforced by centuries-old traditions of precisely such acts, the subjects participate in *Jacquerie* violence, and the system has little choice open to it: either give in or brutally repress the violence. The violence in Communist states of Eastern Europe exhibited against the system has been precisely of such a nature: in the Giu Valley, or at Radom, in Berlin or in Budapest, and it has been precisely such acts that have brought the systems to their greatest crises.

The reactions of the masses to the systemic reality of scarcity has also reinforced the development of fortress and fighter mentality; as mentioned above, life in the developed Communist states is a continuous *bellum omnium contra omnis* for scarce goods, and what goods worth their price are not scarce goods in these states? Consequently, behavior toward each other on *the impersonal level*, i.e., not within family and peer-group settings, is characterized by a singularly large amount of foulness, crudeness, and rudeness. One is struck by the overall "lumpenproletarianization" of behavior in all its manifestations, especially on the lowest levels of society and this is one of the least attractive elements of the "successes of the system" in personality formation.

It is important to enter the *caveat* that the behaviors discussed above generally stop at the door of the individual's familial residence; the institutional paranoia discussed above permits the double standards to cease at the threshhold of one's intimate relations. Although there have been times and relationships that have been penetrated by the desires of the regime—Pavel Morozov's glorious example replicated by thousands-fold all over the alliance system—in contemporary times, an existing greater privatization has allowed the amelioration of this least attractive trait of the "developed Communist personality" to be left outside of the most immediate primary peer-groups. And this privatization, while enhancing the officially-desired institutional paranoia and cognitive dissonance, may be the best hope for the individual subjects of these states.

Conclusion

In summary, perhaps the picture painted above is too bleak, too gloomy, to be taken as a generalized view of the Communist personality structure. Indeed, in discussions with several members of the Hungarian, Yugoslav, and Polish Party elites, I was struck by their genuine desire to create "decent" people, who act in accordance with decent ways. Regardless of their own desires, however, I would like to contend that the systemic inputs into personality formation are such that these desires are doomed to failure. As long as the system is characterized by the allocation of authoritarian values, by extremist demands, by institutionalized paranoia, by scarcity and ever-growing levels of cognitive imbalance, reinforced by the national character of the people of Eastern Europe, the personality structure of these nations is likely to remain the same for a long time to come.

NOTES

1. Iosif Vissarionovich Stalin, *Kratkaia Bibliografiia*, Moscow: Gospolitizdat, 1947, 227.

2. On the structure of beliefs see Milton Rokeach, *Beliefs, Attitudes and Values: A Theory of Organization and Change*, San Francisco: Josey-Bass, Inc., 1968.

3. James C. Davies, *Human Nature in Politics: Dynamics of Personal Behavior*, New York: Wiley, 1963, 19.

4. M. Brewster Smith, "A Map for the Analysis of Personality and Politics," *The Journal of Social Issues*, XXIV, 3 (July 1968), 17.

5. John J. Honigmann, *Culture and Personality*, New York: Harper and Row, 1954, 28.

6. Arthur A. Murray and Clyde Kluckhohn, "Outline of a Conception of Personality," in Kluckhohn and Murray, *Personality*, New York: Alfred Knopf, 1967, 6.

7. Talcott Parsons, *Social Structure and Personality*, London: The Free Press, 1964, 17.

8. Murray and Kluckhohn, "Outline of a Conception of Personality," 42.

9. Irvin Child, "Socialization," in Gardner Lindzey and Elliot Aronson, eds., *Handbook of Social Psychology*, Reading, Mass.: Addison-Wesley, 1968, v. 2, 678-679.

10. Talcott Parsons, *Social Structure and Personality*, 17-33.

11. Geoffrey Gorer, "The Concept of National Character," *Science News* 18 (1950), 105-122.

12. Ivan Volgyes, "Political Socialization in Eastern Europe: A Conceptual Framework," in Volgyes, ed., *Political Socialization in Eastern Europe: A Comparative Framework*, New York: Praeger, 1975, 3-18.

13. Richard E. Dawson and Kenneth Prewitt, *Political Socialization*, Boston: Little, Brown, 1969, 110.

14. Wasyl Shimoniak, *Communist Education*, Chicago: Rand McNally, 1970, 51-66.

15. For some of the best attempts, see Raymond A. Bauer, "The Psychology of the Soviet Middle Elite: Two Case Histories," in Kluckhohn and Murray, 633-650; Bauer's *Nine Soviet Portraits*, New York: John Wiley and Sons, 1955; Margaret Mead, *Soviet Attitudes Toward Authority*, New York: McGraw-Hill, 1951; and John Kosa, *Two Generations of Soviet Man*, New Haven, Conn.: College and University Press, 1962.

16. Frank S. Meyer, *The Moulding of Communists*, New York: Harcourt, Brace and World, 1961, 10-13.

17. Ralph T. Fisher, *Pattern for Soviet Youth*, New York: Columbia, 1959, 2.

18. *Primernoe Soderzhanie Vospitania Shkol'nikov*, Moscow: Pedagogika, 1971, and Charles D. Carey, "The Goals of Citizenship Training in American and Soviet Schools," *Studies in Comparative Communism*, Autumn, 1977, 180-197.

19. Ivan Volgyes, "Political Socialization in Eastern Europe," *Problems of Communism*, January-February 1974, 46-55.

20. Raymond A. Bauer, "The Psychology of the Soviet Middle-Elite. . .", p. 638.

21. John P. Kirscht and Ronald C. Dillehay, *Dimensions of Authoritarianism*, Lexington: University of Kentucky Press, 1967.

22. Steven Sales, "Economic Threat As a Factor or Authoritarianism: The Case of the Great Depression," Paper presented at the Annual Convention of the American Psychological Association, 1972, reprinted in *The Journal of Personality and Social Psychology*, (September 1972), 420-428.

23. Ross Stagner, "Fascist Attitudes: An Exploratory Study," *The Journal of Social Psychology*, VI I(1936), pp. 309-319; Hans Gerth, "The Nazi Party: Its Leadership and Composition," *The Journal of Abnormal and Social Psychology*, XXXVI (1941), 565-582; Daniel Katz and Hadley Cantril, "An Analysis of Attitudes toward Fascism and Communism," *The Journal of Abnormal and Social Psychology*, XXXV (1940), pp. 356-366; Erich Fromm, *Escape from Freedom*, New York: Holt, Rinehart and Co., 1941; Allen L. Edwards, "Unlabeled Fascist Attitudes," *The Journal of Social Psychology*, XVII-XVIII (1943), pp. 401-411; and T. W. Adorno, et al., eds., *The Authoritarian Personality*, New York: Harper and Brothers, 1950.

24. Maslow's study containing these personality traits is printed in Philip L. Harriman, ed., *Twentieth Century Psychology*, New York: The Philosophical Library, 1946, pp. 234-240.

25. David W. McKinney, Jr., *The Authoritarian Personality Studies*, The Hague: Mouton, 1973, p. 14.

26. On extremism, see Bauer's excellent *Nine Portraits*.

27. Ruth Benedict, "Continuities and Discontinuities in Cultural Conditioning," *Psychiatry*, I (1938), 161-167, esp. 165.

28. Quoted in Erich Fromm, "Individual and Social Origins of Neurosis," *American Sociological Review*, 9 (1944), 383.

29. For the best study, see Leon W. Festinger, Henry Recken and Stanley Schachter, *When Prophecy Fails*, New York: Harper and Row, 1956.

30. *Ibid.*, p. 26.

31. Interview in Budapest, with an instructor in philosophy at the Evening College of Marxism-Leninism, November, 1978.

32. Gerald D. Bell, *The Achievers*, Chapel Hill, N.C.: Preston, Hill, 1973, 84-125 and 39-60.

33. Even important American policy-makers tend to be carried away by this appealing approach; supporting Brezhnev and his position is preferable to the unknown "opposition" that the Soviet leadership always characterizes as eventually aiming to end their liberal policies.

34. Robert K. Merton, "Bureaucratic Structure and Personality," *Social Forces*, 18 (1940), 560.

CHAPTER III

TERRORISM AND LENINISM:
A FEW PRELIMINARY CONSIDERATIONS

WALTER GLEASON

> This has happened several times in the course of history.
> A thing which was conceived in a lofty ideal manner be-
> comes common and material. Thus Rome came out of
> Greece and the Russian Revolution came out of the
> Russian Enlightenment.
>
> —*Doctor Zhivago*

At a few minutes past eleven on the morning of January 24, 1878 a young woman—later identified as Vera Ivanovna Zasulich—approached the Governor-General of St. Petersburg, General Trepov. Zasulich waited in the anteroom to Trepov's office as the Governor received the day's petitioners. When her turn came Zasulich handed Trepov her petition, hesitated for a moment and then pulled out a revolver and shot the General at point-blank range. Zasulich's act inspired a number of would-be assassins in the period 1879-1881. The most notorious case occurred in 1879 when Alexander Solov'ev lay in wait for Tsar Alexander II as the Tsar walked along a promenade in St. Petersburg. As the Tsar came near, Solov'ev raised his revolver, aimed and fired at close range. He missed and then missed again and again, firing five times in all at what must have been a rather beleaguered Tsar. In the same year, the founders of the People's Will, encouraged by Zasulich's deed, formed a conspiratorial party that gave organizational sanction to terror. Modern Russian terroristm dates from this period and took its tone and style from the example set by Zasulich.

Zasulich's reasons for trying to kill Trepov were moral rather than political. She sought to emulate the ideal figures of her childhood, Jesus Christ and the Decembrist Ryleev—figures whom Zasulich cast in heroic poses as sufferers and eventual martyrs.[1] Self-sacrifice took precedence over the cause itself. Once she decided to shoot Trepov she thought she ". . . had freely separated with life and did not think [she] would live any more."[2] When the moment came and Zasulich actually pulled the trigger she immediately let her revolver drop and

[41]

retreated to a corner of the room. No attempt was made to escape This. heroic, sacrificial example was an accurate measure of the character of Russian terrorism. It differed generically from the Great Terror initiated in late 18th century France in its personal, moral bases. Terrorism was not, as will be argued below, inherent in Russian Social Democracy or its variant, Leninism. Certainly Russian terrorism of the pre-1930s vintage cannot compare with the indiscriminate terror that readily became the customary practice of Stalin's regime. Traditional Russian terrorism was *sui generis*.

Terrorism as "the great deed," at once exalted and exalting to its executor, was but one of the traditions of the Russian revolutionary movement, the corpus of ideational heritage that was accepted and refined by every generation of Russian intellectuals during the 19th century. The received knowledge of the revolutionary past served to shape in a quite specific and substantive way the policies the Social Democrats and Lenin could endorse about such issues as terrorism. Indeed, terrorism à la Zasulich led Russian Marxists, especially Lenin, to adopt ideas and methods of operation essentially incompatible with Social Democracy and disavow others quite readily reconciled with the philosophic dictates of Marxism. The history of Russian terrorism is, in part, the history of the Russian Marxists' efforts in not revising the issue of terror to suit Social Democratic theory but construing Social Democracy as the fulfillment of the traditions of the revolutionary movement.

This accent on the heritage of the movement is not simply the abstract constuct of the historian. It is the basis of the question of legitimacy, a question every revolutionary group explicitly asked itself during the last half century of Tsarist Russia. For the Russian Marxists of the 1890s the question of legitimacy was raised with a sense of urgency. Unlike their predecessors, the Social Democrats argued for the advantages of an economic system which Russian intellectuals had never before supported. They voiced the interests of a constituency which Russian thinkers had no prior occasion to represent and viewed these phenomena through the prism of a philosophy that was, after all, German. Russian Marxists were particularly vulnerable to the charge of being "alien" and for that reason particularly interested in claiming a heritage. They made their claim to legitimacy in the course of the great debates with their rivals, the Populists. Aside from the particular issues under debate, each side sought to support its arguments and legitimize its position by laying claim to the heritage of the Russian revolutionary movement.

The lineage of the Social Democrats was established by Lenin in 1897 in his famous article, "What Is The Heritage We Renounce?"[3] No less a critic than Mikhailovskii had charged that Social Democratic violations of Populist theories meant that ". . . these people [i.e., the Social Democrats, w.g.] do not acknowledge any continuity with the past and emphatically renounce the heritage. . . ."[4] To rebut the charge Lenin first unleashed a rather indiscriminate attack on his critic, branding the charge "an absurd fabrication," and then redrew Mikhailovskii's own line of reasoning before discrediting the logic behind the case, i.e., not the original case but Lenin's version of the original. The burden of the charges against the Social Democrats was not, Lenin claimed, their dismissal of Populist ideals. Rather, the issue was the precedent to either Populism or Marxism in Russian intellectual history. He traced the genealogy of both parties back to the 18th century and claimed common ancestry in the persons of the key figures of the Russian Enlightenment. Once the pedigree was established, Lenin defined the Russian enlighteners in quite general terms as advocates of fundamental change in the social and political order, defenders of the interests of the masses and firm opponents of serfdom. Given these criteria, Russian Populists were to be understood as enthusiasts of a regressive, agrarian order already rendered obsolete by industrialization. By way of corollary the Populists' vision of a communal agrarian society was taken as tacit support for the vestiges of serfdom. "Turning to the fundamental views of Narodism outlined above, the first thing we must note is that 'the heritage' has *absolutely no part in them.* There are a whole number of undeniable representatives and guardians of 'the heritage' who have nothing in common with Narodism, who do not pose the question of capitalism at all, who do not believe in the exceptional character of Russia, the peasant community, etc. . . . "[5]

So far Lenin's charges were rather common fare in the polemics of the 1890s. He differed in drawing one key inference from the Populists' alleged betrayal of the peasants and support for serfdom. Specifically, the Populists disregarded the presumed connection between the intellectuals and their constituents, i.e., disregarded the social bases of political activity. To deny this link was to deny realities for the sake of abstractions—and fictional ones at that. This denial allowed the Populists to assume that their utopian agrarian order was recoverable by the initiative of a political party. Here Lenin's polemics with the Populists intersected with the history of Russian terrorism. He intimated in the essay under review what he spelled out fully in "The Tasks of the Russian Social Democrats," also written in late 1897.

There he argued that the Populists' disinterest in social realities led them to reduce political action to conspiratorial action. Comparing the Populists of the 1870s with the Social Democrats of the 1890s, he claimed that

> . . . Blanquist, conspiratorial traditions are fearfully strong among the former, so much so that they cannot conceive of political struggle except in the form of political conspiracy. The Social Democrats, however, are not guilty of such a narrow outlook; they do not believe in conspiracies; they think that the period of conspiracies has long passed away, that to reduce political struggle to conspiracy means, on the one hand, immensely to restrict their scope, and on the other hand, choosing the most unsuitable methods of struggle. . . . This fight must be waged not by conspirators, but by a revolutionary party based on the working-class movement.[6]

Lenin's renunciation of conspiracy created a dilemma. His denial of conspiratorial methods was a disavowal of the terrorist organizations of the period 1879-1881. What had suffered from a mistaken value on voluntarism and an illusory notion about the efficacy of individual effort would, if repeated, be at best quixotic and in any case doomed. Nonetheless, Lenin's opposition to terror was maintained at the price of disinheriting his own movement. He could not disclaim conspiracy and terror without disclaiming the heritage of the revolutionary movement. Hence the dilemma.

These theoretical difficulties were sharpened in the opening years of the 20th century by the second, major series of terrorist acts. Individual terrorists indulged in the heroics of personal combat with the government. In 1901 the revolutionary Karpovich shot Bogolepov, the Minister of Education, and the following year the target was Sipiagin, the Minister of the Interior. Perhaps the most controversial incident occurred in 1902. The Governor-General of Vilna, von Vahl, broke up a demonstration and gave orders for the whipping of a number of the protesters. For his trouble, he was shot at by Hirsh Lekkert. It is accurate to say shot "at," rather than killed, because many Russian revolutionaries of the early 1900s were no better shots than were their predecessors in the late 1870s. More substantively, the organized terror of political parties was restarted with the founding of the Socialist Revolutionary Party in 1900. To compound the Social Democrats' problems, the Russian worker had at last made his appearance as a political actor on the stage. While the famous strikes of 1896-1897 were trade-unionist in character, the second wave, those of 1900-1902, was—for the first time—political. Given these signs of a rapidly developing working class, Lenin and the Social Democrats were confronted with the problem that "great deeds" of terror exercised an enormous appeal among the rank and file of workers, distracting them from the comparatively mundane tasks of party organization. At the same time terror brought on counter-terror; each terrorist act provoked the government to retaliatory actions against terrorists that could nip the incipient labor movement in the bud. Terrorism could no longer be addressed in the philosophical and polemical terms of the 1890s. Nor could the dilemma Lenin created for himself in 1897 be left unattended.

A conventional point is to note that Lenin's reaction to the strikes of 1900-1902 and the new wave of terrorist acts was to accent the role of organization. In a series of articles in *Iskra* and in the famous revolutionary catechism *What Is To Be Done?* Lenin also elaborated repeatedly his theoretical critiques of terrorism. His argument was fourfold. Terror was a matter of tactics, not principle. "Terror is one of the forms of military action that may be perfectly suitable and even essential at a definite juncture in the battle, given a definite state of the troops and the existence of definite conditions."[7] But, terror as a method of operation required its direction by a strong party organization. Terrorism unconnected to organization was inappropriate, random and, ultimately, disorganizing and distractive. Second, terrorism as a tactic was suitable only to the specific circumstance in which the party had organized all its forces, schooled its regulars in matters of philosophy and practice and employed terror as one of its tactics on the day of revolution. Third, individual acts of terror were the work of persons given to their own "infatuation" with the romance of the great deed.[8] These acts of personal indulgence drew their advocates away from the task of establishing links between the organization and its chosen constituency, the Russian working class. The links were, as Lenin accurately estimated, only recently established and could be quite easily broken. Fourth, terror was simply ineffective. A contemporary "Economist" journal, *Svoboda*, advocated terror as a means of "exciting" the working class. Lenin's response was derisive. The government perpetuated such frequent acts of offense against its citizens as to provoke the maximum number of workers. No excitants were necessary. Those unmoved by official misconduct were hardly likely to be roused to action by the heroics of a handful of terrorists. On all four counts terror was no substitute for organization.

This classic case on terrorism provided the theoretical norms with which Lenin hoped to restrain those "infatuated" with the terrorist deed and harness the revolutionary energy of the zealots to the organization. Taken literally, his arguments maintain the link between written constructs and logical causation. His constructions were so arranged as to give sanction to terror only when practiced in a margin whose parameters were narrowly set by theoretical standards. Yet these norms surely did not suffice to limit the appeal of the terrorist act. Lenin's recourse was to introduce additional rationales, generically different from those outlined above and parallel to them, and superimpose these lines of argument on the original ones. The rational level of debate was traduced by reduction to the use of artificial contrasts and symbolic language. In redrawing the lines of debate Lenin disavowed the link between construction and causation, allowed literary imagery to represent rational argumentation, and even came to a new appreciation of the terrorist heroes of 1879-1881 vintage. The burden of his argument increasingly came to rely on symbolism, and on arguments that conformed to the heritage of the Russian revolutionary movement.

The key to these arguments was their simplicity. One claim was that the organizational coherence and ideological purity of the Social Democrats was threatened by a double menace, the Economists and terrorists.

> The Economists and the present-day terrorists have one common root, namely, subservience to spontaneity. . . . The Economists and the terrorists . . . bow to different poles of spontaneity; the Economists bow to the spontaneity of 'the labor movement pure and simple,' while the terrorists bow to the spontaneity of the passionate indignation of intellectuals who lack the ability or opportunity to connect the revolutionary struggle and the working class movement in an integral whole.[9]

How serious a threat to the organization was posed by Economism? Since the strike movement of 1900-1902 was political, the Economists were discredited by the very spontaneity of the working class movement that Lenin feared would give them sanction. The idea that the Economists were a threat to Social Democracy was Lenin's invention and not one that was corroborated by political realities.

As for the terrorists, the pair to the Economists as the Castor and Pollux of revolutionary mythology, their presence was contrived. Lenin could not afford to condemn unequivocally the role of terrorism in the revolutionary movement. To avoid this he added constructions that blocked off into stages the history of Russian Social Democracy.

Then he claimed that this history was the latest stage in the history of the entire Russian revolutionary movement.[10] This blanket claim to "good breeding" put the Social Democrats in the direct line of succession, Lenin noted, from their immediate predecessor, the People's Will.

Note some rather interesting wording Lenin now used to describe the People's Will. Learn from the "old Russian masters"[11] their techniques and organizational stategies, he advised. And, most importantly, keep in mind that the terrorists of the late 1870s should be considered "the glorious representatives" of a by-gone age and "terrorist heroes" in the present one.[12] The wording was too consistently repeated to have been casually chosen. Evidently Lenin was willing to allow for the voluntaristic element—the potency of individual action to direct the course of history—and to a degree which he had explicitly disallowed in the 1890s. What changed in the interim was the need to exalt the revolutionaries of the 1870s as luminaries of the movement and, in the process, transform them into no more than symbolic figures. This characterization served two purposes. Lenin could continue to insist that the People's Will erred on the philosophic point of its disinterest in the social bases to political organization. Yet he also reduced the terrorists to the ranks of preternatural creatures who walked the Russian earth in the seventies and so made a possible claim to lineage on no more than fictional bases. The rhetoric was surely not a matter of deferential comments embellishing the substance of Social Democracy. On the contrary, Lenin's sanction to the role of "terrorist heroes" was a clear adoption of a form of revolutionary action he disavowed in the 1890s as contrary to the fundamentals of Social Democracy. His invocation of these "terrorist heroes" of the 1870s was a literary artifice used to point up the legitimacy of Social Democracy on bases that were themselves as symbolic as they were philosophic. The appeal of Social Democracy was in the process of shifting from argumentation to symbolism.

Another claim to legitimacy was made on the basis of extreme simplification. The cause of the Social Democrats was termed "the correct path," and its rivals were criticized for their "one-sidedness" or "crudeness" or failure to keep to "the course." In short, "the line" was linked to the Social Democrats while all others, undefined, were cited for not meeting an unspecified mark. Consider this exercise in imagery:

> We are marching in a compact group along a precipitous
> and difficult path, firmly holding each other by the hand.
> We are surrounded on all sides by enemies, and we have
> to advance almost constantly under their fire. We have
> combined . . . for the purpose of fighting the enemy, and
> not of retreating into the neighboring marsh, the inhabi-
> tants of which . . . have reproached us with having sepa-
> rated ourselves into an exclusive group and with having
> taken the path of struggle instead of the reconciliation.[13]

The political vocabulary gave the Social Democrats carte blanche to
draw lines of revolutionary affiliation according to what were now
entirely symbolic terms. More importantly the language created its
own reality, one whose characteristics and moving principles could
establish their own dominance. Given this precedence, Russian Social
Democracy was vulnerable to reduction from a philosophy to a cause
and from a set of intellectual premises to a litany of slogans.

These considerations point up the potential advantages of a fresh
look at the relationship between terrorism and Leninism. Lenin had
come to speak the language of revolutionary politics. When he praised
"the terrorist heroes" he laid claim to the revolutionary heritage but
also revealed the potential consequences of doing so. In the years between the revolutions of 1905 and 1917, there was a third major
wave of terrorist acts. Incidentally, one should mention the fact that
in this round of assassination attempts the number of targets actually
wounded increased substantially. Unlike the terrorists of the 1870s
and the early 1900s, those of the post-1905 era were better shots.
Lenin's reaction to these incidents was to remain steadfast in his
earlier opinions. Yet only his unique personal prestige and position
within the party was the effective check against terror unsanctioned
by the party or terror practiced by the party. This check lasted, of
course, only as long as Lenin lived. As the later history of Russian
Social Democracy would document, Lenin's deference to "terrorist
heroes" was a measure of the organization's increasing reliance on
terror before 1917 and especially after the revolution. The terrorist
as hero set the stage for the appearance of the terrorist as ruler. Wor-
shipful regard for the old terrorists could lead to the deification of a
single, contemporary terrorist.

NOTES

1. Rita Kelly. "The Role of Vera Ivanovna Zasulich in the Development of the Russian Revolutionary Movement." Unpublished Ph.D. dissertation (Indiana University, Bloomington, 1967), 14-17.

2. Vera Zasulich, "D. A. Klements: lichnye vospominaniia," in *Vospominaniia.* Moscow: Podgotovil k pechati B. P. Kozmin, 1931, 72.

3. V. I. Lenin, "What Is the Heritage We Renounce?" in *Collected Works*, 45 vols. Moscow: Progress Publishers, 1960-1970, II, 491-534. For the sake of the reader's access to the material the textual quotations are taken from the English language version of the authorized fourth edition. The translation was checked against the original and necessary changes noted.

4. *Ibid.*, 493.

5. *Ibid.*, 514-515.

6. Lenin, "The Tasks of the Russian Social-Democrats," *Ibid.*, 340-341.

7. Lenin, "Where To Begin?" *Ibid.*, V, 19.

8. *Ibid.*

9. Lenin, "What Is To Be Done?" *Ibid.*, 418.

10. Lenin, "A Protest by Russian Social-Democrats," *Ibid.*, IV, 181.

11. Lenin, "Our Immediate Task," *Ibid.*, 217.

12. Lenin, "What Is To Be Done?" *Ibid.*, V, 517.

13. *Ibid.*, 355.

CHAPTER IV

THE TRIUMPH OF HITLER'S WILL

DAVID J. DIEPHOUSE

In September 1934, the film director Leni Riefenstahl joined thousands of devout National Socialists in Nuremberg to make *Triumph of The Will*, her perversely fascinating documentary on the sixth Reich Party Congress. Produced "by order of the Führer," as its credits state, the film opens with one of the most famous sequences in cinema history. For more than a minute the screen remains totally dark, while a synthetic Wagnerian overture swells to become the "Horst-Wessel-Lied," the Nazi party anthem. "On September 5, 1934," rolling titles proclaim, ". . . 16 years after the beginning of the German passion, 19 months after the German rebirth, Adolf Hitler flew again to Nuremberg to review the columns of his faithful followers." The blackness then gives way to a vivid aerial panorama of towering clouds, through which Hitler's airplane descends towards the city, casting a cruciform shadow on the massed Storm Troopers marching in the streets below. With its bold visual passage from darkness into light, its references to passion and resurrection, its strikingly literal image of a Führer coming on the clouds of heaven, this scene establishes a tone of insistent messianism which pervades all that follows. Moving, as one analysis has it, with "the slow, stately rhythm . . . of the imperial or religious procession," *Triumph of The Will* transforms the Nuremberg rally from a stage-managed media event into a vast cultic ceremony. In Reifenstahl's theophanic vision, Hitler's "second coming" as Führer becomes an act of revelation, invested with near-apocalyptic significance. "The party is Hitler, but Hitler is Germany, just as Germany is Hitler!" When Rudolf Hess declaims these words at the end of the film, they carry the force of a binding liturgical formula, a benediction to which the proper response is not "Amen" but "Sieg Heil!"[1]

Triumph of The Will gives us National Socialism through the eyes of a sympathetic outsider, a director who, while dazzled by Hitler's charms, never applied for party membership. It stands as eloquent testimony to the role of messianism in the Nazi ethos and its importance for the shape and purposes of the Nazi state. Like the first German Reich, the Third Reich claimed for itself a holy mission. But if the old Holy Roman Empire invoked the universality of Christendom, Hitler's Reich proclaimed a narrow tribalism which found its fullest expression and *ultima ratio* in the cult of the Führer. The Nazi youth leader Baldur von Shirach compressed the "pure faith" of the new order into a single precept: "My Führer, you alone are the way and the end." Robert Ley, director of the Labor Front, professed that "on this earth we [Nazis] believe only in Adolf Hitler. We believe that National Socialism is the only saving faith for our people." This confessional litany could be lengthened almost indefinitely. Even allowing for a large dose of demagoguery, the high priests of the Hitler cult clearly demanded of their acolytes not merely intellectual assent but unqualified emotional commitment. "We National Socialists have but one thing in common with Christianity," proclaimed Roland Freisler, the sinister head of the People's Court: "we demand the whole man."[2]

Contemporaries early recognized the messianic strain in National Socialism. "Hitler's way," the future *Bundespräsident* Theodor Heuss argued even before the seizure of power, was at heart the aberrant revival of an Old Testament prototype—"Judaism with the premises reversed." Other writers of the 1930s, particularly those with ecclesiastical connections, came to similar conclusions. Even Franz Neumann's classic Marxist analysis left ample room for a view of the Hitler cult as the reincorporation of ancient messianic and thaumaturgical traditions. Once the twelve-year millenium had collapsed and its full horrors began to emerge, the image of Hitler as messiah took on renewed import. Heirs of Goethe like Friedrich Meinecke and Thomas Mann could ultimately conceive of what Meinecke called the "German Catastrophe" only in terms of some mass apostasy from the ethical norms of Western humanism, with Adolf Hitler as a kind of *diabolus ex machina* bidding forth all the hidden demons in the collective German soul.[3]

With the passage of time and the Third Reich's consequent transformation, in Leonard Krieger's phrase, "from experience to history," the focus of scholarly interest has undergone a variety of shifts.[4] Yet the vocabulary summoned to the task of explaining Hitler has changed remarkably little. To some extent, surely, the use of messianic terminology serves an ongoing hortative function. It provides a way of acknowledging that the totality of Hitlerism transcends dispassionate analysis, that the "monstrous provocation" of Nazi inhumanity, as Krieger puts it, "continues to call above history across the years to the common humanity that lives alongside the professional [scholar] in each of us."[5] There also remains an understandable tendency, notably in the Marxist tradition, to treat the Hitler cult with skepticism, interpreting it as essentially a facade for the raw exercise of power. But if recent research has moved towards increasingly sophisticated social and economic models of the Third Reich, it also reflects a renewed inclination to take seriously the Nazi movement's religious pretensions. Social philosophers as divergent in outlook as Jacques Ellul and Richard Rubenstein agree, if for different reasons, that Hitler's Germany in effect shows the process of secularization come full circle. The Third Reich, Ellul has insisted, dissolved conventional liberal distinctions between sacred and secular in a political gospel whose apocalyptic totalism fused the state with an explicit religion of the state. Lately, historians and social scientists have sought to avoid the often circular terminological debates over fascism and totalitarianism by advancing theories that explain National Socialism as a response to intrinsically religous needs and desires. And there is surely more than coincidence in the fact that of the many recent attempts to mate historical analysis with psychology—itself arguably a form of postmodern religious consciousness—one of the best should choose to portray Hitler as a "psychpathic god" whose private neuroses formed the basis of the entire Nazi experience.[6]

The messianic face of Nazism is, in short, a familiar one—so much so, indeed, given the array of available sources and interpretations, that even brief consideration of the topic tempts one to misappropriate Karl Kraus' famous remark: "Concerning Hitler I can think of nothing to say."[7] For all its familiarity, however, the cult of the Führer can hardly be treated as a simple *donnée*, the anvil on which to forge some general theory of history or society. Not the least remarkable aspect of Nazism is its sustained capacity for paradox. An inquiry into the sources and functions of Nazi messianism soon encounters all the fascinating complexities which have made the Third Reich one of the perennial growth stocks in the scholar's research portfolio. If one body of evidence suggests that radically religious elements, including the Hitler cult, deserve to be seen as intrinsic to Nazism, investigations into the "fascism of everyday life"[8] undercut the Third Reich's totalitarian image and suggest that Nazi dogma achieved only limited penetration into the hearts and minds of ordinary Germans. The more seriously one takes Nazi claims to the "whole man," in other words, the more difficult it becomes to countenance the final image of *Triumph of The Will*: a mass of Germans marching lockstep behind the banner of the swastika.

Precisely because the messianic theme is so prominent in the Nazi experience, this apparent paradox invites further reflection. Was the deification of Hitler in fact a central factor of the Third Reich? If so, what specific role or roles did it play? And if, as seems likely, few Germans embraced the new religion of the Führer in all its cultic fervor, what was the wider basis—and what were the boundaries—of the Nazi regime's undoubted popular legitimacy? These and related questions demand a fuller treatment than is possible in a brief essay. What follows therefore makes no pretense to being exhaustive, nor does it claim to open up uncharted conceptual territories. The aim is primarily to sketch out a line of inquiry which, while hardly unfamiliar, nevertheless seems to me not to have been pursued as far as its implications warrant. My discussion will revolve around three interrelated points. I hope first of all to establish that an intrinsically sectarian cult of Hitler was indeed basic to the Nazi mentality and played an important practical role in the development of both the party and the Nazi state. Next I will consider the thesis that this messianic appeal tapped certain impulses in the German historical consciousness which served to give the Third Reich a general legitimacy far beyond the circle of devout National Socialists. Finally, I will attempt to suggest that the tension between these two facets of the Hitler cult— the sectarian and the general—provides one way of understanding not only the regime's mass appeal but also the very real limitations on its power.

I

There is widespread agreement, I think, that a messianic image of Hitler constituted a vital component of the Nazi mentality, and that this Hitler cult had a significant role in the functioning of the Nazi party as well as the Nazi state. In Helmut Hieber's widely-quoted statement, "There was and there is no National Socialism without Hitler. The two are identical . . . . Everything else is simply a misunderstanding."[9] To the extent that this assumes the existence of a reasonably coherent Nazi outlook, of course, it begs a complex and important question. Given its self-professed dynamism and the fact that Nazi leaders manifestly treated ideas as more instrumental than normative, the Nazi outlook can better be sought in the praxis of party and regime than in the platitudes of the Twenty-Five Points or the often obscurantist homilies of Hitler's court philosophers. This is not to say, however, that National Socialist claims to be a genuine *Weltanschauungspartei* were wholly without foundation. On the contrary, the history of the movement from beginning to end reflects the galvanizing force of a central Idea. That Idea—the proclamation of Hitler as a kind of messiah, a divinely-ordained personification of German destiny—was not merely an article of the Nazi faith but its necessary condition. At least by intent, Hitlerism provided the cultic community of true believers with what Edward Shils, in a larger theoretical context, has called a "central zone," the "center of the order of symbols of values and beliefs which govern the society" and which is "felt to be [ultimate and irreducible] by many who cannot give explicit articulation to its irreducibility."[10] Hitler's will provided the Nazi movement with a formative myth on which followers could draw to give meaning to their world and direction to their actions.

The claim that Hitler had somehow been "born to dictatorship" and therefore "called to rule," the appeal to charismatic authority which he himself used at the legendary Beer Hall Putsch trial in 1924,[11] arose out of Hitler's fervent, even mystical confidence in his own historical destiny. Psychohistorians in particular have expended considerable energy attempting to account for the emergence of this sense of private mission. None of the proffered clinical theses, taken by itself, seems wholly convincing. What does seem clear, however, is that Hitler's political road to Damascus involved, in the most literal sense, an experience of conversion, a turning away from a "sense of . . . present wrongness" as well as the "imagination of [a] positive ideal."[12] The resulting identification of private will and national destiny, as Eberhard Jackel has shown, made the apocalyptic radicalism of *Mein Kampf* greater than the sum of its *völkisch* parts, all of them essentially coin of the realm in the intellectual demi-monde of pre-war Central Europe. *Mein Kampf* shows Hitler to be both politician and revivalist, the evangelist for a myth of which he himself was the foremost "possessed servant."[13]

From this perspective the Nazi *Führerprinzip* can be seen as a natural extension of the Führer's charismatic authority. Hitler could claim allegiance as Leader because he was first of all accepted as Prophet: the political shaman who, as a seer guarding the true mysteries of the nation, had mobilized a new myth "to fill the gap left by the unsatisfactory performance of traditional ritual and its rationalistic substitutes."[14] Those who became Hitler's closest disciples underwent conversion experiences of their own, eventually coming to find a sense of personal identity and purpose not in themselves or in prevailing social norms but in the revealed will of the Führer. For many veteran Storm Troopers—not to mention a keeper of the grail like Joseph Goebbels, who flatly confessed "credo, ergo sum"—party membership brought the emotional catharsis of rebirth into a holy community. Goebbels confessed in his diary for 1926 that in Hitler he had found "the natural creative instrument of a fate determined by God." To which he responded: "A star shines leading me from deep misery! I am his to the end. My last doubts have disappeared. Germany will live. Heil Hitler!"[15] Even a less chiliastic personality like Albert Speer would later reflect that in becoming a party member he was "not choosing the NSDAP, but becoming a follower of Hitler, whose magnetic force had reached out to me the first time I saw him and had not, thereafter, released me."[16] The deification of Hitler developed, in short, not only because Hitler himself demanded it, but because it was essential to the faith of the true believers.

If Hitler was Germany's destiny incarnate, as the gospel of the Führer proclaimed, then it followed that the nation would have to be remade in his peculiar image. This meant, in the first place, its transformation from a pluralist "system" à la Weimar into a *Volksgemeinschaft*, an organic national and racial community. Abundant evidence shows that Hitler and his disciples saw the *völkisch* idea, an adolescent pastiche of quack science and gutter philosophy, as the blueprint for a new world order. Racialism conjured up the ideal of a tribal community in which membership was not so much a natural right as, quite literally, a birthright. Like the Old Testament image of a Chosen People—an ironic but hardly accidental affinity—Nazi racialism fused the spiritual and the biological. If Marxism attacked the class divisions of bourgeois society by absolutizing class itself, Nazism did so by absolutizing the rhetoric of community. Although the Third Reich never indulged in systematic social or economic levelling, its official doctrines had the effect of weakening conventional linkages between economic class and social status. Rather than abolishing the old economic and military elites which had assisted it into being, it simply promised those of Aryan blood and the Aryan faith an automatic social status, independent of family ties, wealth, or educational background. That Aryanism itself was a shabby artifice detracted little from its appeal; if anything, it probably had the reverse effect.[17]

Racial standards, however, provided more than just a rationale for egalitarianism and social mobility. By defining membership in the organic community they served conversely to isolate the alien, the weak, and those otherwise designated as impure for quarantine and eventual elimination. The tribal character of the Nazi community not only dictated the fates of the millions reserved for the Final Solution but also produced such bizarre individual cases as that of Christine and Luise Sautter, two Aryan sisters reportedly dispatched to Ravensbrück in 1944 because they no longer wished to be considered German citizens. In a very real sense the concentration camp provided the negative image of the *Volksgemeinschaft*.[18]

The monstrous horror of the camps was sanctioned, in turn, by a second fundamental extension of the Führer's will, namely the conception of life as pitiless, unremitting struggle. From the vulgarized social Darwinism of *Mein Kampf* to the fatalism of the "Political Testament," struggle was a constant *Leitmotif* of Hitler's mental and political development. The Nazi movement presented itself from the beginning as a veritable church militant, promising to supplant a humanist "slave ethic" with the martial discipline of a warrior community, a social order in which collective strength and perseverance, not charity and personal freedom, would enjoy pride of place. Faith without works was dead, Hitler in effect told his oldest party comrades at Nuremberg in 1934. To believe in National Socialism was only a mimimum requirement; the favored few of the new order, the true *alte Kämpfer*, would be those pledged not merely to believe but also to fight.[19] As a Christmas homily to the Hitler Youth in 1938 shows, the Führer's will left no room for goodwill towards men, nor was peace on earth a notable priority. "We will not ask Almighty God to make us free!" the youngsters were exhorted. "We want rather to mobilize ourselves, to work, compete and assist each other so that the hour may come when we can go before him and say, 'Lord, Thou seest that we have changed.... The German people has again become strong—strong in spirit, in will, in determination, strong in the endurance of sacrifice. . . . Now, therefore, bless our struggle for our own freedom, for our German *Volk* and Fatherland!"[20]

As this suggests, the Nazi faith banished God not only from the world of men but also, ultimately, from the Throne of Judgment. By reducing all of life to a dichotomous *Freund-Feind* relationship, the "struggle for freedom" invoked no autonomous or immutable standard of justice, no "laws of Nature and of Nature's God," but only the higher imperative of its own dynamism. "We may be inhuman," Hitler had declared before the seizure of power, "but if we save

Germany we will have repaired the greatest injustice in the world! We may be immoral, but if our people is saved we will have paved the way for morality!"[21] This crudely Nietzschean metamorphosis of values found its fullest expression in the nightmare world of the Holocaust Kingdom. "To have stuck it out to the end and at the same time. . . to have remained decent," Heinrich Himmler delared in his famous speech of 1943 to SS henchmen fresh from the crematoria and shooting pits of eastern Europe, "that is what has made us hard."[22] For a state which recognized strength as the final arbiter of decency and preached hardness as the highest human ideal, war became, almost inevitably, the ultimate civic virtue.

Between Hitler's struggle and Germany's struggle, then, the path is short and direct. Hitlerism was the true wellspring of National Socialism, and virtually all the characteristic features of the Nazi millenium, including its most heinous, followed naturally and inevitably from their source in Hitler's will. Messianism was not simply a technique of totalitarian social control, not simply the product of an exercise in political image-building. This does not mean, of course, that the Hitler cult served no significant functional purposes. Indeed, the charismatic nature of National Socialism made deification of its leader functionally indispensable. Lacking effective ideological or administrative means for resolving the factional conflicts endemic to such a dynamic and unruly movement, the Nazi party derived what internal cohesion it possessed largely from its members' shared acceptance of the Führer's transcendent status, the elevation of his will as the lodestar and final authority for faith and practice. After 1933, by extension, the *Führerprinzip* provided a basic if not always coherent principle for integrating party and state—a principle, moreover, which had the virtue of emancipating the Führer, with his notoriously bohemian work habits, from the confines of conventional bureaucratic decision-making processes. Rather than systematically reorganizing the administrative state, with all its inbred habits and accustomed lines of power, the Nazi movement simply enveloped it and made Hitler its focus of authority. The Third Reich "routinized charisma," in Max Weber's terms, by subjecting bureaucratic rationality to the ultimately irrational dictates of the Führer's will.[23]

In a state which thus literally enshrined the leader's will as law, the inevitable struggle to secure the leader's favor both encouraged and at the same time helped to equilibrate the efforts of party chieftains and traditional civil servants alike to build and buttress their often countervailing empires. This explains in part the apparent paradox of the Nazi "dual state." From one standpoint the Third Reich, with its bewildering maze of overlapping jurisdictions, multiple agencies, and unending political *Kompetenzstreiten*, seems the very antipode of a rigid, centralized dictatorship. From another standpoint, however, it offers a terrifying spectacle of efficiency and organization, which, in the assembly-line world of Auschwitz, reduced even human degradation and mass murder to banal engineering problems, simple matters for the card files of bureaucratic routine. In the Holocaust, ideology and functionality became mutually reinforcing. The Hitler cult, with its spiritual glorification of the bellicose, found its natural institutional expression in the Nazi's permanent warfare state, where normality was defined by the abnormalities of the emergency decree.[24]

The deification of the Führer also served, whether intentionally or not, to distinguish Hitler from more traditional *Herrscher* in the German experience. Attempts to fit Hitler into conventional heroic molds bordered on the ludicrous, as witness the famous Hubert Lanzinger portrait of the Führer in the trappings of a medieval knight. With an ancestry more notable for illegitimacy than aristocracy, Hitler was no royal pretender, nor was he well cast for the role of a military patriarch like Paul von Hindenburg. Nor, for that matter, did he measure up to the style and standards of the academic mandarinate he so richly despised. Even in the regalia of the party he remained physically unprepossessing. The "Hitler No One Knows" portrayed by his court photographer is in fact a fairly nondescript Everyman, at home—albeit in a strangely distant way—in the petty bourgeois world of Sunday excursions and picture shows.[25]

The ordinariness of his person only served to underscore the extraordinary character of Hitler's will. His authority, to which the mesmerizing power of his oratory bore witness, derived not from social pedigree but from spiritual mission, the mission which, as we have noted, transformed Hitler in his own eyes into the image-bearer of the divine, a son of the *Volk* who, lifted up by destiny, would draw all the *Volk* to himself. Here again the christological paradigm is unmistakable. As J. P. Stern has observed, the Hitler cult blended "the impersonal ethos of the Frederician tatoo with elements of a highly personalized Austrian and Catholic liturgy."[26] If it drew its content from a kind of vulgarized nationalism, it found institutional form in a vulgarized Catholicism, exploiting liturgical impulses which had been channelled into political forms because, for Hitler and other true believers, they had found inadequate fulfillment within the church itself.

The political culture of the Third Reich in fact bears the strong imprint of a church Hitler and most of his disciples claimed to have left behind. It is interesting to note, for example, that party publications from the 1930s generally bore a self-conscious official imprimatur whose formula aped the venerable Catholic *Nihil Obstat*.[27] Broadly Catholic, too, was the fundamental Nazi emphasis on deed over word. If *Mein Kampf* can be called the regime's bible, its significance in rallying the masses never remotely approached that of the party's public ceremonials and demonstrations. While Hitler once declared that the Reich could build no religious edifices, only parade grounds, it is hard to see the latter as anything but the indispensable "sacred spaces" of the party's cultic activities. Indeed, the great Nazi rallies resemble nothing so much as the religious processionals of an earlier era, with the old guild formations and civil-religious iconography replaced by the various uniforms and insignia of the new order. In this sense, perhaps, the Lanzinger portrait of Hitler as Knight Templar may be less outrageous than it first appears. Like the church of the Crusades, the Hitler regime understood the talismanic power of a central symbol like the swastika, the "twisted cross" of a new crusader elite. Like the medieval church, the Third Reich could also boast its shrines and pilgrimage centers, its holy orders like Himmler's SS, and its preaching friars, the party orators so important to grassroots morale. The rhythm of the National Socialist calendar closely followed that of the Christian church year, with ceremonial high points in the "holy night" of January 30 (the anniversary of Hitler's appointment as Chancellor), a spring festival on the Führer's birthday, the pentecostal observances at Nuremberg each September, and an All Saints' Day in November to commemorate the original Beer Hall Putsch. Other parallels could no doubt be pointed out, not least of which would be the antidotes for heresy which the regime applied through its secular Inquisition, the Gestapo, and the variety of purgative ordeals perfected at Dachau and Buchenwald.[28]

At its most powerful, the Third Reich accomplished a synergistic fusion of cultic nationalism with the personal cult of Hitler, a fusion reinforced at every level by propaganda and terror, by liturgical devices combining religious ceremonial with the most advanced techniques of mass communication. If Shils is correct in arguing that the "central zone" of any society "partakes of the nature of the sacred" and therefore constitutes a de facto official religion, then Nazism might best be described, with apologies to Ernst Troeltsch, as essentially a "sect-type" of civil religion, at once an offshoot of traditional nationalism and its radical reformulation. Nazism defined the nation exclusively, not inclusively, transforming it into a racially circumscribed holy community at odds with the world at large and accessible only to an Aryan elect. Not surprisingly, more than one scholar has drawn parallels between the Third Reich and the radical millenarian experiments of the sixteenth century. In both eras, certainly, the doctrines of the movement led to a similar end. Like the Anabaptist New Jerusalem at Münster, for example, the Nazi New Order eventually conjured up its own nemesis, uniting once and future antagonists— Catholics and Lutherans in 1535, capitalists and Communists four centuries later—in a commitment to unconditional defeat which transformed the believers' millenium into cataclysm.[29]

II

If one accepts this somewhat synthetic sketch of Nazi doctrines and practices, there remains the question of whether the *Volksgemeinschaft* of Nazi ideals ever in fact became mundane reality. To what extent did Hitler's struggle in fact become Germany's struggle? The answer is more complex than wartime propaganda on either side would lead one to believe. Despite the heavy social orchestration of the Hitler creed, considerable evidence points to the fact that the circle of true believers always remained surprisingly small. For most members of the holy community, it would appear, membership was never more than a nominal affair. Even among those who paid party dues, full devotion to the cult may well have been the exception, as it certainly was for the "Septemberlings" and "March casualties," those who joined for pragmatic reasons after the pivotal party successes in 1930 and 1933. *Mein Kampf* probably deserved its reputation as the least-read bestseller in publishing history; even many in Hitler's inner circle privately admitted to finding it unreadable. The works of other party theorists such as Darré and especially Rosenberg suffered a similar fate.

Far from commanding unqualified allegiance, party dogmas furnished the stuff for a burgeoning repertoire of underground humor. Racial theories proved particularly vulnerable to this corrosive wit. One widely circulated quip defined "Aryan" as the "hind quarters of a prolet-aryan"; another, perhaps the best-known of all, portrayed the ideal Aryan as "blond like Hitler, tall like Goebbels, and slim like Goering." The variations on this and kindred themes were virtually legion. Nor, for all the frenetic outpouring of emotions at stage-managed ceremonies, did the regime ever approach the permanent mobilization of enthusiasm which was its evident goal. Around the *Stammtisch*, resignation and cynicism were more typical than the fanaticism demanded by Hitler. Confidential party reports from every period of

Hitler's rule remark on the absence of popular enthusiasm for official policies, particularly in the countryside. The outbreak of war in 1939, the ultimate rite of the Hitler cult, aroused little of the exhilaration of the "August days" twenty-five years before.[30]

Despite conscientious attempts to impose Hitlerism as a surrogate religion, traditional loyalties and practices proved difficult to eradicate. According to the census of 1940, fully 95% of the German population—including, ironically, the Führer himself—remained taxpaying members of the major Protestant and Catholic churches. A tabulation of baptisms, weddings and funerals in Thuringia during a six-month period as late as 1943 showed that 96% were traditional religious ceremonies and only 4% party rites. Composite figures for the Protestant churches from 1933 to 1939 show a similar if less dramatic tenacity of older habits. The number of couples solemnizing their vows in the church dropped substantially (54% in 1939 compared to 80% in 1930), while somewhat fewer children of Protestant parents were being presented for baptism (a drop from 96% to 89%). On the other hand, the incidence of church funerals actually increased slightly, and the percentage of Protestant youths received for confirmation in the 1930s consistently exceeded the levels of the previous decade. Both Protestant and Catholic youth groups stubbornly resisted total *Gleichschaltung*, particularly at the local level. The latter cases are particularly interesting, since they suggest that the regime's indoctrination efforts achieved less than spectacular results—this despite the image of Nazism as a movement of youth.[31]

But while ordinary Germans for the most part held fast to inherited beliefs and privately ridiculed the pretensions of the Nazi dogma, most of them appear to have marched more or less willingly in step to the drumbeat of the new order. The basis for this nominal loyalty went deeper than the quasi-legal character of the Nazi state or the powerful chemistry of Goebbels and the Gestapo. For a broad cross-section of the population, many observers agree, Hitler satisfied a generalized "hunger for wholeness," a desire to escape the anomie of modern society for the promise of refuge in an older community—to reverse, as it were, the perceived drift from *Gemeinschaft* to *Gesellschaft*. To this end the specific content of the Führer's appeal was less important than its sheer fervency and radicality. As J. P. Stern has noted, "the more it diverges from the status quo, which is the direct source of disaffection, the more the messianic image becomes an object of faith and a powerful source of social integration." Hitlerism deserves the label of vulgar messianism not only in the sense that it was a denatured and secularized variant of messianic traditions, but also in the literal sense that it struck a deep common chord among large numbers of German people.[32]

To some extent impulses favorable to a messianic appeal can be found at work in almost every Western country during the interwar period. In Germany, however, the problems of modernity were both widespread and experienced as peculiarly acute, not only because of the political and economic traumas since the Great War but also, more generally, because these problems bore heavily on the largely unresolved problem of German nationhood. If Hitler's gospel called upon all Germans to become National Socialists, one might say, the good news which many chose to hear was the promise of a long-elusive organic national unity. Essential to this response was Germany's history as what George Mosse had called a "disunited nation," a phenomenon whose ramifications scholars have yet to explore in full. Since the political and ecclesiastical upheavals of the sixteenth century, German national consciousness has been the concomitant not of accomplished nationhood but of an incomplete nationhood, its often hyperbolic expressions reflecting a lack of incontestable symbols of common national and societal identity. Perhaps most evident in the tragic history of German Jewry, the problem of the nation has left its mark in every historical era and on every sector of German society.[33]

The effect of the Reformation and subsequent religious warfare in central Europe was to break down the spiritual homogeneity of the Holy Roman Empire while at the same time fortifying its endemic tendencies towards political and cultural fragmentation. This weighty legacy of particularism had profound consequences for national development even after Bismarck refashioned the imperial idea at Versailles in 1871. The feudal fabric of the several principalities had long hindered not only the formation of a centralized nation-state but also, at least indirectly, the development of a self-confident commercial class. As a result Germany came to build its nineteenth century industrial order on essentially pre-modern foundations, and the federal structure of the Wilhelmian empire did little to resolve the inescapable tensions between tradition and modernity which strained German society. The basic artificiality of Bismarck's unification scheme became evident when its authoritarian superstructure collapsed in the trenches of World War I.[34]

The heritage of particularism affected not only the structure of state and society but also the national consciousness around which these developed. In this context it is customary to stress German thinkers' glorification of the state as an ultimate value beyond ordinary human challenge. The idealist apotheosis of the state, it should be noted, reflected the desire of early nineteenth century nationalists, flushed with the exhilaration of Napoleon and the War of Liberation, to make of their fragmented homeland a unified political entity. Hegel hoped for a strong state in which the German nation would not only achieve physical unity and discipline but also discover its moral and historical destiny. Later generations would make of the state an end in itself, a *Machtstaat* of blood and iron in which Hegel's aspirations were distorted or ignored. This strand of nationalism nurtured the belligerent "unpolitical German" and the proverbial respect for order and authority displayed in "right-thinking" and especially Protestant circles. Germans of this persuasion may have found Hitler and his movement crude and uncultivated, but they also found much to applaud in the order and discipline which the Third Reich appeared to provide.[35]

Moreover, because its formative influences were largely those of the local community rather than the national state, the German idea of unity was also essentially organic in character. Unity typically connoted not merely formal political consolidation but also a communitarian cohesion obviating social and political conflict. This archaic social vision retained its vigor even after industrialization had created a new subculture shaped by the tenets of Marx and Engels. The Nazi movement took deep root in the world of tradesmen and artisans, together with other elements of the *Mittelstand* whose fear of engulfment by mass society went hand in glove with an abhorrence of the proletarian doctrine of class warfare. For these groups, tradition played a vital part in legitimizing the Third Reich. The new state reinterpreted pre-industrial norms in the vision of a disciplined *Volksgemeinschaft*, identified with a charismatic leader who, in Martin Broszat's formulation, "enabled the old monarchical loyalties to be renewed in a concept of leadership closer to the masses and seen as the incarnation of the true will of the people." The Nazi state in effect promised to synthesize Bismarck and Barbarossa, to weld the functional modernity of the Second Reich to the communitarianism and spiritual universality of the First. Its elevation of the values of localism to the status of a national order found expression in the choice of Nuremberg, an old Imperial Free City, to be the holy place of the reborn Reich.[36]

III

Appeals to tradition, therefore, were not simply a device of Nazi propaganda but an intrinsic source of the Third Reich's legitimacy.

Where the sense of such traditions was weakest or most attenuated, as in the factory classes, Nazism found little natural root. Where they were experienced most acutely, as in the Protestant middle classes and the much-analyzed Weimar youth cohort, the Nazi movement exerted self-evident appeal. To some extent the malaise of modernity affected every sub-community in Germany, and it is in part this fact which has bedevilled attempts to explain Nazi successes solely in terms of specific social or economic interests. It is more accurate to say, as George Mosse has recently shown, that National Socialism represented the crystallization and political manipulation of an already existing mass-nationalist impulse, a "new politics" which attracted "not only National Socialists, but also members of other movements which found this style attractive and useful for their particular purposes."[37] The uniqueness of the Nazi version lay precisely in its charismatic leader, the Führer who transcended and thereby promised salvation from the frustrating welter of social, economic, and ideological factions that had become a hallmark of the hated Weimar "system."

Paradoxically enough, however, the very factors which contributed to the appeal of Nazism and helped fuel the cult of the Führer also acted, in many cases, as fundamental checks on the loyalty of the masses. If the implicit Nazi goal was a Germany remade in Hitler's image, as I have argued, I have also suggested that many Germans, perhaps a majority, tended to see Hitler largely in their own private images. They followed him, that is to say, not first of all because they had experienced a full conversion into the sectarian mentality of the true believers but because, for one reason or another, they had found it easy to assume that Hitler was simply articulating their own basic resentments, hopes, and conceptions of society. It follows, then, that where Nazi sectarianism diverged from these conceptions, popular support tended to ebb, and enthusiasm turned to ritual if not outright non-cooperation.

Evidence of this contingent legitimation, as it might be called, is accumulating in the growing body of research on grassroots conditions in the Third Reich. Where the policies of the regime coincided with local traditions or expectations, not surprisingly, they normally met with at least tacit approval, if not always fanatical support. The first stages of the Holocaust, for example, aroused minimal opposition from a Christian majority for whom anti-Semitism, in a host of forms, was an all too comfortable and unreflective cultural tradition. On the other hand, efforts to enforce ideological discipline at the expense of custom and tradition encountered widespread resistance. Massive and sometimes violent protests, for example, met attempts to remove crucifixes from public places or interfere with Protestant and Catholic religious instruction in the schools. The reaction to the Nazi euthanasia program is an often-cited example of how popular values and expectations acted as a check on the regime's pursuit of sectarian ideological goals. Inaugurated under cover of war in 1939, euthanasia was a classic instrumentation of the Führer's will; its only basis an internal Chancellery decree signed by Hitler himself. Although those responsible for implementation tried to keep the program secret, enough traces of their activities soon surfaced to mobilize the opposition of victims' relatives, church officials, and even some members of the state bureaucracy. Private hospitals and asylums, like the Protestant facility in Bethel, mounted campaigns of passive resistance, refusing to release patients or handle the paperwork required by the program. Protestant church leaders as well as the Catholic bishops' conference issued formal condemnation, while mobs of outraged citizens demonstrated against transports to known euthanasia centers. Eventually this resistance had an effect. While "mercy death" never came to a total halt, Hitler did suspend the formal euthanasia program in the summer of 1941.[38]

It is no accident that this and other episodes involved the churches, the largest non-military institutions to escape effective *Gleichschaltung*. The Church's struggle provides a particularly illuminating demonstration of the phenomenon of contingent legitimation, illustrating how the same traditions which on one level led to cooperation with the Nazi order acted, on another level, to temper and delimit support. This was especially true for the large territorial Protestant churches, and, to a lesser extent, for the Catholic hierarchy.[39] As a consequence of the Reformation and particularly the *Kulturkampf* of the 1870s, Catholics held ambivalent attitudes toward the German state, which they tended to identify with Protestantism and Protestant interests. While the isolation of Catholics had significantly eroded by the twentieth century, particularly since the heady days of the Leonine revival and the collapse of the Protestant Hohenzollern dynasty in 1918, the Catholic leadership still saw relations with civil authorities as primarily an exercise in diplomacy. The characteristic expression of this attitude was the heirarch's inclination to seek regulation of church-state relations by means of treaties such as the Reich Concordat of 1933—a policy, it must be said, which developed in close conjunction with the general policies of the Vatican. Subsequent Catholic criticism of Nazi measures was frequent and specific, but in most cases the bishops confined their protests to demands that the church's rights under the Concordat be respected. Whatever the tactical wisdom of this approach, it meant that the loyal Catholic often found himself faced with obligations in two conflicting realms, the religious and the civil, both of which demanded ultimate allegiance. The guidance which the church afforded the individual as believer often proved ambiguous or irrelevant to his circumstances as a citizen.[40]

A different situation developed in the large Protestant churches, which for centuries had considered themselves cornerstones of the German civil order and whose parishes provided the great primary reservoir of support for National Socialism. The warm welcome which Protestant leaders by and large accorded the advent of the Third Reich grew directly out of their own particularistic heritage in the post-Reformation symbiosis of throne and altar. Established at the instance of secular powers, the various territorial churches inevitably functioned as moral guarantors of the state, heralding and enforcing good order and proper attitudes among the populace. Protestantism in many areas became literally a state religion, preaching a gospel which stressed not only salvation but also, and equally, obedience and conformity to the monarchical design.[41]

The collapse of the German dynasties in 1918 magnified the tensions arising out of this historical synthesis of piety and patriotism. Swept up in their own organic vision of German unity, most churchmen conceived of the church itself as a paradigm for society, an all-embracing spiritual community in which, as Otto Dibelius proclaimed in his triumphalist book of 1927, *Das Jahrhundert der Kirche*, political and social cleavages could be reconciled or transcended. Even the most ardent monarchist could see, however, that the church's historic identification with the state had only served to alienate it from large numbers of its nominal parishioners, particularly in the proletarian subculture. Ironically enough, the term "national" or "German socialism" had come into currency through the efforts of churchmen such as Adolf Stoecker and Friedrich Naumann, who prior to World War I had attempted, with scant success, to rescue the workers' movement from Marxism and lead it toward Wilhelmian respectability. After 1918 the churches made many attempts to build bridges to their marginal constituencies. These projects remained largely fruitless, however, because churchmen at the same time were struggling to buttress their traditional status as moral arbiters against the dominant relativism and pluralism of the worker-supported Weimar democracy.[42]

It was this ecclesiastical identity crisis which predisposed many churchmen to the "positive Christianity" of the Nazi program, its perfervid anti-Bolshevism, and its call for the national moral rebirth. Church leaders greeted the Third Reich as a providential opportunity not simply to rebuild the pre-Weimar synthesis of state and religion but to do so within a national community blessed with the order and cohesion denied the Second Reich. The shattering of these fond hopes, as the true face of the regime began to show itself, plunged the churches into a profound theological and institutional crisis, a crisis exacerbated by efforts to impose a uniform national church, with a Nazi-appointed *Reichsbischof*, in place of the existing federation of territorial hierarchies. To varying degrees, clergy and laity alike were forced by circumstances to move in the direction of one or the other of two polar positions, one (the German Christians) openly espousing a variant of the Nazi gospel, and the other (the Confessing Church) holding to the claims of orthodox Protestantism.

To the extent that the Church Struggle arose over the question of the role the churches should assume in defining the Third Reich's "central zone," it is interesting to note that both the German Christians and the Confessing Church, despite fundamentally different responses to Nazi totalism, in fact advocated positions consistent with the long symbiotic tradition of German state Protestantism. The German Christians carried to its radical conclusion the synthesis implicit in the historic principle of *cujus regio ejus religio*, absolutizing national loyalty at the expense of moral and theological autonomy. That Hitler himself found this movement embarrassing if not actually distasteful indicates, I believe, the extent to which the Christian elements of the symbiosis remained normative for the self-professed "SA of Jesus Christ." While willing and eager to modify the meaning and content of their Christianity to accommodate it to the framework of *völkisch* nationalism, the German Christians were reluctant to dispense with it altogether. The Confessing Church, for its part, moved to absolutize a moral position at the expense of cooperation with the state. Essentially counter-political in outlook, the Confessing Church did not so much seek to challenge the civil legitimacy of the Third Reich as to defend the church's claim to autonomy and its historic prerogative of holding the state responsible to Christian standards of ethics. This position, to be sure, became politically consequential in view of the totalistic character of the Nazi regime.[43]

In some cases relgous convictions led individuals and groups to challenge the Hitler cult through direct political resistance. More typical than the Bonhoeffers and Moltkes, however, and certainly more illustrative of the ambiguous tendencies prevailing in German Protestantism as a whole, were the responses of such church leaders as Theophil Wurm, bishop of the Protestant church in Würtemberg. Wurm is a particularly interesting figure because his church was one of the largest Protestant bodies to remain "intact" throughout the Church Struggle, with no open split between German Christians and supporters of the Confessing Church. Determined above all to maintain the historic identity of his church and uphold the integrity of its mission as he understood it, Wurm emerged as an authentic spokesman for the Protestant mainstream. Like a great many conservatives, Wurm had viewed the Nazi movement with more than benevolent neutrality prior to 1933, and although he rejected what he considered the nationalist idolatry of the German Christians as well as their disruptive impact on ecclesiastical politics, he was eager to pledge the church to a major role in the "national renewal" once Hitler came to power. His gradual transformation into one of the most outspoken Protestant critics of the regime came about primarily through his bitter disillusionment with the sectarianism of the Nazi outlook and the regime's increasingly obvious efforts to deprive the church of any substantial influence in the new order. "The tragic thing was and is," he wrote as late as 1944, "that a movement for political renewal, which we welcomed and with which we fully sympathized—in part because we expected it to exercise beneficial influence in a moral respect—proved to be so closely tied up with a folkish counter-religion [*Freidenkertum*]." Not only did the Third Reich fail to enforce Christian morality in public life, but it actively encouraged an ethic incompatible with the church's teachings. This, despite his unwavering patriotism, Wurm could not countenance.[44]

The considerations which motivated Wurm's repeated protests, in public sermons and private letters to national leaders, were simple and direct. As he put it in 1944, "can a believing Christian hope for blessings on a people who have allowed all this to happen, and on a political system that has carried all this out and brooks no criticism of its measures? . . . The real question is whether what . . . is happening is right before God and whether the German people can be saved without its leaders recognizing and making good their wrongs." It was this sense of moral responsibility, clearly, which informed Wurm's famous letter to Hitler in 1943, in which among other things Wurm declared that the extermination of Jews stood "in sharpest conflict with the law of God and in violation of the basic principle of all Western thought and life: the God-given right to human existence and dignity. . . ."[45]

Despite such open protests, and although he had regular contact
with the German resistance, Wurm steadfastly refused either to support or to collaborate actively in any political conspiracy against the
Third Reich. From his standpoint such action was and remained
treason. Moreover, it was as morally dubious as the actions which it
hoped to halt were morally reprehensible, since it would violate the
Christian's call to recognize civil authority, however repugnant, as
divinely sanctioned. At the same time, however, as his frequent letters
to party leaders demonstrate, Wurm firmly believed that the church
had both a right and a duty to admonish even the powers that be
when their exercise of authority departed from the guiding principles
of a Christian society. Wurm's resistance to Nazism therefore took
the form not of political action but of calls for moral renewal—the
same renewal he had long hoped the regime itself would bring about.
He never challenged the legitimacy of the Third Reich, only what he
considered its aberrant practices. That the two were inseparable was
a problem which Wurm, like so many of his contemporaries, never
found an adequate formula to resolve.

Wurm's attitude reflects and confirms the ultimately paradoxical
nature of the Hitler cult. Hitlerism was both the vital center of a
millenarian sect, with a sense of holy mission which led inevitably to
Auschwitz, and at the same time a flexible integrative symbol for a
much wider national community whose loyalty to the Third Reich,
rooted as it was in deep-seated and at the same time problematical
values and traditions, remained largely independent of the crusade to
establish National Socialism as Germany's "one saving faith." This
fact may help explain why postwar denazification policies, as a self-
conscious effort at social re-education, would strike so conspicuously
wide of the mark, and why—purely psychological factors aside—the
"inability to mourn" has been so persistent a feature of political culture in the Third Reich's successor states.[46]

In his oft-quoted speech to SS leaders, Heinrich Himmler called
the Nazi extermination program "a page of glory in our history which
has never been written and is never to be written."[47] It is a ghastly
but revealing remark. Even now, a half century after Hitler's seizure
of power, it is the radical negativity of the Nazi order which remains
its most striking and perplexing quality, overshadowing all of the
conceptual debates and the ever more sophisticated analyses of economic and social developments. The vague rhetoric of power aside,
Hitlerism manifested itself not in any coherent positive ideals but in
its systematic effort to destroy everything which it opposed. It called

upon Germans not to build a new City on a Hill but to reduce to rubble those already standing. It sought equilibrium in a state of permanent mobilization, in escalating assaults against an ever-widening array of foes: unemployment, the Versailles *Diktat*, Weimar democracy, Bolshevism, the old and infirm, above all the Jews. Nothing, in fact, better incorporates the Hitlerian ethos than the war against the Jews, a perverted jihad so total in destructive intent that, as Himmler intimated, its final act would have been to destroy even the traces of its own existence.

For a cult which sought salvation in destruction, self-destruction was a logical destiny. What National Socialism sowed in the torchlight of Nuremberg, it reaped in the firestorms of Dresden and Berlin; after Auschwitz and Stalingrad, Germany itself became the altar at which the Hitler cult played out its final liturgy. With his empire crumbling around him, his most savage visions unattained, and his once loyal band of disciples reduced to mutual intrigues and recriminations, Hitler retreated to his bunker "like some cannibal god, rejoicing in the ruin of his own temples."[48] The last days of the Third Reich may or may not have been, as some have suggested, the conscious acting out of a privately scripted *Götterdämmerung*. What is abundantly clear, however, is that, unlike the Christ with whom he had at times identified, the Nazi messiah sacrificed himself in the end not to bring life but to destroy it. Death itself marked the ultimate triumph of Hitler's will.

NOTES

Some of the material in the essay first appeared, in substantially different form, as an article in *Fides et Historia*, VII No. 2 (Spring 1975); the journal's editor, Ronald Wells, kindly allowed me to use the relevant passages. Among those who provided helpful criticisms of the original paper I should like to thank especially Burton Nelson, Hans Mommsen, and Lawrence Walker. My thanks also to my colleagues Frank Roberts and Dale Van Kley for their comments on the present essay.

1. The quotations are from Richard Meran Barsam, *Filmguide to Triumph of the Will* (Bloomington, Ind., 1975), 28, 65; cf. *Der Kongress zu Nürnberg vom 5. bis 10. September 1934* (Munich, 1934).

2. Shirach and Ley are quoted in Hans-Jochen Gamm, *Der Braune Kult* (Hamburg, 1962), 39, 24, Freisler in *A German of the Resistance: The Last Letters of Count Helmuth James von Moltke*, 2nd ed. (London, 1948), 64. For other examples see Georg Schott, *Das Volksbuch von Hitler*, 4th ed. (Munich, 1934).

3. Theodor Heuss, *Hitlers Weg*, ed. Eberhard Jäckel (Tübingen, 1968); Franz Neumann, *Behemoth: The Structure and Practice of National Socialism 1933-1944*, 2nd ed. (New York, 1944); Friedrich Meinecke, *The German Catastrophe*, tr. Sidney B. Fay (Cambridge, Mass., 1950); Thomas Mann, *Doctor Faustus*, tr. H. T. Lowe-Porter (New York, 1948). For contemporary religious assessments see Reinhold Niebuhr, *Christianity and Power Politics* (New York, 1940), 117-130; Karl Barth, *The Church and the Political Problem of Our Day* (New York, 1939), 41-43; Maurice Muret, "Le Paradoxe du christianisme allemande," *Revue des Deux Mondes*, VIII, Per. 54 (1939), 293-308; Edward Quinn, "The Religion of National Socialism," *Hibbert Journal* 36 (1938), 441-450.

4. Leonard Krieger, "Nazism: Highway or Byway?" *Central European History* 11 (1978), 12. Pierre Aycoberry, *The Nazi Question: An Essay on the Interpretation of National Socialism (1922-1975)*, tr. Robert Hurley (New York, 1981), sets a new standard for analyzing the historiography of Nazism.

5. Krieger, "Nazism," 21.

6. Jacques Ellul, "Les religions séculières," *Foi et Vie*, 69 (1970), 73; Ellul, *The New Demons* (New York, 1975); Richard Rubenstein, *The Cunning of History* (New York, 1975). Recent studies emphasizing the messianic component of Nazism include J. P. Stern, *Hitler: The Führer and the People* (Berkeley, 1975); and James M. Rhodes, *The Hitler Movement: A Modern Millenarian Revolution* (Stanford, 1980). For the psychohistorical perspective see Robert G. L. Waite, *The Psychopathic God: Adolf Hitler*, pb ed. (New York, 1978). Karl Dietrich Bracher, *The German Dictatorship*, tr. Jean Steinberg (New York, 1970), remains the finest general account.

7. Karl Krause, *Die dritte Walpurgisnacht* (Munich, 1967), 9.

8. The phrase is suggested by Franz Joseph Heyen, *Nationalsozialismus im Alltag* (Boppard a.Rh., 1967).

9. Quoted in Eberhard Jäckel, *Hitler's Weltanschauung*, tr. Herbert Arnold (Middleton, Conn., 1975), 19.

10. Quoted in S. N. Eisenstadt, "Charisma and Institution Building: Max Weber and Modern Sociology," in Eisenstadt, ed., *Max Weber on Charisma and Institution Building* (Chicago, 1968), xxx. That Hitler fits Weber's typology of the charismatic leader needs no special demonstration.

11. *Der Hitler-Prozess vor dem Volksgericht in München*, II (Munich, 1924), 89. On Hitler's self-deification see Friedrich Herr, *Der Glaube des Adolf Hitler* (Munich, 1968); Wolfgang Hammer, *Adolf Hitler—ein deutscher Messias?*(Munich, 1970); Walter C. Langer, *the Mind of Adolf Hitler* (New York, 1972), 27-40; Waite, *The Psychopathic God*, 30-36 and passim.

12. The locus clasicus remains William James, *The Varieties of Religious Experience*, Modern Library ed. (New York, 1929), 186-253.

13. The expression is from Eugen Weber, "The New Right: An Introduction," in Hans Rogger and Eugen Weber, *The European Right: A Historical Profile* (Berkeley, 1965), 27. On the development of the Nazi ideology see especially Jäckel, *Hitler's Weltanschauung*; James H. McRandle, *The Track of the Wolf* (Evanston, Il., 1965), 121-145; and Barbara Miller Lane and Leila J. Rupp, eds., *Nazi Ideology Before 1933* (Austin, TX., 1978).

14. Weber, "The New Right," 27.

15. Quoted in Amos Simpson, ed., *Why Hitler?* (Boston, 1971), 136-137; Goebbels' "credo" is quoted in Rhodes, *The Hitler Movement*, 167 and elsewhere.

16. Albert Speer, *Inside the Third Reich*, pb ed., tr. Richard and Clara Winston (New York, 1970), 46.

17. The classic Nazi statement is of course Walther Darré, *Neuadel von Blut und Boden* (Munich, 1938). David Schoenbaum, *Hitler's Social Revolution* (Garden City, N. Y., 1966) remains the most convincing scholarly overview of Nazi social theory and practice.

18. Persönlicher Stab RF-SS, File EAP 16kl-b-12/109, Folder 537 (National Archives Microcopy T-175, Reel 48); see also Ernst Niekisch, *Das Reich der niederen Dämonen* (Hamburg, 1953), 294-295.

19. *Der Kongress zu Nürnberg 1934*, p. 211; cf. Barsam, *Triumph of The Will*, 62.

20. Eberhard Möller, *Der Führer: Das Weihnachtsbuch der deutschen Jugend* (Munich, 1938), 172-173.

21. Quoted in *The Nazi Party, the State and Religion, by Adolf Hitler*, "Friends of Europe" Publication No. 41 (London, [1936]), 23.

22. "Rede des Reichsführer-SS bei der SS-Gruppenführertagung in Posen am 4. Oktober 1943," Doc. PS-1919, *Trial of the Major War Criminals* 29 (Nuremberg, 1948), 145.

23. Weber's conceptual statement is in "The Nature of Charismatic Authority and its Routinization," in Eisenstadt, ed., *Max Weber on Charisma*, 48-65. On the role of charisma in the Nazi party see Joseph Nyomarkay, *Charisma and Factionalism in the Nazi Party* (Minneapolis, 1967); and Wolfgang Horn, *Führer-Ideologie und Parteiorganisation in der NSDAP (1919-1933)* (Düsseldorf, 1972). The character of the Nazi "dual state" is set forth in Bracher, *The German Dictatorship*, 228-236; Schoenbaum, *Hitler's Social Revolution*, 192-233; T. W. Mason, "The Primacy of Politics—Politics and Economics in National Socialist Germany," in Henry A. Turner, ed., *Nazism and the Third Reich* (New York, 1972), 175-200.

24. Rubenstein, *The Cunning of History*, provides a provocative commentary on this point; see also the classic by Raul Hilberg, *The Destruction of the European Jews*, pb ed. (New York, 1979).

25. Heinrich Hoffmann and Baldur von Shirach, *Hitler wie ihn keiner kennt* (Berlin, n.d.). Other examples of the same genre include Schott, *Das Volksbuch von Hitler; Adolf Hitler: Bilder aus dem Leben des Führers* (Altona, 1936).

26. Stern, *Hitler*, 85.

27. "Gegen die Herausgabe dieser Schrift bestehen seitens der N.S.D.A.P. keine Bedenken."

28. Hitler's comment on parade grounds is quoted in Hamilton T. Burden, *The Nuremberg Party Rallies: 1923-1939* (New York, 1967), 152. On Nazi liturgical practice see Gamm, *Der braune Kult*; Klaus Vondung, *Magie und Manipulation* (Göttingen, 1971); Hans Werner von Meyenn, *Die politischen Feier* (Hamburg, 1938); and for a historical perspective George L. Mosse, *The Nationalization of the Masses* (New York, 1975).

29. See Meinecke, *German Catastrophe*, 71, 94; Rhodes, *Hitler Movement*, passim.

30. On humor see Hans-Jochen Gamm, *Der Flusterwitz im Dritten Reich* (Munich, 1963). Representative examples of the newer local-level studies are Edward N. Peterson, *The Limits of Hitler's Power* (Princeton, 1969); Heinz Boberach, *Meldungen aus dem Reich* (Neuwied, Berlin, 1965); Heyden, *Nationalsozialismus im Alltag*; and the documentary project of Martin Broszat, Elke Fröhlich, and Falk Wiesemann, eds., *Bayern in der NS-Zeit* (Munich, 1977-).

31. The statistics given are cited in William Sheridan Allen, "Objective and Subjective Inhibitants in the German Resistance to Hitler," in Franklin H. Littell and Herbert G. Locke, eds., *The German Church Struggle and the Holocaust* (Detroit, 1974), 122; and Ernst Eberhard, "Statistik der kirchlichen Lebensausserungen," in Joachim Beckmann, ed., *Kirchliches Jahrbuch für die Evangelische Kirche in Deutschland 1950* (Gütersloh, 1951), 423-468. Some vital statistics on church life, such as attendance at Eucharist, are incomplete, while no reliable figures are available for the war years. On the attitudes of church youth a suggestive study is Lawrence Walker, *Hitler Youth and Catholic Youth 1933-1936* (Washington, D. C., 1970).

32. Stern, *Hitler*, 96. Excellent brief interpretations can be found in William Sheridan Allen, "The Appeal of Fascism and the Problem of National Disintegration," in Henry A. Turner, ed., *Reappraisals of Fascism* (New York, 1975), 44-68; and Martin Broszat, "National Socialism, Its Social Basis and Psychological Impact," in E. J. Feuchtwanger, ed., *Upheaval and Continuity: A Century of German History* (Pittsburgh, 1974), 134-151.

33. Mosse, *Nationalization of the Masses*, 4. See also James J. Shee-han, "What is German History? Reflections on the Role of the *Nation* in German History and Historiography," *Journal of Modern History*, 53 (1981), 1-23; Helmuth Plessner, *Die verspätete Nation* (Stuttgart, 1959); Franz Herre, *Nation ohne Staat* (Cologne, 1967). The German-Jewish dynamic is treated in George L. Mosse, *Germans and Jews* (New York, 1970); and Fritz Stern, *Gold and Iron* (New York, 1977).

34. For recent interpretations see Helmuth Böhme, ed., *Probleme der Reichsgründungszeit 1848-1879* (Cologne, 1968); Theodore S. Hamerow, *The Social Foundations of German Unification 1858-1871*, 2 vols. (Princeton, 1969, 1972); Hans-Ulrich Wehler, *Das Deutsche Kaiserreich 1871-1915* (Göttingen, 1973); Gordon Craig, *Germany 1866-1945* (New York, 1978).

35. Useful discussions include George C. Iggers, *The German Conception of History* (Middletown, Conn., 1968); and Fritz Stern's essays in *The Failure of Illiberalism*, pb ed. (Chicago, 1975), especially 3-57.

36. Broszat, "National Socialism," 151. The range of interpretations can be sampled in M. Rainer Lepsius, *Extremer Nationalismus* (Stuttgart, 1966); Fritz Stern, *The Politics of Cultural Despair*, pb ed. (Garden City, N. Y., 1965); Heinrich August Winkler, *Mittelstand, Demokratie und Nationalsozialismus* (Cologne, 1972); Mack Walker, *German Home Towns* (Ithaca, N. Y., 1971); William Sheridan Allen, *The Nazi Seizure of Power* (Chicago, 1965); Milton Mayer, *They Thought They Were Free*, pb ed. (Chicago, 1966); Ralf Dahrendorf, *Society and Democracy in Germany* (Garden City, N. Y., 1967).

37. Mosse, *Nationalization of the Masses*, 19.

38. See the general sources listed in note 30. On the ambiguous attitudes towards Jews see Richard Gutteridge, *The German Evangelical Church and the Jews 1879-1950* (New York, 1976); on reactions to the euthanasia program Ernst C. Helmreich, *The German Churches under Hitler* (Detroit, 1979), 312-315; and Guenter Lewy, *The Catholic Church and Nazi Germany*, pb ed., (New York, 1965), 258-267.

39. For recent syntheses see Helmreich, *The German Churches under Hitler*; Klaus Scholder, *Die Kirchen im Dritten Reich* (Frankfurt a.M., 1977-); John S. Conway, *The Nazi Persecution of the Churches* (New York, 1969); Eberhard Bethge, *Dietrich Bonhoeffer*, tr. Eric Mosbacher et al. (New York, 1977).

40. For suggestive analyses see Lewy, *Catholic Church*; Gerhart Binder, *Irrtum und Widerstand* (Munich, 1968); Gordon C. Zahn, "Catholic Opposition to Hitler: The Perils of Ambiguity," *Journal of Church and State* 13 (1971), 413-426; and for a contrasting view Walter Adolph, *Hirtenamt und Hitlerdiktatur* (Berlin, 1975).

41. For an introduction to the vast literature see Georg Kretsch-mer and Bernhard Lohse, eds., *Ecclesia und Res Publica* (Göttingen, 1961); Horst Zillessen, ed., *Volk-Nation-Vaterland* (Gütersloh, 1970): Gerhard Kaiser, *Pietismus und Patriotismus im literarischen Deutsch-land* (Wiesbaden, 1961); Robert M. Bigler, *The Politics of German Protestantism* (Berkeley, 1972); Fritz Fischer, "Der deutsche Pro-testantismus und die Politik im 19. Jahrhundert," *Historische Zeit-schrift* 171 (1951), 473-518.

42. On the specific problems of the Weimar church see J. R. C. Wright, *"Above Parties:"* *The Political Attitudes of the German Pro-testant Church Leadership 1918-1933* (London, 1974); Karl-Wilhelm Dahm, *Pfarrer und Politik* (Cologne, 1965); Daniel Borg, *"Volks-kirche,* 'Christian State,' and the Weimar Republic," *Church History* 35 (1966), 326-336; and Jochen Jacke, *Kirche zwischen Monarchie und Republik* (Hamburg, 1976).

43. In addition to the general accounts cited in note 39, see Gün-ther van Norden, *Kirche in der Krise* (Düsseldorf, 1963); Hans Buch-heim, *Glaubenskrise im Dritten Reich* (Stuttgart, 1963); Kurt Meier, *Die Deutschen Christen* (Göttingen, 1964). For the important theo-logical background see Wolfgang Tilgner, *Volksnomostheologie und Schöpfungsglaube* (Göttingen, 1968).

44. Wurm to "Stadtpfarrer X," Feb. 11, 1944, in Gerhard Schäfer, ed., *Landesbischof D. Wurm und der nationalsozialistische Staat 1940-1945* (Stuttgart, 1968), 354-355. For his own perspective see Wurm, *Erinnerungen aus meinem Leben* (Stuttgart, 1953).

45. Schäfer, *Wurm und der nationalsozialistische Staat,* 165, 357-358.

46. The phrase was introduced by Alexander and Margarete Mit-scherlich, *The Inability to Mourn: Principles of Collective Behavior,* tr. Beverly R. Placzek (New York, 1975), especially 3-68. Suggestive studies of denazification include John Gimbel, *A German Community under American Occupation* (Stanford, 1961); and Lutz Niethammer, *Entnazifizierung in Bayern* (Frankfurt a.M., 1972).

47. See note 22.

48. Thus H. R. Trevor-Roper, *The Last Days of Hitler,* 3rd ed. (New York, 1965), 135. On the role of self-destructive impulses in the Hitler cult see Waite, *The Psychopathic God,* pp. 474-518; and McRandle, *Track of the Wolf,* 146-248.

CHAPTER V

STALIN: UTOPIAN OR ANTIUTOPIAN?
AN INDIRECT LOOK AT
THE CULT OF PERSONALITY

RICHARD STITES

It must seem presumptuous for a historian of nineteenth century Russia to turn his eye to that eminently twentieth cnetury phenomenon—Stalinism; particularly since it has been investigated by so many talented and competent scholarly minds in recent years.[1] But since I believe that, in a way, the emergence of Stalin marked the end of nineteenth century Russian social thinking and an emphatic repudiation of the radical intelligentsia of that century, Stalinism is—among other disturbing and disastrous things—an historical punctuation point. I have organized my discussion around the theme of utopianism in the Russian Revolution, the Stalinist response to this, and the emergence of the Stalin cult. In the first part of this essay, I shall describe briefly the main currents of utopian and experimental thought and behavior derived from Russia's past and worked out in the period 1917-1930 or so and how these were criticized and liquidated by Stalin and his associates. Then I will address the question of Stalin's own brand of "utopianism," its roots, and its implications. At the end, I shall related this to the God-like and father-like *persona* that Stalin and his image-makers projected in the 1930s.

During the post-Stalin thaw, Lev Kopelev recalls,[2] "rosy memories of the twenties" kept bobbing up. The first years of Soviet power were, of course, a time of national agony and political repression. But they were also "heroic years": a time when men and women tried spontaneously to refashion the human condition and remake the world. This was a time when anarchist intellectuals, peasants, and even brigands founded utopian communities which offered freedom and equality for their members and death for outsiders; when utopian fantasy writers constructed fictional societies where people remade and adorned the world with miracles of technical progress and social justice; a time when the militant godless, hoping to bring light and science to the dark masses enshrouded in superstitions, moved out among them with novel modes of communication—theatre, rituals, and ceremonies, surrogate holy days, and personal example— many of them devised with the syncretic sensitivity usually associated with the Christian missionaries.

It was also an age when some prophets believed that the time was imminent and the conditions appropriate for the appearance of a new proletarian morality, characterized by equality between comrades, the abolition of inequality in wages and housing and privilege, the dawn of a new form of communist Eros, the abolition of prostitution and the sexual exploitation of women, and the disappearance of alcoholism, gambling, and vice. For a minority at least, it was a time of "living together" in a socialist order where in student, women's, worker, peasant, and ethnic communes, people shared books, clothing, food, services and tasks as a living demonstration of what society could expect when, in the not too distant future, a network of socialist cities would envelop Russia and provide the psychological and architectural environment for the new communist man, woman and child.

Beginning at various points between 1928 and 1936, Stalin and his associates launched a war on the dreamers and on the dreams of the early revolutionary era. The list of campaigns and casualties in this war could fill many pages: the Anarchists were suppressed and liquidated; the economist and utopian writer Chayanov was purged; utopian science fiction writing ended; seekers of a new atheist religion and a new "proletarian morality" were curbed; the women's movement was abandoned; an orchestra without a conductor was abolished; egalitarianism was scorned and privilege was reinstated; communes in town and country were dissolved; and dreams of futuristic "socialist cities" were extinguished. The major prophets, dreamers and thinkers of the experimental twenties were dead, incarcerated, in exile or discredited.[3] The utopians had sought to uproot autocracy, elite culture, a reactionary church, primitive popular customs, gross inequality, the gulf between people and leaders, savage backwardness of thought, and egoistic individualism—all of this seen as the wicked heritage of "feudal" Russia, the Russia of the tsars. The Stalinists destroyed the utopians and *mutatis mutandis*, created a new autocracy, a new Soviet elite culture, a new dogma, a new political morality of power, a new inequality for a new elite, a new social and psychological gulf between rulers and ruled, a new savagery, and a new *sauve qui peut* individualism.

I

I would like to discuss a few of these utopian experiments and ideas born, in the words of David Joravsky, to help ease the "ambivalent torment" of the cultural revolution.[4] I have chosen utopian science fiction, equality, morality, and populism as those themes of the earlier cultural revolution that showed profound aspirations for a humane transformation of life. At the end of the 1920s, the well-known Bolshevik engineer Gleb Krzhizhanovsky, at a jamboree of Communist Pioneers, compared the coming five-year plan to the fantasies of Jules Verne, grander in scope than even science fiction, but containing the familiar elements: advanced technology, travel and exploration, and heroes of science.[5]

In fact, for about ten years (1920-1930) Revolutionary science fiction, grounded in Western and pre-revolutionary Russian literature, had been offering fantastic pictures of the future, colored by utopian visions. Although some of these novels were anti-capitalist dystopias along the lines of Jack London's *Iron Heel*, most were communist utopian science fantasies, replete with visions of communal life, world cities, high technology, full equality, optimum efficiency—and even prolonged life. In the spirit of 19th century social daydreaming, revolutionary science fiction linked the Promethean surge for technical wizardry and prosperity with demands for social justice. But Yury Larri's *Happy Land* (1930) was the last utopian science fiction novel published until 1954. The whole genre came under attack in the 1930s and the science fiction of the Stalin years changed its emphasis from the social to the scientific, from the grandiose to the detailed, and from the distant to the immediate future.[6] Unless linked to current plans, science fiction had no place in Soviet daydreaming. The Stalinists did not like visions of perfect societies which might then be contrasted to the harshness of Soviet life; and they may have feared the anti-capitalist and anti-exploitative genre as well for the comparisons it might have evoked with Soviet style authoritarianism and exploitation.

One of the major utopian themes of Soviet science fiction, and of the Russian Revolution itself, was equality. By this, its proponents—workers as well as intellectuals—meant not simply political or juridical equaltiy, but some attempt to re-distribute the wealth of the old order and to keep wages, housing, amenities and interpersonal relations on a more or less egalitarian level as far as possible. Communes sprung up in town and country offering distribution of food according to need or on an equal basis. High officials were expected to live modestly and a vast levelling moment invaded housing and other

areas of everyday life. Workers demanded equal wage scales in many
industries. An orchestra without a conductor was formed in Moscow
to celebrate the musicians' equal sharing of labor and performances.[7]
All of this was reversed by Stalin who, in 1934, attacked *uravnilovka*
(Stalin's contemptuous slang word for levelling) as "the petty bourgeois views of our left-wing scatterbrains." Beginning in the early
1930s, academic degrees, terms such as meritorious artist, Hero of
the Soviet Union, and military ranks of the old style were restored
or introduced. All these titles had concrete privileges and economic
rewards attached to them. The wage differential expanded widely.
Housing was distributed according to income and occupation, with
workers crowded into hovels and the elite of Moscow—Foreign Commissariat officials, Metro managers, ballerinas, academicians, police
bosses and Party leaders—occupied the new Stalinist buildings and
clamored for "beautiful" edifices. The new construction complex
at Magnitogorsk had five different dining rooms catering to five different levels of employees and technicians. Student communards
got the anti-egalitarian message very quickly, dissolved their communes and exalted differential piece wages. Recent research has
shown that even labor *artels* (cooperatives), on arrival at a factory or
construction site, were broken up to eliminate feelings of equality
and solidarity.[8]

Another feature of Stalin's counter-revolution in culture was the
abandonment of efforts to create a new proletarian morality. The
story of the "sexual revolution" and its moral overtones has been
told many times before. Its main prophet, Alexandra Kollontai, attempted to fight against the old "bourgeois" double-standard of hypo-
crisy and inequality and against the vulgar "communist" notions of
sex, undadorned by emotions, by advancing her "new morality" of
comradeship, equality, work, collectivism, communal living and
childcare. It was thoroughly repudiated—though never taken seriously or understood—and replaced by the reconstruction of the traditional family ideal, with its glorification of stability, production and
reproduction.[9] The family mystique, as we shall see, was central to
Stalin's anthropology. A less well-known phenomenon was the Stalinist repudiation of efforts to inculcate a morality of "everyday life"
among young communist cadres. Throughout the 1920s, the Komsomol had launched steady campaigns against the "old morality"—
drinking, smoking, womanizing (or its opposite), sloppy work habits,
foppishness, prettiness, and philistine materialism. Against these vices
were opposed a code of behavior that stressed efficiency, hard work,

an almost puritan style of life, sobriety, and asceticism. Around 1928-30, with the five-year plan and the consolidation of Stalin's power, the emphasis in young communist training shifted from puritanism to a work ethic based upon material incentives, downplaying the moralizing of the previous period. Private behavior and the leisure sector of life were made a secondary issue. One of Stalin's chief henchmen, Lazar Kaganovich, ridiculed prophets of a "new communist morality" such as Bukharin, for reducing the work of the Komsomol to "a struggle against smoking."[10]

A little studied feature of the revolutionary idealism of the 1920s was "post-revolutionary populism"—a continuation of the classical *narodnichestvo* of the 19th century in the context of Soviet power. Its main ingredients were: a moral debt of the city to the countryside; the *Smychka*, or union of workers and peasants based on mutual respect; bringing light and culture to "the people," that is, to the villages; and a desire to help ease the transition of the rural-rooted worker into an advanced and efficient worker by patient training and consciousness-raising. By the late twenties, the attitude of the leadership was, in the words of an emigré observer, "a fist in the face of the countryside." Peaceful and patient work by urban elements in the villages gave way to an "all Russian pogrom" against the peasants. Proletarian, Komsomol and Party collectivizers saw themselves as beleaguered heroes fighting for survival in enemy territory, using slogans and metaphors against the mass of peasants that old peasants had once used against the Tsarist authorities! In spite of rhetoric about fighting only "kulaks and their allies," urban workers and youth drafted for collectivization clearly looked upon the rural order and its dwellers with contempt instead of fraternal sympathy. *Smychka* was dead and the regime abandoned the populist-like sensibilities of the twenties in favor of the harshest brand of administrative transformation, driving peasants into collectives and into industrial work with a mimimum of preparation. The historical figure Pugachev, leader of the Cossak-peasant upheaval of the eighteenth century, who had been given unqualified praise for his elemental wrath against the towns and the gentry of bygone days, was in 1931 made the occasion for a warning against those "marxists" who were really populsts in disguise and dreamed of a peasant movement without the leadership of the proletariat.[11]

II

The great experiment of the 1920s was compounded mostly of indigenous popular-religious utopianism of Russian peasants, rebels, sectarians on the one hand, and the Western-inspired socialist utopianism of 19th century intellectuals on the other. Though both contained occasional examples of elitism, impatience with the masses, power hunger, and authoritariansim, they were for the most part characterized by spontaneity, belief in the common people, a rough-and-ready egalitarianism, and the centrality of humane interpersonal morality—whether grounded in a mystical Orthodox Christianity or in a secular atheism. The experiments of the revolutionary years and the 1920s, though sometimes induced by pragmatic concerns, were heir to this dual tradition. These dreams and experiments were eclectic and complicated, to be sure; but in their main outlines and driving force, they were examples of humane utopianism. Stalin's repudiation of this is a negative way of defining Stalin's outlook on human relations in revolution.

And yet Stalin too was a utopian. The utopian tradition in Russian history was made up of three major currents: religious-popular, socialist, and administrative. The last was as much a feature of Russian history as the other two. Administrative utopianism—largely the business of Emperors, generals, and bureaucrats—made a cult of parade-ground symmetries, geometric barracks life, and the "well-ordered police state." It was rooted in the rigid attitude to social order expressed in *Tiaglo* and collective responsibility, the practice of minutely detailed government regulations, and in the whole state tradition. It was, psychologically, the answer to a sprawling, huge and chaotic land empire. The "Gatchina" School" of Russian Emperors—Paul, Alexander I, Nicholas I—made a fetish of ceremonial parades, meticulous order, and machinelike precision. Alexander I was greatly impressed by the order, neatness, elegance, and symmetry of his friend Arakcheev's estate and hoped to remodel Russia on it. He expressed a reforming zeal as well as a compulsion to regimentation when he founded the notorious military colonies in 1810, with their forced evictions, barrack-like rows of houses, iron rules of order, radical reforms, modernized military life, and their stonefaced "dictator," General Arakcheev. His successor, Nicholas I, abandoned the colonies but not their underlying "dream of a beautiful autocracy," a dream of status, devotion, service, honor, "silence," duty, obedience, reverence for leaders, symmetry, and hierarchy.[12]

The authoritarian compulsion to manage and direct, to coerce and dragoon was very much in evidence in pre-Stalinist Bolshevism. But the Bolsheviks of the twenties, including Lenin, allowed their visceral drive for order and power to be curbed by the countervailing forces of humane utopianism and peasant apathy. They often smiled ironically at the former and grumbled at the latter; but they did not crush either. In Stalin's time, and at his own behest, administrative utopia ascended majestically and forcefully to the top and became the ruling vision of the Stalinist managers; and the human engineers replaced the humane designers. The soaring Russian revolutionary imagination was fettered and all energies were deflected into economic construction and political repression.

Utopianism as such was far from dead. It blossomed forth in frenetic form during the first of the massive five-year plans; but it was administrative utopia—with heavy emphasis on change from above, order, hierarchy, minute planning and regulation, control of lives, and movement of people. As in the Military Colonies of the 1810s and 1820s, the accompanying reforms and ameliorations were heavily outweighed by the onerous burdens which the Russian and Soviet people had to bear for the next two decades or more.

Allow me to be more concrete about this notion. At the risk of being accused of extreme reductionism, I shall call its main psychological elements "coldness" and "harshness"—the one relating to rationalism of productive life, the other to the military ethos of combat. The "coldness" of Stalinist economic utopianism was the rejection of warmblooded persuasion, idealism, and spontaneity. It appears again and again among Bolshevik leaders long before Stalin's ascent to power, as in the educationist O. Yu. Schmidt's scheme for extreme factory-like production of specialized workers,[13] in Dzerzhinsky's belief that an efficient human organizational machine (such as the Cheka) could be used to solve any kind of social problem (such as that of abandoned children),[14] and in Lenin's authoritarian views on one-man management. Those who, like the Workers' Opposition faction, believed that the leap to socialism and prosperity ought to be calibrated by the workers themselves were curbed in the 1920s and their remnant was destroyed by Stalin in the mid-1930s.[15] Stalin's economic tsars—both those who perished (Ordzhonikidze) and those who flourished (Kaganovich)—wanted rapid and visible results, and were not concerned about the all-sided development of workers and other toiling members of Soviet society. The Faustian-Promethean strain in the revolutionary dream, common in backward societies,

conquered over the once prominent strain of social justice and equality. Stalin's achievement was to subtract the latter element of the
tradition from his revolution-from-above and exalt the former. Stalin
was the twentieth-century administrative utopian, not a dreamer,
but a vendor of nightmare. In contrasting the classical utopians of
the 19th century with the "new utopians"—systems engineers and
computer scientists—a contemporary observer warns that in seeking
man's "ascendance over nature" the latter augment the danger of
"extending the control of man over man."[16]

There is nothing inherently vindictive or violent about the economic utopianism of the Stalin era or the "systems" utopianism of
the computer age: it is cold, not necessarily harsh. But Stalinism
possessed another ingredient: military force and anger.

> War Communism [writes Robert Tucker] had militarized
> the revolutionary political culture of the Bolshevik move-
> ment. The heritage of that formative time in the Soviet
> culture's history was martial zeal, revolutionary voluntarism
> and élan, readiness to resort to coercion, rule by administra-
> tive fiat (administrirovianie), centralized administration,
> summary justice, and no small dose of that Communist arro-
> gance (komchanstvo) that Lenin later inveighed against.[17]

Stalin never inveighed against it, except in a purely hypocritical and
mendaciously tactical way (the "dizziness from success" statement).
The military culture was his natural milieu, as can be seen by the
psychological ease with which he commanded his commanders. It
was abundantly clear that Stalin never felt self-conscious in front of
his generals. In fact, he berated an unnamed general officer for "im-
modesty, unjustified conceit, and megalomania"![18] Much has been
written on the social hatred of 1917 which helped blow away an ancient order; but the 1930s was a time of even greater social hatred
and antagonism—especially between country and city, between toilers
and the technical intelligentsia. George Steiner has suggested a relationship between the terror of the 1930s and "the hatred which reality
feels toward failed utopia."[19] Perhaps. In any case, there is no doubt
that in the triple revolution of industrialization, collectivization, and
purge, a military language and a martial psychology was in the ascendant. "States are not created by generous heroism and passion," Antonio
Gramsci had written some years earlier. "The essential qualities are
discipline, perserverance, coherence, and scorn for irresponsibility."[20]

Stalin's mobilization made, in Merle Fainsod's words, "the Soviet
population both machine-minded and war-minded."[21] If one compares this achievement (ignoring the human costs) with the Russia of

1914, one will at least be tempted to agree that Stalin had accomplished what anyone in 1914 would have called "utopian." The philosopher Jean Koch, writing in 1946, attempted to classify collective utopian experience as popular, social, and national or military. As religious-communist mystique declined, in the cases cited, it was replaced by a "national mystique"—militarization, "absolute authoritarian communism," and mindless dehumanization, as in modern wartime economies and politics after the recession of an initial patriotic euphoria.[22] Roger Pethybridge's interesting study of the social bases of Stalinism speaks of a "second utopia which began in 1929, an authoritarian utopia, opposed to the utopia of the 1920s and the Civil War period," though he wrongly traces the roots of the latter almost exclusively to European socialist thought.[23] The fact that Stalin's administrative utopia was shot through with contradictions, corruption, inefficiency, and even sloth as had been the 19th century Military Colonies as well) does not detract from the vision and the impulse from which Stalin and his associates operated. Stalin's USSR never came close to resembling the machine-like society of Zamyatin's anti-utopian novel *We* (1920).[24] The horror was in the fact that it tried to build a facade resembling Zamyatin's "United State" behind which lay a morass of mismanagement and an ocean of misery.

Stalin's anti-utopianism was a function of his own brand of utopianism of political, personal, economic, and military power. It was reinforced by the perceived economic imperatives of the regime and its economic managers who found much of the experiment of the 1920s to be trivial and wasteful of time and energy. Both were rooted in Bolshevism's long-standing hostility to spontaneity and uncertainty. But there was also a social basis of the new Stalinist order, a topic that has been much less documented than other matters. Much of the old intelligentsia was slaughtered in the purges; workers of semi-rural origins moved rapidly upward into positions of prominence in the economy and administration—the so-called *vydvizhentsy*; and a huge demographic shift accompanying rapid industrialization and collectivization brought about the "ruralization" of many Soviet cities.[25] It may well be that the tastes, values, ethos, thought habits—in short, the *mentalité sociale*—of the lower and lower-middle classes who vaulted into positions of power and influence were profoundly opposed to the fantasies, the raucous debates, and the extravagant dreams of those intellectuals who had launched their schemes in the midst of a revolutionary maelstrom. The still uncultivated masses may have genuinely preferred the familiar, the philistine, the vulgar,

the safe, the old in culture and way-of-life to the unknown, the experimental, the exalted, the periolous, the risky, the novel. The combination of political authoritarianism, revolutionary industrialization,
social makeup, and xenophobic suspicion of Western ideas[26] was
more than enough to stamp out the fantasies and redirect the energies
of those men and women of the earlier revolutionary years who had
genuinely thought it possible to realize the great social daydreams of
the 19th century. In the place of these, the Stalinist utopians constructed their own fantasy world.

Revolutions can be anti-moderninzing as well as moderninzing.
"Revolution," said Engels, "is the most authoritarian thing imagin-
able."[27] And the authority can be used to retard as well as advance.
It used to be a cliché to contrast Nazi Germany and Stalinist Russia
by saying that the former used a mixture of traditionalist and revolutionary rhetroic to adorn an antimodern revolution whereas Soviet
Russia used progressive rhetoric to accompany its purely modernizing
revolution. In fact the Russian Revolution—particularly in its Stalinist
phase—was very much anti-modern in several senses: the authoritarian
edifice blocked the growth of modern political forms begun in 1906;
the surfacing of the conservative lower classes thwarted some of the
modern visions of the intelligentsia; the re-isolation from the West
choked off sources of "modernist" culture and inspiration; and the
strident howling of a new secular dogma that replaced the crumbling
religion drowned out the voices of originality. Stalin's utopia of the
1930s, with all its military and industrial achievement, its welfare
infrastructure, and its mass education, was in part an archaic throwback to pre-modern forms and myth. And at the center of this archaic
myth system was the cult of Stalin.

III

Harvey Cox, in *The Feast of Fools*, wrote that "there is an unnecessary gap in today's world between the world-changers and the life-
celebrators." The "world-changers" he refers to are the people we
are trying to analyze in this volume—dictators, power-mongers, political leaders of larger-than-life dimensions, whether of left, or right,
or of indeterminate ideological provenance. The "life-celebrators" are
the visionaries of history, whose celebration transcends mere play
since it invokes the universe, the Gods, the past, and the race.[28] Stalin
closed this gap in his political and magical *persona*. This man who
may have been responsible for more deaths than any other single

leader in history nevertheless possessed the formal attributes of a "life-celebrator" as well as of a "world-changer." Personally, of course, Stalin was not a celebrator. There is no evidence of a *joie de vivre*, a warmblooded sensibility to nature and his fellow humans, of spontaneous humor, of wit, of love of the beautiful. He was a man who enjoyed power and savored vengeance, a man of low tastes and coarse habits, especially in the company of his cronies. Beneath the grace and charm that he knew how to assume, lay a personality trapped in fear and loathing of most human beings, a loathing whose darkness was lighted only on occasion in his relations with family, friends, and such "adopted children" as Stakhanovites, aviation heroes, and sports figures.[29] But he pretended to be a "life-celebrator." He knew the power of myth and magic and sensed that his utopia could never be accepted unless he invested himself with an image of colossal proportions—so that he might appear to the Soviet people as a father, a hero, a king, and a God.

In an extremely intelligent and learned anthropological analysis of high culture—particularly the novel—in the Stalinist thirties, Katerina Clark has isolated a central feature of that culture: the myth of the "Great Family." Hers is a rich and complex argument with many subsidiary themes and ramifications, but its main thrust is the image of Stalin as The Father in a society of fathers and sons (women have long been shunted to the side).[30] This is confirmed by all the sources I have read. One of them, a study of national culture of the Soviet minorities, shows how the various portraits of Stalin, executed by painters from the national minorities, change their facial features to resemble the ethnic group in question—a device also used in Lenin iconography.[31] Stalin was the father of all Soviet peoples. A popular book written by a Soviet aviator of the time, Belyakov's *From Moscow to America via the North Pole* (1938) was designated as a moral primer for young children and early adolescents. The picture of Stalin which emerges in the scenes where the pilots are entertained by the leader is one of a man full of warm love for human life, of robust organism (built up through revolutionary struggle), of paternal concern for his airmen, of deep suspicion of specialists and scientists who did not perform miracles, of admiration for boldness tempered by study and expertise (*umen'e*).[32] The word "father" (*otets*, not the familiar *papa*, *batyushka*) was sometimes used as an epithet for Stalin, an epithet he modestly accepted, insisting only that his own "father" and teacher had been Lenin. Though he never assumed a royal or imperial designation, the term *Vozhd* ("leader," equivalent to *Duce*, *Fuehrer*,

Caudillo, Conducatore, Poglavnik, etc.) served well enough. After 1934, Kopelev tells us in his memoirs, the word which had been used for local party bosses became Stalin's alone.[33] In tsarist times, peasants found it difficult to believe that the *Tsar-Batyushka* could be responsible for all their woes,[34] just as in 1905 St. Petersburg workers could not believe that the Father of the Russian People would allow troops to fire on their peaceful demonstration. During the Stalin terror, when communists often went to their deaths shouting "Long live Stalin!", this kind of mythologizing about Stalin's benevolence and fatherly wisdom was actually called "Gaponovism".[35]

When workers' spontaneity and egalitarian euphoria had been repudiated in the midst of the First five-year plan, a cult of hero figures arose, in literature, in industry, and at the pinnacle of politics. Stalin personally headed a commission on the writing of new Soviet history textbooks in 1936; he blamed current books for being too "sociological" and for ignoring the great figures and personalities of the past.[36] How this decision was worked into wartime national-historical propaganda is well known. Popular biographies of Stalin himself portrayed him as a historical hero. A 1939 work, recommended for "adolescents," described his studiousness, early leadership qualities, daring, loyalty to Lenin, and innate modesty. His story resembles both the fairy tale and the heroic adventure of the cheap popular press in the pre-war period, replete with arrests, escapes, attempts on Stalin's life, heroic deeds—at Tsaritsyn especially—and so on.[37] Carefully manufactured folk epics (*byliny*) frankly described Stalin as a *bogatyr*, a chivalric knight of the Revolution.[38]

Since Stalin and his fellow purgers invoked demonology to describe enemies, real or imagined, it was only fitting that Stalin himself become God.

> He took unto himself the tears of the ages,
> He took unto himself the woe of the ages,
> He took unto himself the joy of the ages,
> He took unto himself the wisdom of the ages,
> He took unto himself the strength of the ages,
> He burst into the world like morning,
> And the World calls him Stalin![39]

This Kazakh verse of 1936 by the singer Bek could be matched by dozens of similar examples of folk-worship of the God-man. A cradle song by the bard Djambul—the most famous of all Stalin's poetic worshippers—unveils the God-like omniscience and omnipotence of the great Stalin:

Go to sleep my Kazakh babe;
Knowing hands will care for you.
Stalin looks from out his window—
And keeps our broad land within his view.[40]

Russian Soviet "folk epics" and those in other Soviet languages bathed
the dictator in images of divine sunlight (Joseph-Bright was a conventional epithet for him), saintliness, and holiness; and his immortality
was implied by such phrases as "Stalin's Glory Will Be Forever"[41] All
of this in a land where atheism was the official state belief and
many churches had been closed and traditional religions persecuted.

   The Orthodox Church never brought itself to deifying Stalin, but
in a remarkable letter published early in World War II (November,
1942), the Metropolitan of Moscow and acting Patriarch, Sergius,
greeted Stalin on the twenty-fifth anniversary of the Bolshevik Revolution in the name of the clergy and the community of Orthodox
believers in Russia as "the divinely anointed leader of our armed and
cultural forces leading us to victory over the barbarian invasion."[42]
Cults of the machine, of the people, even of the deceased prophet
Lenin had not succeeded in becoming the emotional and religious
cement of the new Soviet order: the Cult of the living Stalin—God,
man, prince, hero, father—attempted to do so. In erecting his cult,
Stalin did invoke the universe, the Gods, the past, and the race in
one of the most successful myths of the twentieth century.

   By the mid-1930s, "life had become happier" and there was no
longer any need for utopian science fantasies. Stalin was now God,
and the "god-builders" who hoped for a religion of socialism were
gone. The Father's morality and the great family ethos were the un-
official law of the land—and not "proletarian morality." Exaltation
of leader and authority meant the liquidation of egalitarianism and
its teachers. "The best and most precious thing to us on earth," said
a 1937 Karelian oral tale, "is the word of Comrade Stalin,"[43] The
repudiation of the Old Utopias and the celebration of the new—found
expression in the rituals and holiday observances of High Stalinism.
On November 6-8, 1935, Stakhanovite shock workers of proletarian
and poor-peasant background came to gaze in wonder at the magical
world that their "Father" had created. On Red Square the hero
Voroshilov cavorted on horseback and harangued the assembled
troops. The sight of massed weapons, hundreds of warplanes over-
head, and mammoth crowds filled Stakhanov himself with pride and
awe. Hundreds of icons of Stalin were held aloft by the masses of
demonstrators. And after the ceremonies, the worker-heroes were

treated to the brilliance of old Russian culture and a tour of the Kremlin with its palaces and cathedrals, its treasure-laden armory, and those twin monuments to old Russia's pathetic aspiration to strength and power: the Tsar-Cannon which had never fired a shot; the Tsar-Bell which had broken when first struck. In the courtyard, the delegation of workers chanced upon Stalin who introduced himself to an aged woman worker and described himself as "the most ordinary man." The old Russian woman revered him as a holy person. And so did they.[44]

In the concluding chapter of an exceptionally learned and thought-provoking study of Russian myth and its relation to power and people, Michael Cherniavsky had this to say:

> Myths, rather than approximating reality, tend to be in direct contradiction to it. And Russian reality was 'unholy' enough to have produced the 'holiest' myths of them all. The greater the power of the government, the more extreme was the myth required to justify it and excuse submission to it; the greater the misery of the Russian people, the more extreme was the eschatological jump the myth had to provide so as to justify the misery and transcend it.[45]

These words, describing a central element of the Russian past, may serve—without further comment—as a conclusion also to this brief excursion into the repulsive and ever-fascinating world of Stalinism.

NOTES

1. R. Tucker, ed. *Stalinism*. New York: Norton, 1977, contains the best of the recent scholarship.

2. Lev Kopelev, *Education of a True Believer*. New York: Harper, 1978, ix.

3. On the fate of some of these trends, not discussed in this paper, see: Paul Avrich, *The Russian Anarchists*. Princeton, N.J.: Princeton University Press, 1967; Naum Jasny, *Soviet Economists of the Twenties*. Cambridge: Cambridge University Press, 1972; on Chayanov; and S. F. Starr, "Visionary Town Planning During the Cultural Revolution," in Sheila Fitzpatrick, ed., *Cultural Evolution in Russia 1928-1931*, Bloomington, Indiana University Press, 1978, 207-240.

4. David Joravsky, "The Origin of the Fortress Mentality," in A. Gleason et al., eds., *The Origins of Soviet Culture* (in preparation).

5. *Pioner* 20 (October 1929), 7-9.

6. Darko Suvin, "The Utopian Tradition of Russian Science Fiction." *Modern Language Review* 66 (1971), 139-159; Richard Stites, "Utopia and Experiment in the Russian Revolution," Kennan Institute of Advanced Russian Studies Occasional Paper, 1981; R. Nudelman, "Fantastika, rozhdennaya revolyutsiei," in *Fantastika* 1966, vyp. 3 (Moscow, 1966), 330-369.

7. On various strands of egalitarianism in the Russian Revolution, see: Robert Wesson, *Soviet Communes*, New Brunswick, N. J.: Rutgers University Press, 1963; Klaus Mehnert, *Youth in Soviet Russia*, New York: Harcourt, 1933; and "Music and Revolution," unpublished paper by Richard Stites (on the orchestra without a conductor, among other things).

8. David Dallin, "The Return to Inequality," in Robert V. Daniels, ed., *The Stalin Revolution*, New York: Heath, 1972; 2nd ed., 109-117; Nicholas Timasheff, *The Great Retreat*, New York: Dutton, 1946, 319, passim. E. D. Simon et al., *Moscow in the Making*. London, 1937, 143-172; A. Kopp, *Changer la vie—changer la ville*. Paris, 1975, 47; Peter Juviler, *Revolutionary Law and Order*, New York: Free Press, 1976, 41; Mehnert, *Youth*, 66, 76, 249-257. The information about the break-up of labor *artel*s was kindly conveyed to me by Professor Lewis Siegelbaum.

9. For various recent discussions: Gail Lapidus, *Women in Soviet Society*, Berkeley, Calif.: Univ. of California Press, 1977; D. Atkinson, et al., *Women in Russia*, Stanford, Calif.: Stanford University Press, 1977; Barbara Clements, *Bolshevik Feminist*, Bloomington, Indiana University Press, 1979; Beatrice Farnsworth, *Aleksandra Kollontai*, Stanford, Calif.: Stanford University Press, 1980; and Richard Stites, *The Women's Liberation Movement in Russia*, Princeton: Princeton University Press, 1976.

10. P. Gooderham, "The Komsomol and Worker Youth," unpublished paper presented at the Conference on the Social History of St. Petersburg-Leningrad, University of Essex, May, 1981. Cited with permission of the author.

11. The literature on collectivization is large. The best introduction to the subject is Moshe Lewin, *Russian Peasants and Soviet Power*, New York: Norton, 1975. For examples cited here see; *Vestnik, Krestyanskoi Rossii* (Prague) 1 (13), June 1928, 7, 18, 23; *Pozyvnye Istorii*, vyp. I (Moscow, 1969), 209-235; *Pugachevshchina*, 3 vols. (Moscow, 1926-1931) (compare vol. I of 1926 with viii of vol. III of 1931).

12. Richard Pipes, "The Russian Military Colonies, 1810-1831," *Journal of Modern History* (September 1951), 205-219; W. Bruce Lincoln, *Nicholas I*, Bloomington: Indiana University Press, 1979, 27, 52, 69; and Sidney Monas, *The Third Section* (Cambridge, Mass.: Harvard University Press, 1970, 231.

13. James McClelland, "The Heroic and the Utopian," in Gleason, *Origins*.

14. Sheila Fitzpatrick, *The Commissariat of Enlightenment* (Cambridge: Cambridge University Press, 1970), 231.

15. For a convenient summary of this, see R. V. Daniels, *The Conscience of the Revolution*, New York: Simon and Schuster, 1969, chaps. 5-6.

16. Robert Boguslaw, *The New Utopians: A Study of Systems Design and Social Change*, Englewood Cliffs, N.J.: Prentice-Hall, 1965, 1-2, 203-204. For earlier links between Bolshevism and systems analysis, see Ilmari Susiluoto, *The Origins and Development of Systems Thinking in the Soviet Union: Political and Philosophical Controversies from Bogdanov and Bukharin to Present-Day Evaluations* Helsinki: Suomalainen Tiedeakatemia, 1982, Department of Government, University of Helsinki, 1981.

17. Tucker, "Stalinism as Revolution from Above," *Stalinism*, 91-92.

18. Albert Seaton, *Stalin as Military Commander*, New York: Praeger, 1976, 264.

19. George Steiner, *In Bluebeard's Castle*, New Haven: Yale University Press, 1971, 46.

20. Quoted in John Cammett, *Antonio Gramsci and the Origins of Italian Communism*, Stanford, Calif.: Stanford University Press, 1967, 72.

21. Merle Fainsod, *How Russia is Ruled*, Cambridge, Mass.: Harvard University Press, 1953, 404.

22. Jean-Paul Koch, *Le Collectivisme devant l'experience*, Paris, 1948. 109-113, 226 passim.

23. Roger Pethybridge, *The Social Prelude to Stalinism*, London, 1974, 22-67, 104, 117, 241.

24. Evgenyi Zamyatin, *We* (1920), New York: Dutton, 1924, reprint 1952.

25. For various approaches to this complex development, see: Lewin's contributions to Fitzpatrick, *Cultural Revolution*, and to Tucker, *Stalinism*; Fitzpatrick, *Education and Social Mobility in the Soviet Union, 1921-1934*, Cambridge: Cambridge University Press, 1979; and Pipes, *Russia*, passim.

26. On this point see Robert Williams, "The Nationalization of Early Soviet Culture," in Richard Stites, ed., "NEP: Society, Culture, and Politics," special issue of *Russian History*, IX/2 (Summer, 1982).

27. Quoted in Avrich, *Kronstadt, 1921*, Princeton: Princeton University Press, 1970, 230.

28. Harvey Cox, *Feast of Fools*, Cambridge, Mass.: Harvard University Press, 1969, viii, 10, passim.

29. On Stalin's illuminating relationship to Soviet aviators, see two excellent recent treatments: Katerina Clark, *The Soviet Novel: History as Ritual*, Chicago: University of Chicago Press, 1980, 224-229; and Kendall Bailes, *Technology and Society under Lenin and Stalin*, Princeton, N.J.: Princeton University Press, 1978, 381-406.

30. Clark, *Soviet Novel*, 114-135. See also her fascinating contributions to Fitzpatrick, *Cultural Revolution* and to Tucker, *Stalinism*.

31. *Tvorchestvo Narodov USSR*, ed. A. M. Gorky et al. Moscow, 1938, illustrations. For the Leninist origins of this practice, see Nina Tumarkin, *Lenin Lives!*, Cambridge, Mass.: Harvard University Press, 1983.

32. A. Belyakov, *Iz Moskvy v Ameriku cherez Severnyi Polyus*, Moscow: 1938, 14-15.

33. Kopelev, *Education*, 244.

34. On this see: Michael Cherniavsky, *Tsar and People*, 2nd ed., New York: Random House, 1969; Avrich, *Russian Rebels, 1600-1800*, New York: Norton, 1972; and Daniel Field, *Rebels in the Name of the Tsar*, Boston: Houghton Mifflin, 1976.

35. Roy Medvedev, *Let History Judge*, New York: Vintage, 1973, 363; Nadzheda Mandelstam, *Hope Against Hope*, Harmondsworth: Penguin, 1975, 263.

36. Timasheff, *Great Retreat*, 173.

37. *Istoriko-Revolyustionnyi Kalendar, 1939*, ed. A. V. Shestakov (Moscow, 1939), 631-649.

38. Clark, *Soviet Novel*, 148-152. On the recurrent hero element in Stalin's biography, see Tucker, *Stalin as Revolutionary 1879-1929*, New York: Norton, 1973, especially chapters 3-4, 6, 12-13.

39. *Tvorchestvo*, 115.

40. Dzhambul, *Kolybelnaya Pesnya*, Moscow, 1938.

41. *Tvorchestvo*, 124.

42. *New York Times*, November 10, 1942.

43. *Tvorchestvo*, 122.

44. Alexei Stakhanov, *Rasskazy o Moei Zhizhni*, Moscow, 1937, 44-47.

45. Cherniavsky, *Tsar and His People*, 229. See also the important work by Tucker, "The Rise of Stalin's Personality Cult," *American Historical Review*, 84/2 (April 1979), 347-366.

CHAPTER VI

JEAN-BEDEL BOKASSA:
NEO-NAPOLEON OR
TRADITIONAL AFRICAN RULER?

THOMAS E. O'TOOLE

Introduction

Caveat lector! This is truly an "essay" in the sense of something that is tentative, partial, and personal. It questions both the rather widespread view that regimes like that of the former Emperor Jean-Bedel Bokassa of the Central African Empire are simply manifestations of individual aberrations or that they represent a personal dictatorship type.[1] Obviously such an essay requires comparison with others elsewhere in the world, both today and in other periods of history. Yet, even as a case study of a single, rather unique country, it ought to at least raise some important questions.

Located in the heartland of the African continent, Central Africa has known many marauders. Arabic speaking raiders from the north hunted slaves there from the 17th- until the 20th century. Then, beginning in 1877, European explorers, military columns, administrators, and agents of concessionary companies moved gradually into the area despite local resistance to their advance. The impact of slave raids had been great and under French colonial rule the systematic destruction of the indigenous cultures—their economies, communities, and traditions continued. In 1899 France divided the territory into twenty concessions, all but two of them going to private companies. All commercial transport at the time moved either by foot over long routes through Chad or by boat following equally tedious river routes, so the remaining two concessions were reserved by the colonial government for recruitment—impressment, actually—of the much needed "porters" and boatmen.

As in the Belgian Congo, the company agents moved in with a ruthless disregard of the local peoples. Missionaries reported famines in villages where all the able-bodied men had been dragged off to gather rubber under the "supervision" of guards and sharpshooters, leaving subsistence food crops untended at home. Besides rubber, the production of which declined after the 1920s, cotton and coffee were soon cultivated commercially by European companies. By the 1930s, gold and diamonds were also being produced.

Politically, the territory, called Ubangui-Shari in the colonial period, moved to representation in the French Assembly as a part of France, then to autonomy within the French community (1958) and finally to independence (1960). Through each of these changes in political status, however, dependence on France never diminished. Occasionally, events in France have, in turn, been influenced by events in this rather undistinguished African nation. For instance, it is quite likely that the continued presence of French troops to maintain David Dacko in power in the Central African Republic played at least a minor role in giving France a socialist president in May, 1981. Yet, whatever one's opinion of French interference in the internal affairs of Central Africa, it would seem highly unlikely that the French had deliberately chosen Colonel Jean-Bedel Bokassa in December, 1965 to lead their client regime.

It is true that, for better or worse, French colonial policy generally sought to produce some few people who identified emotionally with France and French culture and, in addition, received material benefits from this French connection. It is also true that Bokassa, like the first major post-colonial Central African leader, Barthelemy Boganda, and his successor David Dacko, was a member of such an essentially bi-cultural minority. Bokassa was raised, like Boganda, in Catholic missions and had risen through the colonial forces into that relatively privileged group, who having fought bravely for France, could be considered as assimilated. Hence one could pose the "outrageous hypothesis"[2] that Bokassa, if not a political creation of the French, was, at least, a result of France's cultural hegemony which still persists over much of former French West and Equatorial Africa.

Those whose Gallic sensitivities are injured by such an audacious view might posit an extremely different perspective. Rather than seeing the heavy hand of French cultural imperialism in Bokassa's megalomaniacal regime, one could posit the equally "outrageous hypothesis" that Bokassa was simply a normal and natural persistence of traditional African patterns, patterns which France's best attempts have not been successful in stamping out.

This essay seeks to examine these two "outrageous hypotheses" with the aim of somehow going beyond the more usual conclusion that Bokassa was simply an alcoholic and psychotic madman.[3] The

facile parallels usually pointed out between his rule and that of Du-
valier in Haiti, Idi Amin in Uganda, and Macias Nguema in Equatorial
Guinea obviously require at least this tentative attempt.

The French Heritage[4]

The December 4, 1977 coronation of Bokassa I as Emperor of the
Central African Empire is an event virtually unprecedented in recent
history. Unlike Juan Carlos, whose enthronement as king of Spain
two years earlier had antecedents in Spanish history, Emperor Bokassa
patterned his coronation on an external model. Drawing neither on
the precedence of indigenous Central African kingdoms such as
Wadai or Darfur, nor even other African kingdoms and empires in the
twentieth century like Ethiopia and Morocco, Bokassa apparently
imitated the pomp and style of Emperor Napoleon I's coronation in
1804. Virtually nothing African remained in the extravaganza directed
by this individual who held a French passport and was a French army
veteran. Bokassa had even once stated that he loved de Gaulle as a
"papa" and that he has a true "relative" in former President Valéry
Giscard d'Estaing.[5]

There is considerable historical precedence for Africans who rose
through the French military system paying at least subconscious recognition to the "Napoleonic legend."[6] Few of those, though, were
afforded the chance to emulate their hero with as fine a degree of
detail as Bokassa.[7] In the coronation regalia, for example, Napoleonic
touches extended to such minor points as the golden bees embroidered
on the imperial mantle and two laurel fronds bracketing the imperial
initial. "B," of course, replaced "N." No exception was the language
of Bokassa's court—French, rather than Sango, the *lingua franca* of
the country. The only concession he made to African practice was
the use of Bokassa I as his imperial title rather than Jean I or Jean-
Bedel I, as would have been the European practice.

The pomp and majesty of the coronation ceremonies are said to
have cost a third of the nation's $70 million budget for the year. For
some days prior to the ceremonies, 600 of the 2500 guests invited to
attend were treated to meals at leading restaurants and lodging in the
best hotels or in South African constructed housing provided at imperial expense. This hospitality was even to have included Didier I, the
eleventh "king" of the legal fraternity at the University of Poitiers,
had he chosen to accept the invitation Bokassa had sent in response
to Didier's tongue-in-cheek request.

The day of the coronation the emperor rode in a brand new en-
closed coach to the "coronation palace" (the stadium) drawn by 14
of the 16 imported Normandy horses which had survived the shock
of such a massive climate change. The imperial throne of red velvet
trimmed in gold and backed with a huge gold eagle awaited him.
Empress Catherine wore a dress entirely of cloth of gold while the
emperor wore an ankle length tunic and shoes of pearls.

With the heavy crown, its golden eagle glittering in both hands,
Bokassa I crowned himself Emperor of the Central African Empire
shortly after 10:30 a.m. on December 4, 1977. Clad in a 30-foot
crimson velvet, gold-embroidered, and ermine-trimmed mantle which
weighed over 70 pounds, sword bucked on and ebony staff in hand,
he pledged his oath to continue the democratic evolution of the empire. He then crowned his kneeling empress. From here the affair
was off to Notre Dame de Bangui where the archbishop officiated at
High Mass, bestowing the Kiss of Peace on the Emperor. The papal
nuncio read a personal greeting from the Pope and the "Te Deum"
completed this stage of the ceremonies.

A full French-style dinner for some 4000 guests was held at the
Renaissance Palace in the center of Bangui that evening. Dancing to
waltzes played by the French navy band, the royal couple, he in
marshal's uniform and she in Parisian evening gown, opened and closed
the affair. The next day a three-hour military parade of troops clad
in Napoleonic, or at least French, style was the main event followed
by another, only slightly less formal dinner.

On December 14 the imperial government was constituted with
Ange Patassé as prime minister. Bokassa then retired to the walled
imperial court at Berengo about 50 kilometers from Bangui. This
imperial seat was no Versailles. Still under construction, it resembled
at once a military camp, a cheap tourist motel, and a missionary
compound with its own light industries. By March 17, 1978 the emperor was forced to attempt to resume direct control of the army
and on July 14 he dissolved the Patassé government. A new government with Henri Maidou as prime minister was formed on July 17.
By January 1979 demonstrations against the imperial regime were
widespread. Bokassa retaliated by participating in the killing of about
100 demonstrators in April. World opinion, mobilized at first by
Amnesty International, then Central African opposition movements
in exile, and finally an African inquiry commission, condemned Bokassa's regime. On September 21, French troops replaced Bokassa
with former president David Dacko. The empire was over before it
could really be tested.

A Traditional African Polity

The historical study of the Central African Republic is still very much in its infancy. Confusion still exists as to the proper names to give various ethnic groups and nowhere is this confusion more marked than in the Lobaye area in the southwestern part of the country. The once widespread view that Africa had no past still tends to be accepted for this part of the continent by all but the most persistent scholars.[8]

Recent research suggests that the Bobangui, a large scale trading confederation, had taken control of the west and center of the present-day Central African Republic with trading ties to the Nile basin as early as the seventeenth and eighteenth centuries.[9] Even though nineteenth and twentieth century slavery and colonial rule disrupted this trading monopoly, its existence persisted as a potential source of solidarity. Also, a number of relatively large scale political entities had existed in other areas of Central Africa before European domination. Yet, neither the Zande hegemony on the Upper Ubangui nor a number of Muslim ascendancies in the north were ever really more than temporary affairs superimposed over the "ordered anarchy" which had persisted among most of the Central African people for centuries.

Anyone who wishes to understand present day Central African politics must first accept the reality and probably functionality of most Central Africans' persistent and deep-seated opposition to the very notion of the state. Western thought is, of course, permeated with the notion that the state is an evolutionary advance over non-centralized polities. But for the Baya, Mandja, Banda, Sara, and other smaller ethnic groups who constitute all but a fraction of the present day population of Central Africa, opposition to the state has been a long term response to the military, slave trading, and concessionary regimes that for centuries sought to impose themselves upon these peoples. Having once escaped state domination, few Central Africans were eager to be re-incorporated into polities whose only real effects were usually heavy-handed exploitation.

During the colonial era, the social structure of most of Central Africa continued to be based on social and economic units which were significantly larger and more comprehensive than the extended family. These units, or "clans," sometimes smaller than 100 people, could and did unite with others for relatively short periods and for specific purposes. "Blood brotherhood," marriage, and the cross linkage of age groups formed in initiation societies drew together relatively large numbers of these units. Furthermore, trade agents, war leaders, ritual authorities, and arbitrators with wide powers had, for centuries, been selected to perform specific functions for strictly limited periods. The large and small scale resistance movements against colonial oppression, including the Kongo Wara (War of the Hoe Handles, 1929-1931),[10] which were a constant factor in early twentieth century Central African history may have been based upon such traditional leadership functions and linkages.

Boganda, the original founder of the Central African Republic, himself realized the crucial importance of linking the traditional "clans "clans" as the basis for political activity in the immediate pre-independence period. His first political party in 1949 was based upon age grade considerations and his earliest organizational attempts were trading cooperatives. In this he was closely following the patterns of the Bobangui trading diaspora some of whom he numbered among his ancestors. Even his January 10, 1951 arrest and subsequent imprisonment by the colonial administration which ultimately gave him widespread publicity was precipitated by his function as arbitrator in a trading dispute. Likewise, in the Berberati riots of April and May 1954, Boganda was even accepted as arbitrator by the Baya population since he had come to be seen as ritually strong against the even worse alien French oppressors. Boganda's grandiose dreams of a United States of Latin Africa were probably the result of his inability to create a viable hybrid between the highly centralized colonial system he inherited and the persisting segmentary realities. His fear that Central Africa was doomed to poverty unless it was unified into a single production unit drove him finally to reject his own intuitive grasp of Central African realities and seek a unified Central African Republic made up of Ubangui-Shari, the Congo Gabon, and Chad. Thwarted in this by both French and African opponents, Boganda died on March 29, 1959 before his attempts to work out a viable plan for the severely limited Ubangui-Shari colony's transition to the Central African Republic.

His place was subsequently taken up by a former teacher, David Dacko. Dacko, like Boganda and Bokassa (who were both from the village of Bobangui on the river southwest of Bangui),[11] was a member of a very mixed ethnic group of one-time Bantu speakers called Mbaka who had returned to the Lobaye forest in the nineteenth century as the Bobangui trade declined.[12] Dacko, though, was even more cut off than Boganda from grass roots support, and he lacked

Boganda's charismatic appeal. Yet, like his ancestors who had survived the ravages of the slave trade by forming client relationships with stronger allies, Dacko manipulated control of the central government with the help of French commercial interests. As far as most Central Africans were concerned this was simply another imposed government of, by, and for the *Mounjou Voko* (black white) elite supported by French subsidies. Claiming the seemingly laudable goal of stamping out "tribalism," Dacko attempted to create an even more oppressive regime than that which had existed under colonial rule. Seeking support from the very small educated elite for having "driven out" the French, he, nevertheless, left all key posts in the capital and the administrative centers throughout the country in French hands. In order to do this he was forced to create an enormous expansion of civil service positions in order to find places for African supporters of his regime. Unfortunately, the spoils of misappropriated funds which his trading ancestry would have distributed widely among their lineages and clients were retained by only the few who sought only their own gain rather than that of their respective corporate groups as tradition would have dictated. Throughout Dacko's public and private statements during his first year of office runs a schizophrenic theme: some vague lip service to African socialism and the realities of corporate solidarity through the stacked *Mesan (Mouvement pour l'évolution sociale de l'Afrique noire)* organization. Finally by December 1965 in keeping with the historical custom among Central African peoples, Kacko went off into the "bush" of his own volition having proven himself incapable of performing adequately as trade agent, war leader, ritual authority, or arbitrator.[13]

Bokassa, easily perceived at the outset as a "traditional war leader," assumed office proclaiming a re-establishment of equality and protection against a purported "Red Chinese" threat. Rewarding the army, denouncing the previous regime and promising a limited time in control to perform the specific task of "normalizing" the situation, Bokassa began with considerable popular support. Personally intervening in the mundane affairs of "his people," he contributed his first month's salary as president to the Bangui hospital, set up and subsidized two national dance bands, personally paid Central African butchers' debts to Chadian cattle herders in order to assure meat supplies, and made popular radio speeches every day. Bokassa's rule definitely began in a manner that the ancestors of Central Africans would not have criticized.

Soon enamored of power, though, Bokassa personally took a number of cabinet portfolios. By 1969 he became alarmed at emerging opposition and summarily executed a major rival, Alexandre Banza, the man who had handled the logistics for the 1966 coup that had brought him to power. Banza was accused of plotting against his superior.

Like his predecessors, Bokassa worked closely with businessmen, building his own holdings until he possessed shares in every national enterprise and had a monopoly on internal trade. In addition, he established in 1970 a state apparatus for collection, purchase, and sale of all commercial agricultural products—a system of enterprises that had become largely Bokassa's personal business, while farm laborers continued to work for nearly nothing.

Disobedience at any level brought swift prison sentences, and the jails were notoriously full and unpleasant. But until January 1979 Bokassa's reputation as a harsh ruler stemmed from a handful of specific incidents. In 1971 he honored Mother's Day by freeing women prisoners and executing three men accused of murdering women. Two years later, goaded by a break-in at his palace, he personally led an assault on convicted robbers in a nearby prison. Three inmates died as a result of the beating received at the hands of Bokassa and his guards. Later the president decreed penalties involving successive loss of ears and hands for repeated robbery convictions. Bokassa had also dealt harshly with those suspected of mounting coup attempts, two of which were in fact planned in 1976. Widespread massacres or pogroms, however, were not generally a part of Bokassa's regime, and various officials jailed on one suspicion or another were later often returned to government jobs. Ex-president David Dacko, for example, reappeared in 1976 as a personal advisor to Bokassa.

The Emperor tried to wangle aid from every quarter. France, the United States, the Soviet Union, Romania, Yugoslavia, and South Africa were all involved in projects. An Israeli advisor helped with the diamond trade and relations with South Africa. An Arab consultant helped raise oil money. North and South Korea, East and West Germany, Taiwan and Peking all had amicable contacts with Bokassa.

France, however, remained dominant. The budget leaned heavily on a $15 to $20 million French subsidy. Diamonds, which accounted for up to 50 per cent of exports, were extracted by French as well as other foreign companies. Similar arrangements were made for the uranium which began to be developed in the late 70s—an asset that was expected to increase foreign earnings by 50 per cent when production really began.

The empire took shape with little effective challenge at home. However many snickers the idea provoked in foreign capitals, Bokassa's

empire was largely made possible by those who did the loudest laugh-
ing. And the new imperial image could hardly disguise the reality,
which is so much a part of political life in most of France's former
colonies—that of a small elite umbilically tied to Paris and turned away
from their own people. As one might suspect, French consultants
and craftsmen also took a prominent role in preparing the multi-
million dollar coronation.

Bokassa had imposed on the world, and most particularly on the
Central African and French taxpayers, the burlesque and expensive
comedy of a coronation, the smallest details of which were copied
from that of Napoleon I. Under the pretext and the law of non-
interference in their internal affairs, the international community
seemed to accommodate itself to this tragi-comedy.

The May 14, 1979 revelation by Amnesty International of a
massacre of children at the Ngaragba prison, with the personal participation of the "mad emperor," finally, in the middle of the International Year of the Child, upset world opinion. The August 16, 1979
confirmation that these atrocities had taken place, following the
publication of the report by a commission of experts established by
the African heads of state, equalled a condemnation of the tyrant.
Finally the French moved to place David Dacko back in power and
on September 20, 1979 they staged a bloodless coup which restored
to power basically the same regime which Bokassa had overthrown
on the last night of 1965.

Conclusion

It does not seem to misrepresent the data too much to see Bokassa
as exhibiting many aspects of "traditional" African rule as long as
one realizes that this was never a single static category. Focusing on
his increasingly brutal behavior as his regime continued and on the
unAfrican empire, though, begs the question. Brutality à la Nguema,
Amin, or even Shaka is not a necessary or widespread African tradition in spite of superficial analysis to the contrary.[14] Rather the traditional trader, warrior, religious, or broker roles function to help
place and maintain leaders in power over the remnants of an inherited
French administration in Central Africa as long as the ruler fulfills
some of the traditional demands of his constituents. When he fails to
do this, they become unmanageable or unpredictably beyond un-
acceptable bounds, and they are overthrown.

The hybrid regime which held power until September 1981 was
incapable of fulfilling the growing demands of the country's urban

population which today regards all governments with an attitude of in-
difference and mistrust. It remains to be seen whether the military
group now in power will do any better than the "traditional" rulers who
having learned sufficiently to manipulate colonial and neo-colonial
forces to achieve their short-lived and somewhat marginal power positions, allowed Bokassa to achieve his power.

Given the very limited access for upward social mobility in Ubangui-
Shari, it is not surprising that those groups which had the best access
to French culture became the teachers, priests, and military-cultural
brokers. These groups had access to "traditional" government patterns which had evolved in the late eighteenth and early nineteenth
centuries in response to slave trading and other client-patron inter-
faces. Well into the nineteenth century coalitions of big traders had
shared power in the Lobaye and Sangha areas of present day Central
Africa. These coalitions would unite under a single leader as long as
his trading contact with other peoples up and down the rivers of the
middle Zaire and the Ubangui river basins were valuable. Leaders
whose access to the economic resources of the colonial administration seemed strong were thus in a good position to act as political
and economic brokers for their corporate groups under the colonial
and neo-colonial situations right up to the present.

Just as most rural Central Africans seem themselves as members
of a local community or of a descent group, the shifting congeries
of people in charge of the Central African state, particularly that
comparatively small ruling group at the highest levels of government
and party, had come to constitute a national or state descent group
or "clan" with many Bobangui-type patterns intact. This group, in
keeping with time-honored Central African custom, accepted a leader
for as long as this leader could meet specific needs. When the leader
was no longer needed, he was abandoned. It was the group which
collectively persisted in a self-conscious manner. Though any one
member's position was precarious, the group as a whole did control
the state, and by means of that control, controlled much of the economy as well. Seeing Bokassa, or any other leader as a permanently
entrenched power-holder is obviously misleading. In fact, much of
the apparently bizarre behavior of both Dacko and Bokassa can only
be explained as their attempts to find sources of legitimization of
power which transcend the ruling "clan." Their attempts to legitimize
their authority by appeals to Boganda's messianism, Napoleonic
pomp and majesty, mass terror, or external troops all have the same
inherent weakness; they are not part of the average Central African's

world view. In order to build a more humane and satisfactory life for the majority of Central Africans neither a French model nor a lip service nod toward some general African values will suffice. At the end of his rule Bokassa was neither Napoleon nor a "traditional" African ruler. He was a man without policy goals and prescriptions who played a subservient role to external economic interests for as long as these interestes were not too embarrassed by his growing megalomania and ineptitude. When the cost of maintenance for his personal whims came up against spiraling costs in his land-locked resource-poor country he proved expendable to those outsiders. Likewise, when the standard of living and entrenched power position of the ruling "clan" appeared threatened by opposition from more ideologically committed Central African groups, this *bourgeoisie* descent group again chose a leader who could serve as arbitrator with their French trading partners. Dacko, like Bokassa, served as long as he was functional and did not threaten the status quo on either side. It appears that Mitterand's government was not interested in continuing this balance and Dacko was again removed. Whether the new military regime offers a more legitimate Central African nationalism still remains to be seen.

NOTES

1. Christian P. Potholm, *The Theory and Practice of African Politics*, Englewood Cliffs, N.J.: Prentice-Hall, 1979, 183-205.

2. Robert S. Lynd, *Knowledge for What?* New York: Grove Press, 1964, 202-208.

3. Though personal correspondence and statements by personal acquaintances of the Emperor might bear this out. See, for example, Pierre Kalck, *Historical Dictionary of the Central African Republic*, trans. Thomas O'Toole, Metuchen, N. J.: The Scarecrow Press, 1980, xv.

4. William B. Cohen, *Rulers of Empire: The French Colonial Service*, Stanford: Hoover Institute Press, 204-206.

5. See *Africa News*, Vol. IX, 10 (September 5, 1977), 8; and Ronald Koven, "Bokassa's Version of Giscard Link: Portrait of Paternal Relationship," *The Washington Post* (Sunday, May 17, 1981) C1.

6. See Samuel Decalo, *Coups and Army Rule in Africa: Studies in Military Style*, New Haven: Yale University Press, 1976, passim.

7. The view of the coronation presented here is from three main sources. Interviews with first hand observers; John H. Crabb, "The Coronation of Emperor Bokassa," *Africa Today*, Vol. 25, 3 (July-September, 1978) 25-44; and Jeff B. Harmon, "His Former Majesty, Bokassa," *Harper's Magazine* (May 1980), 34-39.

8. Joseph C. Miller, *Equatorial Africa*, Washington, D. C.: American Historical Association, 1976, 3-6.

9. Robert W. Harms, *River of Wealth, River of Sorrow: The Central Zaire Basin in the Era of the Slave and Ivory Trade 1500-1891*, New Haven: Yale University Press, 1981.

10. My unpublished paper, "Kongo Wara—The War of the Hoe Handle: A Central African Protest Movement, 1928-1931," presented at the African Studies Association Meeting, October 21-24, 1981.

11. Kalck, 1971, pp. 75, 93, 154; and Dennis Cordell, *A History of the Central African Republic*, Bangui: Peace Corps, 1975, 25.

12. Jacqueline M. G. Thomas, *Les Ngbaka de la Lobaye*, Paris: Mouton and Company, 1963, 254-258.

13. Kalck, 1971, 28; and Pierre Kalck, *Histoire de la République Centrafricaine*, Paris: Berger Levrault, 1974, 330-331.

14. Ali A. Mazrui, "The Resurrection of the Warrior Tradition in the African Political Culture: From Shaka to Amin," in *Soldiers and Kinsmen in Uganda: The Making of a Military Ethnocracy*, Beverly Hills: Sage Publications, 1975, 195-214.

CHAPTER VII

STRUCTURAL LOGIC IN AUTHORITARIAN PATTERNS
IN THE THIRD WORLD:
THE CASE OF NASIR, QADHDHAFI AND QASIM

PETER GRAN

This essay argues that in the case of several Arab countries current research in social structure and social dynamics casts some doubt about assumptions which have been accepted for a long time by the modernization school concerning authoritarian regimes. I refer specifically to the correlation between the existence of parliamentary systems with multiple political parties, liberal ideology, and democracy in a broadly-based sense.[1] The analysis of social structure by means of political economy of these three countries reveals that the "Liberal Age" (1860-1950) was far more repressive to the majority of the citizenry than was the period of "dictatorship" which followed. But the fact that large masses of people including workers identify themselves with aspects of what dictators do, has ipso facto confirmed the validity of the older paradigm. Isn't it logical that a clever politician can appeal to an uneducated mass? Yet in the three cases under consideration, it is far from being a question of elite domination of a passive population or of brain-washing. There is too much spontaneous political participation. Nor is it clear in the case of the Arab countries that history will favor a fuller development of capitalism, thereby progressively mitigating a "traditional" authoritarianism, i.e., one can scarcely speak of a single path in history of which England or Germany could serve as a model.[2] Our hypothesis of the less regressive character of the dictator in state capitalist regimes, while new to Arab studies, is well-established in Latin American studies and seems applicable to Arab studies.[3]

By using the Arab world as a basis to test this hypothesis, it is possible to add some new considerations without detracting from the attempt to build a model for Third World political studies grounded

in a shared socio-economic context. A feature of the political systems
which, while not unique to the Arab World, is found there commonly
is the autoritarianism peculiar to regimes which collect their surplus
primarily as rent and therefore do not need to interact with the majority of their subject populations. All these states are characterized
by weak institutions[4] and by a lack of incentive to push for fuller
capitalist relations of production. Paradoxically then the oil rich
countries are more vulnerable[5] than many states which have little or
no wealth.[6] Yet evidence abounds to show that these trends do not
reflect innate capacities as much as structural factors. Oil rulers regu-
larly invest their money shrewdly in Europe and America while remaining rentier capitalists at home content to see a very slow pace of
change. These oil rich states represent a variation of the general
model leading to and then away from state capitalism. Their authoritarianism is given a separate treatment.

The Rise of Nasir, Qadhdhafi and Qasim — A Political Economy Explanation[7]

Nasir,[8] Qadhdhafi[9] and Qasim[10] were junior army officers who
led or were prominent in the struggle for political independence of
Egypt, Libya and Iraq. This paper combines them for the sake of
making a series of generalizations about the state capitalist regimes
of the Arab world of which they are prime examples and at the same
time it separates them to show the specificity of their individual cases.
This emerges most clearly when one looks at the type of society which
existed prior to the revolutions, a period often called the Liberal Age.
Through a consideration of the historical dynamics of the Liberal
Age in each case, one arrives at state capitalism. A study of the structural logic of each type of regime leads to a discussion of authoritarian rule per se in the final section of the paper.

Liberal Age is used to characterize Arab and other Third World
states in the period from the middle of the 19th century to the 1950s,
a period often beginning with colonialism and terminating with independence struggles, a period marked by an integration of the Third
World into the world market. The term Liberal Age is chosen in preference to "rentier capitalist phase" and "semi-feudal" phase because
these terms imply a teleological coming of a full development of
capitalism in the Third World, something which may or may not
come about. Liberal Age places the emphasis on politics, which is
helpful given the theme of authoritarianism. But it permits us also to

group together several social formations with their dynamics and to portray their destruction by and replacement with state capitalism. In writing about the Arab World, I am of course also following the precedent of Albert Hourani and others who have long used "Liberal Age" to point out how liberalism constituted a phase of history, the colonial phase. I differ from the Liberal school of Professor Hourani in my emphasis on the internal Arab bases of liberalism over the European influence in the development of the ideology and its political forms.

From the middle of the 19th century, Europe supported the development of a class of large landlords in the Arab World. This class derived its wealth from the sale of cotton, wheat, and later oil as raw products on the world market. This agrarian ruling class had replaced an older class of rulers of the Ottoman period which had also drawn their wealth from land and trade but as tribute and for local consumption. During the classical Ottoman period, the ruling classes of the Ottoman empire, particularly those in the Arab provinces of the Empire, had been composed of Muslim merchants as well. The Liberal Age saw the destruction of the Muslim merchant position; the new Arab, landed, ruling-class turned to Greeks, Jews and Americans who had an entrée in the European market which Muslim merchants did not. Muslim merchants and producers were often force to move into the provinces and secondary towns, or to the hinterland of the newly-formed states. To the present day these Muslim merchants have opposed the rise of the modern secular liberal national culture; many have supported the Muslim Brothers, an organization seeking a political solution not unlike Khomeyni's.

The conflicts which existed within the Arab ruling classes of the 19th century were those between the small inner coterie of holders of very large estates in and around the royal families on the one hand and a larger number of landholders, often called provincial notables, on the other. The conflict within this class took the form of the notables championing a liberal constitutional form of government in which the whole ruling class would have one man-one vote while the royal families of the three countries, backed by the colonial authorities, opposed liberalism and rallied forces which would accept royalism. The economic aspects of these conflicts are particularly well-studied in the case of Egypt. In Egypt the fluctuating value of cotton and the high cost of investment in irrigation placed many notables in debt or on the verge of being in debt. The notables continuously struggled with the government seeking to equalize access to government credit, to water rights, and to other services which were largely dominated by the royal coterie. By the 1930s in Egypt, and Iraq, a segment of the notables began to diversify its activities; some members of their families became involved with industry. The dominant form of industrialization was always closely aligned to primary goods production. In Iraq and Egypt, the notables also championed national development through public education. Their belief was that an educated, salaried, managerial class, knowledgeable in agronomy and business methods, would greatly increase the profits on their lands and that a law school would produce graduates who would protect their profits. Thus a part of the ruling class encouraged the establishment of secular universities, open to those who could pay a modest but still substantial fee.

The decision to pursue capitalist development was not greeted in the political circles of the colonialists or among the royal families with any enthusiasm. Indeed, the new institutions of higher learning soon became centers of nationalist opposition to foreign domination, and the student movement a political force. In all three countries the new educational opportunities led to the rise of a salaried petty bourgeois class tied to the fortunes of the state. This class became important in Egypt after the First World War, in Iraq by the 1940s, and in the cities of Libya by the 1960s. This class was composed of teachers, soldiers, police, social workers, government functionaries in the much expanded central bureaucracy, and skilled workers. The petty bourgeois grew far more rapidly than did the ruling class; it numbered in all countries in the hundreds of thousands if not millions. While this class by definition lacked an independent economic base, it assumed a growing influence in determining the course of events before the respective revolutions. First, the Pasha class had to give up control over more and more aspects of daily affairs as life became more specialized. This was particularly the case in technical areas where the new professional elite had a monopoly of the relevant skills. Second, the petty bourgeoisie had power in certain institutions, such as the newspapers, publishing houses, schools, and universities; third, this class had influence which could be translated into power in the streets, through the weight of its numbers in the capital cities; fourth, they had real power in the army on the level of the junior officers. The three leaders of the revolts were junior officers. With the rise of modern industry and capitalist agriculture in the Egyptian case, there developed a working class. It engaged in extensive strike activity both authorized and unauthorized. Around the workers grew up a strong Communist movement. Since the industrial sector was relatively small, this might have been contained by the government, but simultaneously, peasant struggles erupted on the estates of absentee landlords. It was this multi-sided struggle which created the real crisis of the Liberal Age permitting the petty bourgeoisie to become spokesmen of the nation.

The collapse of the Liberal Age was also brought about by short term economic crises and political scandals. Let us turn to these conjunctural dimensions of the Egyptian Revolution of 1952. Economic stagnation in the agricultural sector returned after World War Two. The revolution in synthetics took a deeper cut in the cotton clothing market; the Egyptian ruling class did not have access to European and Japanese advances in chemistry. They were trapped without an adequate market either for raw cotton or cotton clothing which they could manufacture. World War Two itself had a very significant impact on Egypt. While the Middle East Supply Center located in Cairo benefited a few businessmen, the masses were expected to support the Allied war effort with extra labor. By the end of the war, there was considerable unrest among peasants and workers from this demand. The "threat from below" was matched by a picture of apathy if not corruption or worse in the Court and in the political leadership of the ruling Wafd party.

One suggestive corruption incident, the Defective Arms Deal of 1948, had a profound consequence for the fate of the Royalty and the Liberal Age. In 1948, during the first Palestine War the Egyptian petty bourgeoisie was solidly pro-Palestinian and pro-Arab. The monarchy and important elements of the ruling class either were indifferent to Arab causes or, perhaps, were even sympathetic to the Zionists. King Faruq permitted the Port of Alexandria to be used as a depot and entrepot for the Zionist movement organized through the synagogue of Alexandria.[11] One author hypothesized that Faruq was obliged to cooperate since he was still repaying a Rothschild loan taken out by his ancestors. In fact, however, the loan was fully paid in 1948, so the leverage from that quarter could not have been great. In any case, British policy during the war was so chaotic that one could hardly suspect coherent colonial pressure.[12] At the same time, pro-Arab support in Egypt on the verbal level was considerable. But, the King was able to stall Egyptian participation in the war and engineer the famous "defective arms" deal. Much of Egyptian weaponry would not work.

To understand the position of the king, and the whole tradition of royalist authoritarianism which he represented, it is necessary to examine more closely the workings of the rural structure. The confrontation between the king and the urban population should not be overstated. Beginning in the 1840s, a system of rural administration was created in which one or two rich peasant families administered their village on behalf of an absentee landlord, who owned the land. These rich peasants served the state as village headmen. Above the village headman, there stood the regional administrative apparatus. In the 20th century, the village headman had a lot of power. He had the only telephone, had the right to choose the young men to be drafted and to decide the organization of village work. His power, thus, guaranteed that the fallahin would work and produce the cotton crop. The rich peasant families attempted to prevent other families in their villages from challenging their dominance. Such a challenge could come about only through the control of land. Therefore, bitter struggles took place between the rich peasants and the group which had some land, but were not rich, the middle peasant. The technical distinction was that the rich peasants owned enough land to employ others to work for them while the middle peasants owned some land but had to work it themselves. The vast majority of peasants in every village were poor peasants, i.e., they were landless or owned tiny parcels which did not provide them with a living. Thus, they had to exist on day labor. A few peasants owned animals which they rented out, or they performed other specialized services which gave them some power. Migrant labor was brought in on a seasonal basis for harvests.

While the poor peasants were the overwhelming majority they did not constitute a direct political challenge to the regime. They were mainly concerned with day-to-day existence. It was the middle peasant who could pursue the connection between his own frustrations and the inequity of the existing system. But the poor peasant could exert pressure on the system through work slow-downs. The system, which was based primarily on "absolute extraction" from the peasant naturally had recourse to extreme authoritarianism. One of the greatest works of Egyptian literature portrays this system in its last phase. 'Abd al-Rahman al-Sharqawi's *The Earth* concerns the rise of the middle peasants in a village in Egypt in the 1940s.[13] The novel showed that, as the regime experienced conflicts with workers, peasants, and students, it could not simultaneously block the rise of the countryside; many villages destroyed the rich peasant class before the Revolution. In these struggles women played an important part.

The impact of the money economy forced a greater and greater need for cash on the villager. This posed a severe threat of fragmentation

on village and family life and it is on this level that the struggle of women has been particularly important in trying to preserve tradition and
the family. It is quite noteworthy how peasants resorted to having
a maximum number of children in the hope that some of the children
would live to grow up and would succeed in finding work. Despite
the high infant mortality rate, the population of the countryside shot
up dramatically in Egypt since the late 19th century. Ironically the
upper classes clamored for birth control only when this rural wave
swept into the cities.[14]

The last parameter to consider in explaining the rise of state capitalism is the impact of the world economy on the local economy.
The economy of the British Empire was one in which the small firms
of Britain, many of which produced luxury goods, profited through
the sale of their products to the wealthy classes of the Arab World and
India. The position of the United States on the world market was quite
different. The U.S. stressed large scale organization and mass-produced
items. A percentage of English industry did reach the monopoly
stage but compared to the United States it was much slighter.[15] After
World War I, the more powerful American monopolies led by oil
broke into the British colonies in the Middle East. In the Middle East,
the American oil companies struggled fiercely with the British to get
into British-controlled oil fields. A very severe economic competition
existed between two ostensible allies. As World War II drew to a close
and the Cold War dawned, a new more expansive role of the U. S.
government emerged. It made use of the CIA. 'Abd al-Nasir, one
writer claims, received help before and after the Revolution from the
CIA. Nasir allegedly created his modern police force and secret police
with CIA help.[16] American corporations, working covertly had more
flexibility than they did through the traditional state department
apparatus, which was bound by treaties.

1952 State Capitalist Revolution in Egypt

The Egyptian Revolution of 1952 brought about a number of important changes. It was a revoution within capitalism; the class basis
of the government shifted to include the petty bourgeoisie; the central latifundist component was liquidated. Parallel to these developments came a wave of nationalizations which created a large and important public sector. The beneficiaries of the revolution were the
industrial bourgeoisie and segments of the petty bourgeois class. To
a lesser degree the small capitalist farmers were also beneficiaries of
the changes. The large absentee estates were attacked through land
reform laws.

How complete was the change? Our information on the success of land reform is still fragmentary. On the one hand, it is clear that land was taken away from many families; later it was noticed by many observers that the large landlords still managed to get important jobs in the ministries of Agriculture and Agricultural Reform. Observers noted that landlords registered their land in the name of peasants who did thereby not gain power over the land. On the other hand, the policies which were carried out in the economic sphere reflected the new forces in power. The agricultural capitalists enacted a series of state-supported programs: Liberation Province was one of the largest land reclamations in the world, and the coop scheme created a pool of new resources in the villages in the form of technology and credit resources. These projects were, of course, firmly under the thumb of the peasants and provincial notables. The industrialists too made their weight felt. The state spent a major part of its revenue on industrial projects, e.g., in Hulwan and in Mahalla al-Kubra. The petty bourgeoisie gained many benefits as well. The state committed itself to a massive program of education and social services as well as to the support of culture. Petty bourgeois intellectuals, army officers and trade union bureaucrats administered these programs.

As the new configuration evolved and more and more industrial products were produced, the problem of lack of a domestic market, which had plagued Egypt in the 1930s, recurred. Here we find the leadership tried to solve its economic problems through its foreign policy. Nasir had a very outward-turning foreign policy in the 1950s and 1960s. He described it in terms of three spheres—the Arab world, Africa, and all the Third World. He made attempts to ally himself with a range of neighboring states which, very importantly, had little or no domestic industry. These attempts involved him in a number of conflicts. One conflict was the war in Yemen; in Yemen an Egyptian alliance with Yemeni merchants eventually threatened the shaky political structure of the Saudi oil world. Another type of conflict was waged against the principal industrial rival, Israel. Everyone knows that Nasirism was anti-Israeli. Nasirism charged the Jewish state with imperialism and with oppressing the rights of the Palestinians. (Israel did not become primarily a Jewish-Muslim issue in Egyptian eyes until the failure of Egyptian state capitalism; namely, the Sadat open-door period, the period in which industry collapsed.)

The political structure of Nasirism was based on a cross-class political alliance (petty bourgeois, and bourgeois) within which the bourgeois component always had the upper hand. As with other such regimes, it relied on a single party structure and on a charismatic front man. The role of the single party was to blur to the maximum degree possible conflicts which were ongoing within the government and which went on between the government and society at large. The position of 'Abd al-Nasir both in Egypt and throughout the Arab world was obviously significant. Many people identified their hopes with him in a very genuine way. Few could resist his fabulous speaking ability which could cross class lines, especially his quick wit. Although Nasir was more popular and more long lasting than most other Third World leaders of his period, one must suppose that the structural determinants which affected all such leaders affected him as well. The single party, the Arab Social Union, was composed of constituent blocs, on one level the industrialist, on another the capitalist farmers. The influence of the industrialists and capitalist farmer in the government can be judged by the fact that the government tried to coopt workers and peasants, making it illegal for them to strike. On the highest level of decision-making, the fundamental compromise between the contending elements was that each would grant power to a Nasir-type figure so long as he could walk a tightrope never permitting the interests of one class to rise out of proportion to its real power. This type of regime seemed to be quite stable when one class clearly predominated, but there are numerous examples where, as in Syria and in parts of Latin America and Africa, that the contending elements were so close in their relative strength that it was too hard to be a political figure dominating them mediating their differences.

In such a case regime would follow regime without bringing any noticeable structural changes in society. The other extreme existed in the case of Franco as an individual, and in the case of a number of parties which ruled for a long time, e.g., the Labor party in Israel, the Congress party in India, and the PRI in Mexico. Here one finds a gerontology of heroes.

Various factors contributed to the continuing viability of state capitalist regimes in the 1950s-1960s. The external ones were of course those inherent in the world system. The two superpowers of the post-war years were America and Russia; each had interests in the Third World and each sought to mold a number of regimes to fulfill those interests. Sometimes this involved direct competition for the political sympathy of a given country. In such cases Russian support (as in Egypt, Iraq and Libya) took the form of encouraging the Public Sector and of the offer of assistance for the development of primary industrialization. For the United States the range of concerns was somewhat broader. In the Middle East, the overwhelming American concern was always cheap oil; American policy has normally been subordinated to that goal.[17] Ideology has played a part in the policy of both governments although more so for the United States with its free world ideology. Not only had the United States supported any initiatives of the private sector which were visible, it has often withheld critically needed loans, machine parts, or markets from public sector regimes. This was somewhat offset by Russian support but, in general, American policy has been more effective in the Middle East than that of Russia.

Nonetheless, by the 1970s internal problems sapped the vitality of many state capitalist regimes. Generally speaking, these problems manifested themselves as class conflicts. They took various forms reflecting the specific conditions and possibilities of the age. One feature of the period was the huge demographic shift from country to city; another was the continuing rural overpopulation and stagnation. According to classical theory the ascendancy of the industrial bourgeoisie intent on the rapid development of personal wealth would have led to the growth of a politicized industrial working class. This would have been the case but the demographic shift referred to above influenced politics in a new way. The industrialists quickly saw that their meager resources would be exhausted, as they had been in the 1940s, if they tried to confront the growing working class massed on an assembly line à la Europe. Instead, they turned to farming out the bulk of production as piece-work to sweat shops. In little tin shacks in crowded quarters of Cairo thousands if not millions of people labored in squalor with primitive equipment. The owner of each sweat shop with his work force of a handful of men bid for the work; if need be he augmented his labor force through a labor contractor or by word of mouth, and delivered his finished pieces to the gates of the modern sector factory where a medium size work force completed the assemblage or finishing touches. Not surprisingly the modern sector work force became an aristocracy of labor, moderate in its politics. Neither the Russians nor the Americans seemed to oppose the trend toward sweat shop industrialization in Egypt. Since the 1970s a number of USAID officials have shown interest in this small-scale industry, citing its efficiency.[18] In sum, the 1970s marked a regression away from class formation, back toward absolute extraction of surplus from the workers, as was the case in the Liberal Age.

The political consequences of De-Nasirization were predictable. It happened before. The Muslim Brothers, a political force in the

1930s whose fortunes had waned after 1952, reemerged. When large numbers of people migrated to Cairo and Alexandria, quadrupling in a generation the population of these old cities, a radical religious leadership resurfaced in the so-called traditional sections of society. In the 1950s, a strong secularist government declared the Muslim Brothers to be illegal, by the 1970s the government could not command the cultural loyalty of the society with the same vision, nor did it have the power to stifle the opposition by force. Secular culture held out no promise to those working in sweat shops or to the merchants of provincial towns caught in the flux of world market conditions. Not surprisingly when Nasir outlawed the Brotherhood in Cairo, it was able to retreat to its stronghold in the provincial towns, where such sentiment had had a powerful influence among merchants and others for the past century. The downfall of Nasir presented the Brotherhood a chance to return to Cairo, which it did, reorganized in a number of small underground groups. The new structural model for these groups would appear to be the small-scale production workshop with all its secrecy over wages and work conditions. Such would appear to be the case for such violent groups as Takfir wa-l-Hijra which has assassinated a number of people including the late President Sadat.[19] But how could the Egyptian government have been caught off guard? Was it pure greed for cheap labor? One might also surmise that this great lumpenproletariat was an indispensable weapon in the government's hand against the working class (based in trade unions) and the secularists. The gains of workers and women achieved during the Nasir period were quickly eroded in the Sadat period despite Jihn al-Sadat. Many prominent secular intellectuals were forced into exile, protesting the breakdown of basic liberties and the rise of authoritarian repression on all levels. In sum for Egypt, political authoritarianism appeared to ebb and flow with the division of labor adopted by capital. The state capitalist period was the least regressive.

Libya and Iraq: Modifications of the Argument

Libya and Iraq share in common a great abundance of oil wealth which distinguishes them from Egypt. There are of course important differences between them as well. Oil-based economies have a number of political forms from republicanism to royalism but they have in common a reality that the state and the ruling class need not concern themselves with the development and reproduction of society. The only work force required is a small number of oil workers and a few managing technocrats. The phrase "need not" is misleading in that the direction of history is not in the hands of any one class. But the forms of leverage of the masses against the state are quite different than in Egypt or in any state which has large-scale productive ventures. The state which attempts to arrogate to itself authority as the Iraqi state has, confronts an ongoing problem of legitimacy. It may bemoan the archaic structure of society but if it seriously tried to integrate tribes, peasants and ethnic regions into the polity, the power base of the ruling party would be threatened. In Libya, an authoritarianism of the state rooted in oil wealth confronts a juridical decentralization of three partially autonomous regions.

To begin on a modest scale, let us examine the ways in which the generalizations and patterns of causal links would need to be modified to explain the rise of Qasim and Qadhdhafi from the point of view of demography, the impact of the world market and social structure. For the Liberal Age, one obvious difference was the demographic layout of these much smaller societies and the effect which this had on social structure. In both cases semi-nomadic conditions existed in wide areas of Iraq and Libya; where sedentarization existed, as with the Marsh Arabs, tribal solidarity remained as strong as other affiliations. Homogenization of the population which is common in creating nation-states did not progress far. In both cases the scale and density of population was quite low compared to Egypt as well as many other parts of the Third World. These factors combined to lower the expectation of foreign capital or local capitalists about rapid development. Redeployment of the labor force would not necessarily bring increased profit.

In the case of Libya the motivations of the dominant European power, Italy, had very little to do with Libya *per se* (oil had not yet been discovered); in the case of Iraq, British interest was in oil from the beginning. Another main difference was that where the whole of Egypt could be profitably turned into an export-oriented economic unit for the British, this was clearly not true in Iraq. The Middle Euphrates land in the center of the country was well-irrigated by the Tigris and the Euphrates rivers and could produce wheat. Along the southern coast, date plantations were lucrative. The North was less useful. There remained numerous archaic elements, like the Marsh Arabs of the South, in a slowly evolving and disarticulated state.

The impact of the world market on Libya and Iraq took different forms and made different demands than in the case of Egypt. Oil was and is crucial to Western economies, and from the First World War it was crucial to the British navy. The British decision to change from coal to oil in the navy in 1910 was obviously in the background of the most crucial engagements between the German and Turkish forces on the one hand and the Arab and British on the other; the result was British victory, the creation of the British mandate of Iraq and an oil monopoly for BP.

From the beginning, the British faced many difficulties governing Iraq in the face of a strong nationalist opposition. The only way to halt national development was to build up the power of the feudal elements to offset the modern urban classes which were anti-British. This tactic worked for a generation but thereafter the movement of people to the city mentioned above turned the struggle in the direction of nationalist victory. Whereas in Egypt the British had some incentive to see the development of the infrastructure both for agriculture, and even for industry, in Iraq, the need for oil prevented the British from taking any unnecessary risks. Libyan development was retarded by the Italians as well, not because of oil, but because of the needs of settler colonialism.

For Italy, the reasons to colonize Libya had more to do with solving domestic social problems than making a profit for Italian industry.[20] It is true that capital for the projects came from a large bank which spearheaded heavy investment, the Banco-Roma, but the support for colonization also came from the latifundist south, a region which would normally not follow the Northern lead. From the late 19th century onward, the southern landlords faced growing unrest on their estates; they believed that only by ridding themselves of a significant number of peasants could they retain their position and gain profits.

When the Italians came to Libya they barricaded themselves into settler camps guarded by the army. There was not much obvious wealth to confiscate; the Libyan resistance was considerable; the Italians unlike the British in Egypt had few if any allies in Libya. This explains the style of conquest and the different nature of the colonial ideology from that which one found in Egypt or Iraq. After killing a third or a half of the Eastern Libyan population, Italy, like England, became embroiled in World War II. In 1945 as a member of the Axis, Italy's claim to overseas colonies was regarded as null; however, none of the victorious colonial powers wanted Libya, so Libya was declared independent under King Idris. It was only then that oil was discovered. By the late 1950s some Libyan developments began in the cities. Once oil was discovered in Libya, the United States supported the monarchy. The revolution of 1969 brought down the monarchy.

The Liberal Age ruling classes of Iraq and Libya were fragmented as the inner circles controlled the oil while the outer circles held power over tribes, regions and commerce. This is the case if we start our account of Iraq in the 1930s. The disunity of the outer circles gave the ruler specific opportunities of dominance. This encouraged the playing off of the poor and disaffected of one region against those of another. The massacre of the Assyrians, the endless struggles with the Kurds, did not lead to new class formation and higher integration but followed a cyclical pattern according to the needs of the King and BP. This uneven regional development also exacerbated urban demographic problems. In the Iraqi case, oil wealth benefited the royal family and a class of grandees who came from families of inherited wealth, most of whom lived in Baghdad; the middle provinces were also the most fertile. The result was that South Iraq, a poor region, saw the greatest migration moving north to the slums of Baghdad. The government in Baghdad was more narrowly based than Egypt's had been. It was not heir to any nationalist tradition; it was a monarchy which was the creation of the British in opposition to the nationalists. The monarchy did not want to develop the country at a rapid rate; it identified itself with conservatism in its education program, in the development of the Iraqi military, and in all those sectors which affected the petty bourgeoisie. At the same time, the growing value of oil made development more possible; these contradictions contributed to the collapse of the regime. A similar situation prevailed in Libya which went from poverty after the war to increasing wealth through oil.

The ideological demands of the rising petty bourgeois classes of Libya and Iraq can be distinguished from those of Egypt as can the programs which they set out to enact when they came to power. The Egyptian petty bourgeois which support Nasir called for the end of the monarchy and the British control. The stagnating industrial program would then march ahead or so they believed. For the Iraqi petty bourgeois class, the struggle against the totally parasitical monarch led them to side with the masses and to denounce capitalism. The frustrations of this class, much of it serving as junior officers who saw no service, may partly account for their intense feelings.[21] The Libyan demands also went beyond the abolition of the monarchy to economic and social justice. In Libya's and Iraq's revolutionary regimes the skyrocketing oil revenues initially blunted the class issue in national politics. A dramatic effort by the revolutions to build housing for the poor in both countries led to a guarantee of a home for everyone in Libya and to a forced but effective resettlement of the southern Marsh Arabs (the Shurughis) who had come to Baghdad. An authoritarian nationalism (Ba'thism, Libyan Arab Nationalism) became ascendant; sweatshops did not develop.

The state capitalist period in Libya and Iraq date from their revolutions, 1969 and 1958 respectively; it was at those points that the petty bourgeois could share in power effectively. In contrast to Egypt, Libya and Iraq did not have an important industrial bourgeoisie; this also made their revolutionary rhetoric more radical. What existed in place of an industrial bourgeoisie was a collection of rentier capitalists with landed interests and some rich merchants. There was not even a large number of notables as in in Egypt. In addition, there were many elements such as tribal chiefs and regional powers, whose relation to central authority was problematic. In Libya and Iraq the tendency toward *de facto* or *de jure.* decentralization manifested itself at once and contributed to the radical and anarchist sentiment of the time. In Iraq the central government embarked on a series of fruitless wars to capture Kurdistan. Kurdistan, 23 years later, remains autonomous in a *de facto* sense. It is one of the bastions of the current internal enemy of the Ba'th Party, the Daw'a Islamiya. In Libya these regional differences were spelled out on a *de jure* basis in the constitution which created a state with strong federalist tendencies, the first in the Arab world. The Libyan Jamahiriya, like the Iraqi state, both under Qasim (1958-1961), and then later under the early Ba'th Party rulers, could never pursue centralism effectively despite great wealth. Both governments have followed their developmentalist mandate through the importation of labor, through the purchase of turnkey plants, and through the subsidy of local enterprises. In the capital cities, new suburbs of the rich have appeared to the embarrassment of the "socialist" state. Like Zamalek in Cairo, the rise of Hayy al-Andalus in Tripoli and Mansura in Baghdad appear to mark the challenge of the bourgeois class emerging in full flush, in a disarticulated state.

The political leadership of these two countries, al-Qadhdhafi in Libya and Saddam Husayn in Iraq have a marked populist style in their political personalities. They tour their countries, dine with peasants and tribespeople yet in every way reflect the balance of forces which exist. In fact, they represent the new oil bourgeoisie of the cities. Given the relative balance between contending forces the political leadership in these countries appears often to be inconsistent, and unsophisticated; but both, at times, have frightened the Egyptian leadership and other status-quo regimes by their sharp political analysis and their lack of dissimulation.

Conclusions

Political Economy as a rising paradigm in the social sciences needs to provide answers to questions of general intellectual and moral concern. Human freedom and political authoritarianism are examples of such problems. For a long time, perhaps since antiquity, they have been defined in terms of a culture which took only the elite seriously. Greece, we learn, was a democracy but also a slave state. The task of political economy is to absorb the insights of the previous formulation but to broaden the range of application so as to include the relevant totality which is the domain of socio-economic analysis. At this stage in the development of the paradigm, there is a gap between the political vocabulary and the socio-economic analysis. This gap has given rise to some of the most intense political and philosophical conflicts of this century between the more "political" adherents, the "permanent" revolutionists and their opponents who argued for the objective conditions of revolution based on stages of economic development. This was of course the conflict of Trotsky and Stalin and subsequently of many others.

Political economists in Latin American studies have developed the concept of authoritarianism in a way which appears useful for Third World studies. First they distinguish it from fascism and other totalitarian systems which were based in the industrial class structure of the advanced countries. Second they attempted to find a logic for it and to describe who benefited from it and in what ways the system progressed. A number of writers concluded that this authoritarianism was less oppressive than the one class political systems which sometimes followed the "authoritarian" state capitalist regimes. The rule of Peron in Argentina and the Cardenas and post-Cardenas periods in Mexico are well-studied examples of this transition from state capitalism toward class rule. This essay makes the same attempt to use classical political concepts in the political economy framework; it attempts to apply them to three Arab countries.

The argument made for a diversified political economy framework is not that Arab states and Islamic culture are inherently different than states and cultures in Latin America but rather that, apart from Egypt, some necessity exists to analyze the oil-producing states according to their own specificity. This need for specificity does not negate the utility of the more general concept of Liberal Age or state capitalism but it does permit a focus on states which do not extract their surplus from the labor of their working classes. This latter type of state was termed in the case of Iraq and Libya disarticulated as its relation to society was remote and often coercive. While it was possible to offer some examples where the coerciveness of the oil state is essentially the same, whether it was royalist, e.g., Saudi Arabia, or republican, e.g., Algeria or Iraq, this essay also sought to distinguish between Iraq and Libya while maintaining them as a category separate from Egypt. The course of the Libyan independence struggle led to a *de jure* federalism which resulted in a more democratic way of life for the Libyans on many levels than the Iraqis have, who have a *de facto* regionalism of the North. As with the first part of the argument, the second also stressed the objective characteristics or constraints of political behavior, here authoritarianism. The novelty of the first part lay in the emphasis on the ebb and flow of authoritarianism from its linkage to the shifting division of labor. The novelty of the second part was the economic analysis of the state's relations to the people. Of course, objective economic factors do not encapture the political moment in its entirety.

Notions of freedom and authoritarianism are scarcely separable as well from a concept of man. It might be well in anticipation of many future studies to note what notions of man have come down to political economy from the past and how they have affected our use of terms such as freedom.

Two main traditions of thought about man exist in the United States. There is the notion of Locke which postulates that man's fulfillment as an individual is the Homo Faber, working to achieve his property in harmony with the greater good of the state and society. The second tradition, that of Rousseau, disputes that. From Locke emerges behavioral psychology. But where Locke postulated that man has a nature which was developed through his environment, the modern behavioral psychology finds man to be totally self-created, or created by how others perceive him. In other words it does not root man in history or necessity. In this latter view, man differs from the beast because he can overcome his environment through intelligence. The latter school prevails in the liberal universities. It contributes quite directly to the American analysis of dictatorial regimes, like those of the Arab world.

In practice the American yardstick for the existence of freedom in any state is the measure of democracy and personal liberties. These terms are rooted in the psychological theories mentioned above. History and the logic of structure have not played much of a role. An Arab woman who has an arranged marriage constitutes an offense to these Western ideas because her true nature is in her independence from the web of family connections whose mediations she accepts in making this decision. Here clearly the observer abandons behaviorism and the relativistic morality which has grown up by its side in favor of a universal, if American, human nature. However, it would seem that little is gained by teetering between these two extremes of total relativism and a human nature made on an assembly line. Here a political economist would suggest that one could modify a universalist approach to a social science issue, i.e., human nature, without abandoning it, by retaining the specificity of social class and of the broader historical conditions. Within these boundaries, it is possible to speak meaningfully of freedom or lack of freedom. To return to the Arab woman, it would not occur to her in our hypothetical case that she was going to exist apart from her own family and her husband's family. Family politics would determine in many historical conjectures the kind and amount of leverage she would have the rest of her life so that their participation in her marriage decision is part of their becoming party to it. This woman may very well have reflected on the advantages of education and a job but if she lived around the Mediterranean or in parts of Latin America in periods of economic stagnation she may quickly have come to the conclusion that what the workplace offered her was far worse than the struggle to maintain herself as a housewife.[22] In times of growth and rapid development, it is a cliché that women appear enthusiastic about education. This is happening to Saudi women at the moment.[23] But it is clear that the topic of freedom or lack of freedom now has lost its Arab flavor, it applies equally to the struggle over the ERA. The issue is class specific.

But "men dominate" or "the Soviet army stands over its citizens" goes the traditional discourse on authoritarianism. In fact, Arab women or the Soviet people grant power and legitimacy far more ambiguously than we usually recognize. If a significant number of people pay lip service to a supreme central authority it then can function with some degree of impunity. The Soviet state capitalized no doubt on the very real threat of the extinction of the Russian people from the Nazis to impose Great Russian control more deeply on the lives of millions of people. These people were confused about dealing with contradictory problems.

In the post-War period, to stay with the Russian example for a moment, that success at social control has diminished in many re-regions. The West now cheers the breakdown of Empire, and the rise of Islam. An interesting hypothesis would be to test if states like Russia, the prototype of state capitalism, were ever particularly strong in and of themselves, merely through the possession of the means of violence, or if in fact a test would show that power was always widely diffused and moved fluidly between men and women and different levels of society, except in times of crisis when it became very centralized. To those who run the central state institutions, the possibilities of international emergencies may have a personally overwhelming appeal.

For the Arab regimes which we covered, the most precise meaning of the term "authoritarian" would derive from specific social conditions rather than directly from the regimes. Political participation is a factor. Authoritarianism in the Liberal Age preceding the revolutions was more widespread despite parliaments and constitutions than after the revolutions, because for the great majority the Liberal Age was a transitional era. Village life and self-reliance broke down, the ravages of the market economy arrived. Many people caught between these two systems were very adversely affected, especially poor women. State capitalism as a system took cognizance of many of the social problems and state policies pulled a number of people out of the problems in which they and their families had been suffering. The abrupt transition from tribe to market laborer in Iraq in the Liberal Age led to violence on a scale unknown in the 18th or early 19th century; clearly Iraq is a society still reeling from the shocks of these dislocations. Assuming the new context of the state capitalist regimes, the word authoritarian has to change its meaning: it applies to government policies aimed at groups suppressed by the regime in order to create the surplus. One thinks of the control of the landless peasant exercised by a willing urban citizenry through the state. Clearly a large per cent of state capitalist societies can make a society terribly authoritarian for certain minorities as well. Still there is no question that state capitalism[24] judged from the perspective of the vast majority marked a great step forward toward freedom and participation and away from authoritarianism in the vulgar sense. The ideology of the Liberal Age was too restricted to play any role outside of the small privileged groups who owned all the property whether European or Arab. Clearly a detailed argument of the history of the authoritarian side of liberal ideology needs to be developed in Middle East studies.

NOTES

1. Modernization theory developed many of its contemporary features during World War Two. The first attempts to define the Non-West were influenced by the growth of distinguishing self and others which grew out of the War. While this turned out to be an enduring feature of American political studies of the Middle East, many of the categories once applied to the study of under-developed countries found their way back into the study of America in the 1970s as conditions deteriorated. An early Middle East example is Daniel Lerner, *The Passing of Traditional Society: Modernizing the Middle East*, Glencoe: Free Press, 1958. Lerner's roots can be found in earlier books like Hannah Arendt, *The Origins of Totalitarianism*, New York: Harvest/HBJ Books, 1951; and Karl Popper, *The Open Society and Its Enemies*, London: G. Routledge and Sons, 1945. The application of modernization theory to America, note the confusion in meaning created, is Samuel Huntington, Jr., *American Politics: The Promise of Disharmony*, Cambridge: Belknap Press, 1981, or Samuel Huntington, Jr. et. al (eds.), *The Crisis of Democracy: Report on the Governability of Democracies to the Trilateral Commission*, New York: NYU Press, 1975.

2. Samir Amin. *Unequal Development: An Essay on the Social Formation of Periphery Capitalism*, New York: Monthly Review Press, 1976.

3. Mexico under Cardenas developed a large public sector, state capitalist system. It had an ideology of corporativism. A recent essay on this subject by Robert Kaufman, "Mexico and Latin American Authoritarianism," in Jose Reyna and Richard Weinert (eds.), *Authoritarianism in Mexico*, Philadelphia: ISHI, 1977, argues in a vein which is very applicable to the Arab world. For example, he speaks of the breakdown of the populism of the Cardenas era and the rise of new authoritarianism (the technocratic elite, the reliance on orthodox and liberal economics, the priority on growth over social welfare, high technology and inappropriate industrial strategy). These points are quite applicable to Egypt under Sadat, and they are beginning to become relevant to Iraq in the late 1970s. Kaufman's formulation is superior to even a sophisticated modernization theory approach, e.g., Gino Germani, *Authoritarianism, Fascism and National Populism*, New Brunswick: Transaction Press, 1978, because given the internal dynamic in political economy the meaning of structure is much richer. Finally, if one compares Kaufman's formulation to a contemporary Marxist formulation, e.g., Florestan Fernandes, *Apontamentos sobre a teoria do Autoritarismo*, Sao Paolo: Editora Hucitec, 1979. Kaufman's rendering is less mechanical. Fernandes theorizes at great length about the periphery state and the transition of socialism. This appears to be a generalization and a universalizing of Lenin's theory of the uneven development of Russia. Do all states on the periphery have Russia's chance for socialist revolution?

4. A. W. Singham (ed.). *Non-Aligned Movement in World Politics,* Westport: L. Hill, 1977.

5. Samir Amin. *Arab Nation,* London: Zed Press, 1978.

6. Peter Evans. *Dependent Development: The Alliance of Multi-National, State and Local Capital in Brazil,* Princeton: Princeton University Press, 1979, ch. 1.

7. "Political Economy as a Paradigm for the Study of Islamic History." *International Journal of Middle East Studies,* 11 (4), 1980, 511-523.

8. In Egypt the political economy position arose as a critique of the official left as one finds it in 'Abdel Razeq Hassan et al., *La Voie egyptienne vers le socialisme* (Cairo: n.d.), and the Western modernization theory in its various indigenous forms, e.g., Henry Habib Ayrout, *The Egyptian Peasant,* Boston: Beacon Press, 1963, (the original French edition was 1938). In these notes I will emphasize works written in or translated into European languages. Another modernization work is Gabriel S. Saab, *The Egyptian Agrarian Reform, 1952-1962,* New York: Oxford University Press, 1967; among political economy works of note are Hossam Issa, *Capitalisme et sociétés anonymes en l'Egypte,* Paris: R. Pichon et R. Durand Auzias, 1970; the best-known political economy works in English are Mahmoud Hussein, *Class Struggle in Egypt 1948-1970,* New York: Monthly Review, 1974; Nawal el-Saadawi, *The Hidden Face of Eve, Women in the Arab World,* London: Zed Press, 1980.

9. There are several competent modernization school interpretations of Libya. Henri Habib, *Politics and Government of Revolutionary Libya,* Montreal, 1975; Ra'fat Shanbur, *Power and Concept of the Libyan Revolution,* Lausanne: Ed. Mediterranéenes, 1977; Omar I. El-Fathaly et al., *Political Development and Bureaucracy in Libya,* Lexington: Lexington Books, 1977; the political economy critique of modernizing theory has not developed too far, see Ruth First, *Libya, the Elusive Revolution,* Middlesex: Penguin, 1974. The reasons for the weakness of the political economy cannot simply be laid to the lack of material, cf., Aghil Barbar, *Government and Politics in Libya 1969-78: A Bibliography,* Monticello, Ill.: Vance Bibliographies, 1979, nor to the lack of adequate scholars. One suspects that a fundamental preoccupation with centralism that runs through political economy (and modernization theory) may simply be less applicable to Libya. Political economy could potentially be developed to stress the dialectic between region and central state far more than it has. Libyan proverbs suggest a vast gulf between the central state intellectuals and the world of the people, cf., 'Ali Al-Misrati, *Al-Mujtama' al-libi fi Khilal amthalihi al-sha'biya,* Tripoli, 1962 (Libyan Society from Its Proverbs). Since the Libyan Revolution, the Markaz Jihad al-Libi has collected a great deal of oral history material. This is published in the *Journal* of the Markaz.

10. For Iraq, Hanna Batatu, *The Old Social Classes and the Revolutionary Movements in Iraq*, Princeton: Princeton University Press, 1978, eclipses everything so far; the Iraqi writers on the modern period have emphasized the nationalist movement.

11. Ahmad al-Ghunaymi. *Jews and the Zionist Movement in Egypt, 1897-1947*, Cairo, n.d., in Arabic.

12. Martin Wilmington. *Middle East Supply Center*, Albany: SUNY Press, 1971.

13. 'Abd al-Rahman al-Sharqawi. *Egyptian Earth* (Novel) Trans. by Desmond Stewart, London: Heineman, 1962.

14. Wendell Cleland. *The Population Problem in Egypt: A Study of Population Trends and Conditions in Modern Egypt*, Lancaster, Pa.: Science Press, 1936.

15. Sam Aaronvitch. *The Ruling Class: A Study of British Finance Capital*, London: Lawrence and Wishart, 1961. For more recent trends reflecting the mergers, see *Big Business...* , New York: Holmes and Meier, 1975.

16. Miles Copeland. *The Game of Nations*, New York: Simon and Schuster, 1970.

17. An introduction to American Middle East foreign policy: Joe Stork. *Middle East Oil and the Energy Crisis*, New York: Monthly Review, 1975.

18. Mona Hamman. "Labor Migration and the Sexual Division of Labor," *Merip*, no. 95 (April 1981) 5-11; more generally Chris Gerry and Ray Bromley (eds.) *Casual Work and Poverty in Third World Cities*, New York: Wiley, 1979.

19. Saad ad-Din Ibrahim, "Anatomy of Egypt's Militant Islamic Groups: Methodological Note and Preliminary Findings," *International Journal of Middle East Studies*, 12 (4), 1980, 423-453.

20. Richard A. Webster, *Industrial Imperialism in Italy, 1908-1915*, Berkeley: University of California, 1975; Claudio Segre, *Fourth Shore: Italian Colonization of Libya*, Chicago: University of Chicago , 1974.

21. For a comment on the link between the attempted coups by junior officers and the Palestine issue see Muhammad Muzaffir al-Adhami, *Nationalist Dimensions of the 1941 Ma'iss Revolution in Iraq*, Baghdad, 1980, 8 (in Arabic).

22. Ester Boserup. *Women's Role in Economic Development*, London: Allen and Unwin, 1970. Still the best general work on the deterioration of women's condition in the Third World as capitalism develops.

23. Soraya al-Torki, "Family Organization and Women's Power in Urban Saudi Arabian Society," *Journal of Anthropological Research*, 33, 1977, 277-287.

24. Farhad Kazemi. *Poverty and Revolution in Iran: The Migrant Poor, Urban Marginality and Politics*, New York: New York University Press, 1980, contains interesting information for this perspective.

CHAPTER VIII

POLITICS, HISTORY AND NATIONALISM:
THE ORIGINS OF
ROMANIA'S SOCIALIST PERSONALITY CULT

VLAD GEORGESCU

Few modern ruling classes have encouraged in recent years a personality cult similar to the one practiced today in socialist Romania; we should also add, that in the past, surrender to the powers of one single leader has hardly been a characteristic of the East-European, not to speak of the Romanian, political elites. In Romania, the traditional pattern has been to have rather strong and dominating elites: these were the boyars until 1858, and the political parties representing the landlords and the bourgeoisie after that. These elites were usually much stronger than the executive power represented by the princes or the kings. The existing power structure never favored the development of a personality cult. Even domineering personalities like the two Brătianus had to accept the fact that their power was limited: Romanian political tradition lacks any messianic approach, any missionary or visionary zeal. The constitutional system adopted in 1866, and the fact that from 1866 to 1927 the country was ruled by only two kings (both moderate personalities favoring the constitutional regime), as well as the existence of several social and political groups effectively counterbalanced each other, and were probably the reasons why the emerging modern Romanian society was spared the experience of a regime based on the personality cult.

As elsewhere in Eastern Europe, the very basis of the system introduced in the 19th century was challenged during the 1930s; the old political parties and social elites continued to run the country along the traditional lines and no cult could be perceived as far as their leaders were concerned. However, Romania's third king, Carol II, succumbed to the authoritarian temptation and proclaimed his royal dictatorship in 1938. General, later Marshal, Antonescu replaced it in 1940 with his own military dictatorship, which lasted until 1944. From an institutional point of view, both were personal regimes, very

[129]

different from the ones which had existed since 1866; nevertheless, in neither case did the dictators, who both ruled for a very short period of time anyway and under rather adverse international conditions, try to establish a personality cult similar to the one existing at that time in Italy, Germany or Russia. Their personal dictatorship was mainly political, their aims were limited. They were conspicuously lacking in any philosophical background; the role of the past, of history, both as a model and as justification was not essential. At no point did these first Romanian dictators, or as a matter of fact, any East-European dictator, pretend to be a guiding light. Their entire system of values, their *forma mentis*, the aims they were pursuing, were all opposed to a political mentality which would have singled out one of them as the source of universal knowledge. Dictatorship was perceived just as a temporary political instrument, meant for achieving some practical goals, not the changing of the entire fabric of society.

If some sort of personality cult has to be found in inter-war Romania, the only place to look would be the rising Iron Guardist movement. The legionnaires did not want to change the world, but they had a philosophy, simple as it was. Their goals were beyond a mere political change. Like all their European brethren, their policy was teleological and the remodeling of the world did not stop with the present and the future but was running deep into the past. For the first time in Romanian history, a political group tried to remodel the past according to its own perceptions, ideology, and political goals.

The most striking fact about the legionnaire approach to the past was that it rejected the traditional concepts on which Romania's nationalism has been based for at least three hundred years, namely, the concept of the Roman origin of the people. For the Iron Guard, Rome was just another example of Western decadence. The Roman conquest of Dacia had not been a progressive event; quite the contrary, it prevented the natural development of the superior genetic characteristics of the natives. The less civilized but morally superior Dacians were to be preferred to the mollified Latins; the Romanian right proclaimed its will to return to the sources and achieve society's rebirth through what was called "the revolt of our non-Latin essence."

The reshaping of society was, thus, supposed to take place not by following some general abstract schemes but in accordance with an axiological pattern born with the beginning of time and specific only to their country. This was obviously too much of a task for the old leadership, patterned after the traditional political values; a new image emerged, independent but similar to the same one emerging within the other European rightist or fascist movements. The image of a leader appeared with almost supernatural qualities, capable of changing the course of history, willing to take his people's fate into his hands, convinced of having to fulfill a historic mission and with no doubts whatsoever about the way to achieve it. Such a leader was supposed to be the embodiment of the best national traditions, somewhere between a fairy tale character and the old, legendary princes. The powers he had been blessed with, all God-given, were similar and comparable to the elements of nature. He was usually compared with the sun, the mountains, the eagle, the oak; in the legionnaire system of values, such a chosen personality was more than a leader: he was a hero.

This heroic approach was constantly used to enhance Codreanu's image and present him as the instrument of providence, the only man capable of bringing about needed change. After the "captain's" assassination, the same approach was used to portray the movement's new leader, H. Sima.[1]

The legionnaire personality cult had nevertheless a short life. The Iron Guard was capable of overthrowing a weak royal dictator but was no match for the tough general who seized power in September 1940. The supernatural and heroic leader went into hiding in January 1941, taking with him the first real attempt at creating a personality cult in Romanian political life.

Theoretically at least, conditions for the emergence of a new cult returned to Romania after the war; the new social and political totalitarian pattern had all the potentials of breeding the same kind of heroic and providential leadership image it had given birth to half a century earlier. But it did not. In Stalin's Eastern Europe there was room for only one cult, and even those most eager to imitate his style, had to content themselves with the role of lieutenants.

The first communist Romanian dictator, Gheorghe Gheorghiu-Dej seems to have accepted such a place with ease. He wasted no time in pointing out Stalin's greatness and genius as well as the "objective" obligation: every communist had to try to imitate the model as closely as possible. It had been Stalin after all, wrote Gheorghiu-Dej in 1949, who had performed miracles: "old Russia, a country backward economically, predominantly agricultural, has become in an unbelievably short period of time an advanced industrial country, the most civilized country in the world, with the best educated and cultivated people in the entire world. Soviet industry has now the most modern world

technology. . . . Soviet agriculture has become the most advanced
agriculture in the world, with the highest productivity and the highest scientific and technological level."[2]

It is still an open question if by making such statements, Gheorghiu-
Dej was sincere or only shrewd but from the point of view of our
topic this is not relevant. Relevant is only the fact that the satellite
status and the personality cult were antinomic terms, impossible to
conciliate. A real cult could flourish only in socialist countries where
some degree of political independence has been achieved and where
the ruling classes did not always have to acknowledge Soviet pre-
eminence.

When the architect of Romania's maverick course died in 1965,
the ruling class was seemingly moving domestically towards a Tito-
type solution, willing to use its newly acquired margin of maneuver
to put some distance not only between its foreign policy and the
Soviet state but also between its internal options and the Soviet
model. The infighting between the apparatchiks and the technocrats
over the country's internal evolution lasted until the early 1970s. It
ended with the victory of the nationalistic but strongly Orthodox
hardliners. The technocrats surrounding prime minister Gheorghe I.
Maurer were gradually eliminated, as was the prime minister himself.
After a couple of more hesitating years a presidential regime was introduced in 1974 based on the strident cult of the president.

"Life shows," as a much-used Marxist formula likes to proclaim,
that with no exception, the communist elites which have decided to
challenge total Soviet hegemony and achieve some sort of political
autonomy, have finally resorted to the regime of the personality
cult, as the most useful instrument of maintaining their power. This
was true in Yugoslavia, as it was in Albania, North Korea, China and
North Vietnam. Only in Yugoslavia was the cult moderated with the
passing of time. In all the other cases it increased with every new
step taken towards weakening the ties with Moscow. It looks as if
socialist independence inevitably breeds the personality cult, making
domestic change, modernization, and liberalization even more difficult to achieve than in the dependent socialist regimes.

The case of Romania could give us some answers about the question, why a communist independent elite supports a regime which is
sometimes more Stalinist than the Soviet model itself? This is even
more difficult to understand since the personality cult regimes are imposed after some degree of independence has been achieved. What

makes these parties want to escape the Soviet political influence while at the same time are eager to stick with the past Soviet domestic pattern?

The autonomy of the Romanian Communist Party, at that time the Romanian Workers Party, was won in the early 1960s over the problem of economic independence, that is over the right of the R.C.P. to go on with the orthodox Marxist path of modernization and impose a crash course of industrialization. Being independent meant the continued enforcement of the Soviet economic program, which Khruschev had planned to reserve only for the northern tier of his bloc. His plans of the early 1960s called for the transformation of the southern tier, including Romania, into an agricultural and raw material supply area.

Relative Romanian independence was won by a coalition of two main forces, one representing the old but nationally-minded communists[3] and the newly risen technocrats, the other representing a group of young, nationalistic, and ambitious apparatchiks led by Nicolae Ceauşescu. The technocrats were in favor of a moderate rhythm of industrialization and more liberal internal policies, aimed mainly at reforming the inherited Stalinist structure. Under their rule, the country would have probably used its greater diplomatic margin of maneuver to slowly move towards the Yugoslav domestic system. The victory of the independent minded but neo-Stalinist apparatchiks put an end to their timid reforms. The Romanian communists continued to keep their distance from the Soviet Union while at the same time rejecting any kind of internal reforms except strictly administrative ones. Internally, they moved back to the classic Stalinist pattern of economic development. The paradox of this policy was that a more and more autonomous country was based domestically on a more and more Sovietized regime.

The decision to continue imposing Stalinist economic policies had long-lasting effects upon the country's political regime. Instead of moving towards a progressive, liberal and decentralized system, like the Yugoslavs and the Hungarians, the Romanians moved in the opposite direction. The new ruling class had a strong sense of its "historic" mission, it wanted to go not only far but also fast. As in any Sovietocracy it was convinced that the truth had been revealed to it and that it had the right to impose and enforce any kind of policy in order to bring it closer to fulfillment. Forcing and concentrating all the resources and energies into a few chosen fields could not possibly be accomplished through the relatively liberal policies of the late 1960s and early 1970s. The very pattern of modernization adopted by the apparatchiks made quite impossible, even without taking into consideration any other reasons, the rise of a more open and human socialism.

The neo-Stalinists showed great ability in pushing around and finally eliminating both the old converted Stalinists and the technocrats, that is the group which had actually engineered the independence and the reformist course introduced after 1964. In many ways, they represented the new ruling caste, limited as far as the decision making process was concerned to a small number of individuals, bound, at least at the top, by many family relations. Most of them had a predominantly peasant background. They were sharing a more traditional set of values, were opposed to Western culture and were afraid of its potential impact almost as much as they were afraid of the Kremlin's influence. It was this group which gained control over the party first, then over the state apparatus. This group imposed the regime of the personality cult. It was considered to be the most suitable instrument for achieving the ambitious economic program while at the same time maintaining a safe and unchallengeable power monopoly.

The great socialist personality cults have usually been built around rather uncharismatic personalities; Stalin was the first and most striking example and Ceauşescu fits well into that category. It would be almost irrelevant to repeat his many alleged qualifications and qualities or the long list of praises that are chanted whenever his name is mentioned; he is God and genius, sun and eagle, indestructible as a rock, architect of undreamed-of achievements; he happens to be a Romanian but he has long ago transcended any ethnic boundaries to become part of mankind's eternal glories. It was, thus, only natural for the archeologists to discover the first *homo sapiens* not far from his native village.[4]

In fact, all this does not sound terribly new or original. From Stalin to Hoxha, from Mao to Kim-Il-Sung, not to mention several non-Communist cases like Hitler's, Bokassa's or Khomeini's, all such cults resort to the same type of rhetoric. They all bless the dictator with the same supernatural and inborn qualities. What makes the Ceauşescu case somehow different is the fact that the "guiding light" complex has been extended to most of his family. His wife is presented as one of the world's leading scientists, his daughter is a renowned mathematician, his two sons are both rising stars in the field of theoretical physics, one of his brothers is a prolific historian, another is a great biologist. These "characteristics" exist obviously besides their current political duties. Mrs. Ceauşescu is a Vice-Prime Minister and is in charge of the party's personnel policy. Her son Nicu runs the communist youth organization; brother Ilie supervises the army's political department, being what the Soviets used to call, a political commissar; Ion, the biologist, is running the State Planning Committee.

The family seems to be directly in charge of some of the most important state, party and army positions; it shares with the President not only the political burden but also the aura of intellectual excellence and cultural superiority. Such an enlarged cultural complex is a specific characteristic of the Romanian personality cult and is seldom found in other socialist or non-socialist cults.

One of the striking facts about the 20th century personality cults is their lack of original thinking. Regardless of the claims, the "guiding lights" had little to add to the existing ideological Marxist edifice. The Romanian cult makes no exception. Officially, Ceauşescu's contribution to the "thesaurus of Marxist thinking" is hailed as "priceless" and "inestimable" but the many volumes published under his name show little else but a very eclectic thinking, made even more superficial by the conscious attempts at diminishing the importance of its Soviet roots. Ideologically, the Romanian cult was indeed placed into an agonizing dilemma: how to maintain a Stalinist regime without paying tribute to the Stalinist ideology? How to enforce the Soviet economic pattern, without accepting the Soviet political and ideological presence? Forced into such a dilemma because of the Soviet character of his independent regime, the Romanian ruling class had to resort to the only available ideology and practice aggressively what all political elites have used in times of crisis, that is, nationalism. Nationalism was of course not new on the Romanian political scene. It had been cultivated, advocated, used and misused long before the rise of the personality cult. There are nevertheless some essential differences between the boyar and bourgeois nationalism and the socialist one.

The former ruling classes had practiced a predominantly political nationalism, with rather precise goals, aimed at the creation of the national and united Romanian state. After 1918, it was aimed at defending the gains of the Great War. It had had an overwhelmingly external character and had been concerned first of all with neighbors who were perceived to be threatening the national identity and unity of the state.

Because of its strong anti-Russian character, this type of nationalism was considered very dangerous by the emerging communist regime and targeted for destruction. One of the first moves of the Communist party, once it achieved total control over the country in 1948, was to destroy the very institutions the old nationalism had been built on, that is, the academy, the educational and research system, and the intelligentsia itself.[5] National and nationalism became outcast terms,[6] as was cosmopolitanism.[7] The first ones were identified with the bourgeois heritage, the second linked to Western imperialism.[8] It was in the name of this new patriotism, called "socialist internationalism" that the party proceeded with rewriting the history of the country and remodeling the past according to the new political realities. The Roman origin and the Latin heritage were almost completely denied, ethnically the Romanians were declared to be Slavs and even the orthography was changed to accommodate the new theory.[9] In order to emphasize this Slavic character and diminish the Roman one, România became Romînia.[10] Reading the pre-World War II historians, like Iorga, became a serious offense, regardless of the fact that Iorga had been assassinated by the Iron Guard in 1940. Practically all non-communist intellectuals—who had been communist in a country where the party itself had less than 1,000 members in 1944—were dismissed as bourgeois, forbidden, their works taken out of the bookstores and libraries, and expelled from the educational programs.[11] There is no doubt that such a cultural surgery, organized by academicians like M. Roller,[12] had a long-lasting effect upon the country's cultural life and was responsible for its visible decadence.

These philo-Slavic and pro-Russian "scientific" excesses were the first ones to disappear when Gheorghiu-Dej began his drive for autonomy. The teaching of the Russian language lost its privileged place in schools, the Soviet-Romanian research institute, the Soviet bookstore and the Romanian-Russian museum were closed. Most of the "bourgeois" intellectuals were rehabilitated, as were the Roman and Latin cultures. A wave of official anti-Russianism swept the country in 1963 and 1964, cleverly orchestrated by the Gheorghiu-Dej group.[13] The Romanians' initial reaction was cautious, the "dialectical" turnaround was so sudden and dramatic that many greeted it with suspicion. It was only when the "declaration of independence" was made public in April, 1964, that its real motives were finally understood.

Gheorghiu-Dej had no time to build his own personality cult. He died in 1965, having ruled for less than a year as an autonomous leader. It might not have been built at all. The fact is that in 1965 the party's new leadership had most of the options open and an opportunity for relatively free maneuvering that few other East European elites ever had.

Ceauşescu became party secretary in 1965, president of the State Council in 1968, and president of the republic in 1974. These years were conspicuously lacking the nationalistic approach which was to become so typical for his later style. His speeches as well as the official party documents ignore almost totally the past, making only rare and marginal historical references. From 1965 to approximately 1971, historians could say and write more or less whatever they wanted, without being too much afraid that their findings about the Romans, the Slavs or the Dacians could have a political significance. As a result, Romanian historiography experienced a short period of relative freedom and autonomy, something it had lost after the assumption of power by the socialist regime in 1944.[14]

For most analysts, as for most Romanians, the sudden nationalistic upsurge of 1971 as well as the neo-Stalinist approach to domestic issues expressed in the so-called "July theses" came rather as a surprise.[15] Today the "theses" could be seen as the final stage of the power struggle between Maurer's reformers and Ceauşescu's hardliners. But in 1971, the lines were not yet clearly drawn. Not before 1974 did the neo-Stalinists achieve complete victory. It was only then that the 11th Party Congress officially sanctified the president's personality cult and the nationalistic ideology on which it was based.

"The Program of the Romanian Communist Party, for the building of a socialist, multilaterally developed society and for the advancing of Romania towards communism," adopted by the Congress has a long (18 pages) historical introduction. It is, in fact, a theoretical background of the new cult. This was the first time that a communist party program spelled out so clearly its interest in the past and its will of rewriting it according to its own perception. The verbiage was still Marxist but that was about all which was left of it. Under a misleading socialist rhetoric, the program was actually promoting a history-oriented nationalism, aimed primarily at justifying the cult of the president.

The most striking characteristic of the new philosophy was its genetic, some might call it racist, approach. The Romanians seem never to have changed or evolved, their inborn qualities have been the same from the age of the Dacians, to the builders of socialism. A crazy "Thracomania" contaminated official Romanian culture after 1974. It was asserted that Romanians have always had some sort of superiority over their less fortunate neighbors and certainly over the Slavs whose place in the country's history was almost totally ignored. The party did not want them to be part of the Roman ethnicity. A

very clear attempt was made at eliminating from the process of eth-
nogenesis everything which might have spoiled the initial Thracian
and Roman character of the people. Such a purifying approach was
almost as much of an exaggeration as the Slavomania had been in the
1950s. For political reasons the party was rewriting now the same
past it had once remodeled, albeit in the opposite direction.[16]

The reason for this new genetic and megalomaniac perception of
the past is not difficult to understand and it is part of the president's
own perception of his place in history. When he visits Transylvania he
likes to be greeted by people dressed like Dacians. In Moldavia, he re-
views not an army of workers or peasants but hundreds of individuals
imitating Stephen the Great's (1457-1504) cavalry. In Bucharest, the
grandiose ceremonies organized in the Stadium of the Republic are
opened not by a worker carrying the hammer and sickle but by Tudor
Vladimirescu and his *pandours* (gendarmes). And the museum of the
history of the party does not begin with the Romanian socialist
movement but with the conquest of Dacia by the Romans.

There is no doubt that the president considers himself much more
as a descendant of the old princes and heroes than as a follower of
the several obscure Soviet citizens who ran the party as general sec-
retaries in the interwar period. The "princely" mentality is also witnessed by the fact that alone among the 20th century presidents, he
chose to carry a sceptre at his presidential inauguration.

Apart from any other immediate and practical reasons, the Party's
nationalism should, thus, be seen as a projection of the personality
cult complex. It is not political nationalism; it has no outside goals
to achieve, it is not even concerned with the Russians any more or
with the problem of independence, as it should be. After some initial
but strictly controlled anti-Russianism, any references which might
upset the big brother have been banned and today not even the word
Bessarabia can appear in print. The Party's nationalism is not interested in such a question any more because from the point of view of
the personality cult there is nothing to gain from it. The obsession
with the Thracians and *homo sapiens* stems from the fact that it projects into the past a magnified image of the leader. In order to be
great, greatness has to be concerned not only with the future, with
the promised land, but also with the past. The roots, too, have to be
grandiose. This is probably the psychological explanation of the historically oriented nationalism of all contemporary socialist personality
cults. They have nothing to do with politics, little to do with the nation, they are hardly interested in history or nationalism. The only
thing that matters is the global image of the "guiding light."

Almost all the extreme 20th century personality cults have flourished in societies claiming to belong to the socialist system. Such an intriguing fact has to be explained and the easiest answer would be to consider the cult as a natural, inbred symptom of socialism itself. Socialism has indeed the potential of giving birth to the personality cult, mainly because its elite rules over a classless society and cannot identify itself with any social background and force. It lacks social determination which would make it open to the moderating pressure of a diverse social body. In countries where the ruling group still represents a social class, such as those in pre-world war Eastern Europe or in today's Latin America, the regime can be dictatorial but the temporary leader would never be able to establish a viable personality cult. In countries where the ruling party represents only a political not a social elite, the cult has been almost always imposed.

But the mere fact that socialism has in its social structure a potential for the rise of the cult does not entirely explain why as a political regime, the personality cult did flourish only in some socialist states. Considered as a social and economic system, socialism had actually given birth to a variety of political regimes, ranging from Hoxha's and Ceauşescu's cults, to Kadar's enlightened despotism, from Honecker's absolutism to Jaruzelski's military dictatorship and to Yugoslavia's semi-democracy. Choosing a certain political regime within socialism's framework is more or less an option the ruling elite can choose for itself.

As far as the regime of the personality cult is concerned, if some degree of independence from the Soviet Union is a clear prerequisite, the real reason for its imposition has to be found in the internal approach to the problem of development. The independent socialist countries which, like Yugoslavia, have moved away from the Soviet economic pattern have considerably softened the leader's cult. From a cult, very similar to Stalin's, Tito's image has gradually moved towards a grandfatherly figure, used more as a symbol than as an everyday political tool. In Romania, the change moved in the opposite direction. The decision to stick with the Stalinist economic policy gradually ended the liberalizing process started after 1964, and led to the restoration of a typical neo-Stalinist, although autonomous regime, characterized by an extreme personality cult. Like Stalin, the president is supposed to be both "guiding light" and "grand helmsman," which means that he is involved in the everyday economic, cultural, social, and political processes. Such an "undemocratic centralism" adds considerable burden to a system already plagued by its unworkable economic pattern of development. Strange as it might look, the obvious signs of economic crisis and social unrest have made the cult even more strident. The people are constantly assured that the helmsman has all the answers. But these answers all look not only familiar but distressingly similar to the ones given in the bankrupt 1950s. Because of the genius complex, there is little chance to see the helsman confessing that the options might have been wrong and initiating a new course. The regime of the personality cult seems to have succeeded in blocking in Romania, as in all the countries in which it has been installed, any foreseeable mechanism of change.

So far, no regime of the personality cult has ever been overthrown during the lifetime of its founder. But no personality cult has survived the founders. In both Russia and China, the process of desacralization began almost immediately after the ending of the grandiose farewell ceremonies. The cult proved to be as much of a burden for the respective countries as it was for the ruling elites. It is entirely reasonable to think that this will also happen to the still existing personality cults. Because even in the land of socialism, politics have to be based, once in a while, on some kind of common sense.

NOTES

1. Here are some samples of the rhetoric surrounding Horia Sima's short-lived cult: "Horia. . . is bigger than the mountains. He has the look of an angel and the sword of an archangel. Horia is the light, he is the will," *Glasul Strămoşesc* (Sibiu) December 15, 1940; "He stood up in the middle of the tempest. His convictions never wavered," *Muncitorul Legionar*, January 15, 1941; he is "the eternal pilon of the nation," *Biruinţa*, December 15, 1940.

2. Gh. Gheorghiu-Dej, *Articole şi cuvîntări* (Bucureşti 1960), 265.

3. Nobody would deny today that L. Pătrăşcanu's communism had a rather national character, but Gh. Gheorghiu-Dej is also on the record for having made remarks which might have cost him dearly. See especially his volume *O politică românească* (Bucureşti 1946).

4. In the volume presented to the president in 1979 on the occasion of his anniversary, he was proclaimed "providential man," "torch," "genius," "legendary soul," "sunrise," "oak," "eagle," "helmsman," capable of turning "the heavy wheels of history" and to be "the architect of contemporary history." For a more detailed list of qualities bestowed on this "man chosen by history" see Vlad. Georgescu, *Politica şi istorie. Cazul comuniştilor români, 1944-1977* (München, 1981), 59-60, 150.

5. The old Romanian Academy was abolished in June 1948 and replaced by a new one with all the members handpicked by the party; in the same month a new educational law forced out of the universities most of the "bourgeois" professors; many spent years in prison where some of the best known, like Gh. Brátianu, for example, were actually killed. All the existing historical institutes were closed and their journals replaced with one single, centrally controlled review. It seems that the anti-intellectual repression was harsher in Romania than in most other "people's democracies," *Ibid*, 12-13.

6. The term "national" was banned even in sports; the former national soccer championships became republican soccer championships.

7. Leonte Ráutu, for more than 20 years the regime's chief ideologist, published an attack on cosmopolitanism in 1946; the intellectuals were accused of treating their Western counterparts as "colleagues instead of class enemies" and of having failed to unmask "rotten cosmopolitanism," L. Rautu, *Impotriva cosmopolitismului şi obiectivismului în ştiinţele sociale* (Bucureşti 1946), passim. In 1981 after his daughter expressed the desire to emigrate to the West, Ráutu lost all his party positions, including his seat in the Central Committee.

8. The Soviet Union "has won the right to teach all the others the traits of the new man," *Patriotismul în literatura sovietică* (Bucureşti, 1957), passim. To help build such a "new man," several manuals of patriotism were published in the late 1940s and 1950s, such as *Patriotismul* (Bucuresti 1947), and *Patriotismul socialist şi internaţionalismul proletar* (Bucureşti 1955).

9. The Slavicized orthography was introduced in 1953. See the decree in *Mic dicţionar ortografic* (Bucureşti 1953), 5-6. If we would believe the linguistic journal *Limba română*, 6, 1954, the old orthography had become "intolerable," "a great concern for the working class and a state problem."

10. Both *â* and *î* express the same sound but the first rendering was closer to Latin while the second one to the Old Church Slavonic and the Cyrillic alphabet. Romînia rebecame România immediately after Ceauşescu's coming to power.

11. The list is too long to be worth mentioning. Typical for all these intellectuals' misfortunes was the case of Titu Maiorescu, one of the fathers of modern Romanian culture. Unfortunately, he had also been a Kantian philosopher and, even worse, a conservative prime-minister. These were more than enough reasons to declare him a "royal court valet," a "cosmopolitan without fatherland," servant of the "clique of oppressors;" S. Bratu, *Fantoma lui Maiorescu* (Bucureşti 1957), passim. C. Ionescu-Gulian, *T. Maiorescu* in "Studii," 2, 1950, passim., *Din istoria filozofiei în Romãnia*, I (Bucureşti 1955), passim.

12. M. Roller ran the academy and the "historical front" from 1948 to 1956, as a sort of local Zhdanov. His *Istoria României*, first published in 1947, became the new bible of "socialist patriotism."

13. The "Cartea Rusă" bookstore was closed in 1959, immediately after Soviet troops left Romania; the institute and the museum had the same fate in 1963. A violently anti-Russian volume called *K. Marx: Insemnări despre români* was published in 1964 and most historical studies adopted an anti-Slavic tone. Several formerly persecuted intellectuals became members of the academy in 1963 and the cultural exchanges with the West were resumed.

14. The "historical front" was actually almost completely disbanded, putting an end to the old Stalinist system of publishing collective works, expressing only one single point of view. Several histories of Romania were actually published during the early 1960s and their interpretations were unusually divergent; Vlad Georgescu, *op. cit.*, 41-43.

15. The thesis revived the forgotten rhetoric of the 1950s and the tone of "ideological firmness"; N. Ceaușescu, *Expunere la consfătuirea cu activul de partid din domeniul ideologiei*, in *România pe drumul construiri societății socialiste multilateral desvoltate*, VI (București 1972), passim.

16. For an excellent analysis of the present obsession with history and its continuous remodeling to fit the party's political needs see S. Fischer-Galati, "Myths in Romanian History" in *The East European Quarterly*, XV, 3 (Fall 1981).

CHAPTER IX

THE DESPOT AS THEOCRAT:
AYATOLLAH KHOMEINI AND ISLAMIC FUNDAMENTALISM
IN HISTORICAL PERSPECTIVE

MAJID TEHRANIAN

"He could have done in Tehran what Jesus did in Jerusalem and Mohammed did in Mecca . . . . But he missed his chance."

—Abdol-Hassan Bani-Sadr
The deposed president of Iran,
speaking in an interview about
Khomeini, September 1981

There are few contemporary political leaders who have attracted as much attention, curiosity and bewilderment as Ayatollah Khomeini has in the world. At first glance, Khomeini appears as an historical anachronism. He does not fit the ordinary image of a twentieth-century dictator. He defies the ordinary explanations for a despot's craving for absolute power. He is too old (81 years in 1981) to be considered in search of personal power; too frugal in his living style to be viewed as a fortune hunter; too independent of his family ties to be accused of building a dynasty (his son is ideologically too liberal, while his grandson has defied his policies); too divisive in his leadership style to be suspected of constructing a modern political party; too much of a traditionalist to be considered as the architect of a modern totalitarian state.

Andrew Young, the United States Ambassador to the United Nations, called him—in a moment of enthusiasm in 1979—the equivalent of a modern saint. Dariush Sayegan, an Iranian intellectual, likened him to Mahatma Gandhi. Oriana Fallaci, the Italian reporter/novelist, has viewed him as a "shrewd fanatic."[1] Mansour Farhand, former Iranian Ambassador to the United Nations who served early under Khomeini's regime, has labelled him "criminally insane."[2] Contemporary novelist/reporter Naipaul has perhaps captured Khomeini's contradictory images most poignantly in his reactions to two photographs of the leader he encountered in Tehran. The first showed Khomeini, "as hard-eyed and sensual and unreliable and roguish-looking as any enemy might have portrayed." The second revealed "his old man's eyes held victory. No frown, no gesture of defiance, no clenched fist: the hands were the hands of the man of peace, the man at peace."[3]

To understand Khomeini and his place in history, we are clearly in need of some historical perspective. Psychological categories and subjective impressions tend to lose their poignancy and relevance with the rapidly changing circumstances. Indeed, the first two of the above characterizations of Khomeini have been already recanted by their authors, while the last three will probably seem remote with the passage of time. The purpose of this essay is therefore to focus on the phenomenon of Khomeinism rather than on Khomeini, to examine the roots of Islamic fundamentalism of which Khomeini is a vital part, to review the Sh'a Islamic Ulema's revolutionary role in Iran, and finally to put Khomeini's doctrines of political legitimacy and political leadership in that historical context.

The Historical Roots of Islamic Fundamentalism

Islamic fundamentalism, or perhaps more accurately "puritanism," is not a novel religious phenomenon in Islam, although its current political and ideological manifestations are new.[4] Fundamentalism is a religious concept in Christianity which has perhaps no counterpart in Islam. By contrast, Christian fundamentalism is an ultraconservative movement, whereas Islamic fundamentalism or puritanism is a peculiar mélange of modernity and tradition, radicalism and obscurantism—more analogous to Christian Puritanism and its historic roots than to Fundamentalism. To live strictly according to the rule of the *Shari'a*, the Divine Law of Islam, has been an aspiration commonly shared among the Muslims for centuries. In contrast to the New Testament, which is a record of Divine Revelation, the Qur'an is considered by Muslims as *The Word* of God to be obeyed completely and unconditionally. The *Shari'a* is thus founded on four pillars: Qur'anic injunctions, the *Sunna* (tradition) of the Prophet, *Qiyas* (or principle of analogy), and *Ijm'a* (or the consensus of the Muslim community). While the first two are givens, the latter two have provided considerable room for interpretation and have led to the development of at least four different generally acknowledged schools of law in Sunni Islam (the majority sect) and one in Shi'a Islam (the minority sect primarily practiced in Iran, Iraq and Bahrain).

There has been, of course, always a difference among the five competing schools in their relative adherence to a strict versus a liberal interpretation of the *Shari'a*. The current puritanical revolutionary movement in Islam, however, cuts across that division and may be dated back only to the mid-nineteenth century.[5] In response to increasing Western penetration, a Pan-Islamic movement spread rapidly throughout the Muslim world in the second half of the nineteenth century that should be considered as the political and religious forerunner of the current upheavals. This represented a threefold response to a threefold challenge from the West. In reaction to the external domination of the West, it called for Islamic unity (Pan-Islam) to resist military, political and economic subjugation. In response to the internal domination of Western supported oligarchies and governments, it mobilized the masses for a series of liberal, nationalist and constitutional revolutions that occurred in Iran, Turkey and Egypt at the turn of the century. In recognition of the decline and decay of religious faith, undermined both by superstitious accretions as well as secularist tendencies, it also called for a new vitality and purification of the *Shari'a*. While there was considerable agreement among the *Ulema* (the learned men of Islam) and the faithful on the first two objectives, the third program proved far more difficult than initially believed. Some shrewd and yet conservative members of the *Ulema* (such as Shaikh Fazlullah Nuri in Iran) readily recognized the inherent contradictions between a divinely revealed legal system (the *Shari'a*) and the emerging constitutional forms of secular legislation for which members of the *Ulema* had agitated. Others, like Mohammed Iqbal in Pakistan and Muhammad Abdul and Rashid Rida in Egypt, opted for a reformation of the *Shari'a* along a modernist path and outside the political sphere.

The Failure of Secular Ideologies

In the meantime, the secular ideologies of progress imported from the West (Nationalism, Liberalism, and Marxism) continued to penetrate the Muslim world.[6] In the political sphere, this meant the establishment of secular nationalist regimes (Attaturk in Turkey, Reza Shah in Iran, the Wafd in Egypt) which tried to replace the *Shari'a* with Western systems of law and justice, secularize education, and modernize the entire fabric of society, including changing the position of women. In the economic sphere, the creation of centralized nation-state systems led first to the construction of economic infrastructures (transportation and communication, power, and banking systems) and subsequently to the introduction of import-substitution industries and the increasing dependence of the national economies on to the international capitalist market. In the cultural sphere, the penetration of Muslim societies by imported Western cultural arti-facts and mass media led to increasing levels of ideological conflict among the competing traditional and modern world views.

The secular ideologies of progress have largely failed to capture the imagination and loyalty of the masses on several grounds. First and foremost, these ideologies were foreign imports and lacked indigen-ous historic roots. The individuals and social groups that served as carriers of nationalism, liberalism and Marxism have often represented social and cultural elites, themselves alienated from their own cultural traditions through years of Western residence or Westernized educa-tion. Second, the increasing hegemony of the two world political and economic systems (capitalism and communism)—as represented by the military, technological and economic domination of the United States and Soviet Union—has increasingly left little room for the autonomy of the liberal/nationalist or Marxist/nationalist movements. As illustrated by the cases of the Shah's regime in Iran, the Marxist regime in Afghanistan and the Nasserist and Sadatist regimes in Egypt, an independent course of development in the so-called Third World has proved difficult if not impossible. The Third World may thus be considered as more of a fervent hope on the part of the less developed countries than as a historical reality. Last but not least, the mobiliza-tion of vast numbers of traditional Muslim peasants into the cities in search of employment and identity alongside a demographic revolu-tion that has created a youthful population (more than 50 per cent below the age of 20), have created ripe revolutionary conditions. The secular ideologies of progress, however, have not been able to provide this transient, alienated and exploited segment of the popu-lation with those delicate ties of ontological security and social iden-tity that a traditional religion can.

Fundamentalism as Counter-Modernization

The combination of these factors, in addition to a radicalization of the *Ulema* and a rising popular nostalgia for the lost innocence and cohesion of the past, have brought about an ideological revolution in the Muslim world that is at once revolutionary and obscurantist. What is going on in that world, however, is not without historical precedence. Most countries going through the initial phases of industrialization have experienced the phenomenon of counter-modernization, which might be called "the Rousseau effect."[7] It was perhaps the French romantic revolutionary philosopher Jean-Jacques Rousseau who first articulated a theory of counter-modernization. His formulation of the sense of popular disenchantment with the depersonalizing, alienating and abstracting effects of modern industrial society provided a revolutionary political philosophy that called for a radical attempt to recapture the innocence of "the noble savage" and the natural harmony of a Golden Past. Jefferson's call for rural democracy, Gandhi's advocacy of return to cottage industries in India, and Ayatollah Khomeini's zeal for a return to the purity and justice of pristine Islam are different ideological expressions of similar sentiments.

The road to hell is, however, paved with good intentions. The past, even if it were ideal, cannot be brought back to life. Efforts to do so through persuasion (as in the cases of Jefferson and Gandhi) will lead to romantic ideological lip service (as exemplified by the canonization of Jefferson and Gandhi in the United States and India). Attempts to recapture the past through violence and coercion (as in the case of Iran) will ultimately result in a complete breakdown of society and all traditions of civility—including those of Islam. In this sense, Ayatollah Kohmeini will be perhaps as effective in demythologyzing Islam as the Shah was in demythologyzing monarchy in Iran.

To say this, however, is not to consider fundamentalism as a political and ideological phenomenon that will soon wither away. The strengths of Islamic fundamentalism come from the conditions of foreign domination, elite exploitation, socio-cultural dislocation, mass mobilization and a continuing failure of the more progressive political ideologies and leaderships to provide viable alternatives. The Muslim world stands today in the twilight of tradition and modernity, suffering from the obscurantisms and inequities of both. Despotic modernization, either imposed by colonial or post-colonial secular elites, has often displaced traditional society without necessarily substituting a new rational and humane order; it has undermined the self-sufficiency of the indigenous economy without providing for productive interdependence; it has destroyed the legitimacy of the old polity without constructing a new peace and justice; it has homogenized and depersonalized the old cultural patterns without a new sense of cultural autonomy and creativity. The obscurantism and timidity of traditional societies are thus mixed with the greed and ceaseless anxieties of modernity to produce atomized societies held together by the fears and shame of backwardness.

The Ulema*'s Revolutionary Role in Iran*

This increasingly dualistic structure of Muslim society, economy and polity revealed itself perhaps above all in Iran in the ideological situation of the country prior to the Revolution of 1979.[8] We can best examine the salient features of this dualism in terms of the two competing religious and secular ideologies, structures, and processes of social communication, living autonomously side by side with immense frictions wherever and whenever they collided.

Secularization in Iran, as in the rest of the Islamic world, has faced the formidable obstacle that Islam recognizes no separation between spiritual and temporal authority. Muslims of all sectarian persuasions believe that Prophet Mohammad established an ideal Community of Believers in Medina within the short period of ten years from his exodus in 622 to his death in 632.

In Islam, it is not the birth of Mohammad which is celebrated as the beginning of the Islamic Era (in contrast to Christianity, which is dated from the birth of Jesus), but rather the "hegira," the Exodus of Mohammad from Mecca to Medina, together with a small band of his disciples. Muslims of the Sunni faith extend their conception of the Ideal Islamic State to the period of rule by the four "khulafa al-Rashidum" (the Rightly-Guided Successors of Mohammad), while the Shi'a maintain that succession rightly belongs to Mohammad's cousin and son-in-law Ali, the fourth Sunni Caliph of Islam, and his direct descendants.

The differences in doctrine have been of considerable historical importance up to this day. Because the Shi'tes have often been in minority, they have generally provided in Islamic history an ideological vehicle against the established powers and favorable to revolutionary action. Shi'ism was declared a state religion in Iran and gained a majority position during the sixteenth century. But its doctrines remained potentially revolutionary against any unjust temporal ruler.[9]

In matters of ideology and organization, Shi'ism continues to be distinct from Sunni Islam in two important respects. First, the doctrine of *Inamat* in Shi'ism transfers the *temporal* as well as the spiritual authority of Ali to his direct descendants. Among the Ismaili Shi'ites, that authority has been transferred through the seventh Imam, Ismail, to his present descendant, the Agha Khan. In Iran, however, it is the "Twelver" Shi'ites who dominate. For them, the transfer of power ceased with the disappearance of the twelfth Imam and is held in abeyance until he returns to save the world. In the meantime, however, all temporal power is considered to be illegitimate, to be tolerated only when and if it is exercised in accordance with the rule of the *Shari'a* as judged by the body of the *Ulema*. Shi-ism gives the *Ulema* considerable veto power over the temporal authorities. It also maintains the eschatological hopes for a second coming of the Mahdi, the twelfth Imam. Time and again, Mahdism has served revolutionary purposes in the Islamic world.

Secondly, the *Ulema*'s position of strength in Shi'a doctrine is supplemented in Iran by the strength of the country's religious organization. Given the right cause, this communication network can mobilize vast numbers of people (as we have seen in Iran's three revolutionary movements in this century, including the Constitutional Revolution of 1905, the oil nationalization movement of 1950-53 and the Islamic Revolution of 1979), each imbued with religious indignation and inspired by a single-minded purpose.

The traditional autonomy of the *Ulema* from the state, buttressed by their independent sources of income from religious endowments and taxes, placed them very close to the mood of the people and presented them as a powerful counter-elite. Historically, the *Ulema* used this power to act as mediators between the ruling elites and the masses. However, their close association with the Bazaar merchants and the liberal intelligentsia had always provided them with strong claims to political power. Under the Pahlavies, however, the relentless policy of Westernization and secularization increasingly alienated the *Ulema* from the monarchy. The *Ulema*'s religious, educational, legal and charitable institutions, wrapped into one integrated system, were considerably weakened by the encroachments of a secular and secularizing state.

However, another feature of the *Ulema*'s religious organization—namely, its polycentrism—gave them both the power to resist this repression and the ability to act when and if a unifying issue arose. The opportunity came after the bloody riots of June 1963 led by Ayatollah Khomeini and the radical *Ulema*. The *Ulema* and the monarchy were popularized as symbols for two diametrically opposed visions of the future of Iran. These two visions differed on almost every possible ground. The Islamic vision stemmed from an impulse to return to the purity and sacred justice of pristine Islam. The secular vision attempted to revitalize the pre-Islamic memories of Iranian nationalism in order to recapture the power and glory of Iran's imperial past. Not only did both visions thus clash in their reconstructions of the past but also in their utopian images of the future. The Islamic vision has been inextricably tied to Iran's cultural association with the Arabs and the rest of the Islamic world. The secular nationalist vision, however, wished desperately to wipe away all memories of Iran's subjugation to the Arabs, to purify the Persian language, and to revive pre-Islamic memories and political symbols. The responses to the Western challenge have also been markedly different. Secular nationalism has rejected Western political domination but has accepted and indeed welcomed Western cultural values. In extreme cases, the former is enamoured of Western influences to the extent of what is called Westomania ("gharbzadegi") while the latter feel threatened by the West to the extent of xenophobia. All these ideological rationalizations derived from the increasing gulf that separated the life styles of the Westernized elite and the generally religious masses.[10]

A central element of the Pahlavis' cultural policy was the reconstruction of Iranian historical consciousness around the memory of its imperial past, and the destruction of everything that might stand in its way. The choice of the dynastic name of "Pahlavi," after Iran's dominant pre-Islamic language, was itself symbolic. The organization of an Academy of Iranian Languages to purify Persian (primarily from Arabic); the return to the grandeur and massive architectural style of the Achaemenids; the forced adoption of Western clothes, breaking the continuity of the country's traditional religious and lay clothing styles; the celebration of Persian kinghood on the 2500th anniversary of the Persian Empire and the 50th anniversary of the Pahlavi dynasty; the changes of calendar, first from the Islamic lunar to the Persian solar and then from "hegira" (1355) to "shahanshani" (2535), were all aspects of the same policy of revived purification. Memories of the constitutional revolutionary period, and of the period of 1941-53, when a quasi-liberal parliamentary system was in operation, were severely repressed. The only major books on the history of the Masaddeq era that remained in circulation were those of the Shah's autobiography, *Mission for My Country*, and a few histories which glorified His Majesty's role in the recapture of Azarbaijan and in the nationalization of oil.[11]

A nation without historical memory is a nation lost. Thus historical memories cannot be altogether suppressed. Persians have never had to rely entirely on historical documentation for their memories. This is why Ferdowsi's epic poem, *The Shahnameh*, and the legends of the martyrdoms of Hussein and so many other saints, are part of

Iran's oral tradition of vivid drama and meaning.[12] But the cultural policy of historical vivisection did lead unwittingly to historical schizophrenia. The 50 per cent of the population that was illiterate and the 50 per cent below the age of 20, by and large, lost the memory of the liberal constitutionalists; but they were reinforced in their memories of the martyrdom of legendary heroes, while simultaneously acquiring a religious and quasi-Marxist revolutionary ideology through informal networks and underground publications.

In this context, therefore, it was no wonder that for leadership, Iranian society turned to a sector least affected by the corrupting influences of modernization, namely the *Ulema*. Because the *Ulema* under the Pahlavis had been progressively stripped of their control over the legal, educational, charitable, and endowment (*Waqf*) institutions while still retaining their spiritual powers through the mosque and *minbar* (the pulpit), they had both the cause and the means to stir the opposition. Twice in this century, the *Ulema* had entered into an alliance with the bazaar merchants and the liberal intelligentsia in campaigns to limit the monarchy. In both of these cases (the Constitutional Revolution of 1905-11 and the oil nationalization movement of 1951-53), it was the liberal intellectuals who led the way and the *Ulema* who provided the mass support, but the situation had radically changed in the meantime.[13] The riots of 1963, taking place in protest against "the White Revolution," were the harbinger of the new politics to come. They were organized and almost exclusively led from Qom with Ayatollah Khomeini as its leading spokesman. They had been preceded by a visit paid to Qom by the Shah, in December 1962, during which he had castigated the radical *Ulema*, as "obscurantist, backward, and lice-ridden," to be crushed if they resisted his enlightened reforms. This was followed by the referendum of January 1963 which seemed to have won his six-point reform program a popular test, to be rejected in the following June by massive riots. The last vestiges of rapport between the monarchy and the radical *Ulema*, which had supported each other since the coup of 1953 against the common threat of Communism, was ruptured. For the moment, the radical *Ulema* seemed to have been isolated from their allies among the bazaaries and the liberal intellectuals who, represented by the National Front, acted bewildered during the riots of 1963.

This was the beginning of a relentless struggle between the radical *Ulema* and the monarchical regime, characterized by bitterness and venom. In interviews conducted by the author with some leading religious leaders in 1974, the issues emerged quite clearly.[14] To the

Ulema (though not a monolithic and homogeneous group), it seemed that the entire trend of Iranian society was going against their sense of truth, goodness and justice. Their arch-enemies, the Bahais, the secularizing technocrats, and their foreign advisors were ruling supreme in every niche and corner—the court, the armed forces, *Savak* (the secret police), important branches of the civil bureaucracy, and the burgeoning financial and industrial enterprises. Having usurped the educational, legal, and charitable institutions from their hands, the monarchical regime was intent on taking their prerogatives away even in family and religious matters. The new Family Law of 1967-74 introduced measures that undermined some of the fundamental tenets of Islam on marriage and divorce. The grant of rights of suffrage to women, in 1963, the organization of the Women's Corps in 1968, the appointment of women to highly visible public offices, but above all, the display of a decadent life style and permissive sexual relations grieved the *Ulema*. The organization of a Religious Corps in 1971, the drafting of theology students for religious services under the auspices of the military, the plans for the organization of an Islamic University in Mashhad, the change of calendar from Islamic hegira to the Imperial Shahanshi, the introduction of daylight saving time that trespassed the *Shari'a* time, all were further indications of the arrogance of the new omnipotent state. These measures were deeply resented by all factions among the *Ulema*, but it took the political, economic, and moral exhaustion of the new secular society and the determination and persistence of the Khomeini faction to dismantle the monarchical power.

It was not, however, the *Ulema* alone who rejected the secular trends. In a national survey conducted in 1974 among some 5,000 of a cross-section of Iranian society, the dominance of religious beliefs and attitudes was pronounced.[15] In another survey conducted in 1974 among three traditionally secular and secularizing social groups in Iranian society (namely, the communication elite, the professional broadcasters, and the university students), the trend towards strong religious sentiments was already unmistakable (for a composite view of the findings, see Table 1). More than 60 per cent of the students and 30 per cent of the elite and broadcasters, responding to a list of twelve ideological orientations, had expressed a preference for a *fundamentalist Islamic* position. The response was all the more remarkable because of the categorical nature of the expressed ideological position and the prevailing repressive official attitude towards religion: All individual and social problems can be resolved with the

TABLE 1

Ideological Orientations (Percentage of Individuals by Category Who Agreed with Stated Ideological Position) in Order of Their Strength of Support

Ideological Position	Communication Elite	Professional Broadcasters	University Students	Average of three groups
	%	%	%	
Egalitarianism	83	82	85	83.3
Secular Nationalism	81	86	78	81.6
Islamic Modernism	82	77	82	80.3
Liberal Nationalism	78	77	69	74.6
Islamic Mysticism	68	67	79	71.3
Fatalism	58	57	63	59.3
Technocratic Nationalism	55	55	55	55.0
Pristine Nationalism	64	72	74	48.6
Islamic Fundamentalism	30	30	62	40.6
Opportunism	13	17	46	25.3
Nihilism	18	14	16	16.0
Cynicism	16	10	19	15.0

Source: Majid Tehranian et al., *Communications Policy for National Development: A Comparative Perspective* (London: Routledge & Kegan Paul, 1977), 275.

help of the divine law of Islam. If everyone were to abide by it, human laws would become unnecessary. The highest preferences, however, were accorded to an egalitarian position close to the spirit of Islam: In order to become a developed society we should strive to achieve a fair distribution of wealth and of income and abolish present social and economic inequities.

Between 82-85 per cent of all three groups had identified with this position. By contrast, *Islamic Modernism* gained the support of 82 per cent of the elite and the students, and 77 per cent of the broadcasters:

The mystical and legal traditions of Islam should be pre-
served. But it is the duty of all Muslims and particularly
of the *Ulema* to maintain harmony between religious
precepts and modern spiritual and material needs. In this
way Iran will play an ever-increasing role throughout the
entire Islamic world.

Sufism (Islamic mysticism) trailed behind Islamic modernism
with a 67-68 per cent support among the elite and broadcasters and
a 79 per cent support among the students. The Sufi position with its
non-doctrinaire emphasis upon purity of intentions held that:

Islam's teachings enlighten us on the true goals of life,
but piety alone cannot solve our problems. To be successful in the search for truth, we should embrace the mystical insights of the Holy Koran and the traditions of the
Prophet and his Rightful Successors.

Nationalism in four of its varieties in Iran was the second most
important set of ideological tendencies to follow the strong Islamic
preferences among all three groups. It was, however, the secular and
liberal varieties (represented by the National Front) which elicited
the highest support. Secular Nationalism found the greatest favor
among broadcasters (86 per cent), followed by the elite (81 per cent)
and the students (78 per cent):

We have at our disposal all the essential material and human resources required for rapid development, as the
past few decades have amply demonstrated. But to join
the ranks of the fully developed countries we ought to
keep separate the religious and political spheres. We may
have to do away with some of our old traditions and accept social and economic reforms.

By contrast, Liberal Nationalism was slightly less favored among the
elite (78 per cent), broadcasters (77 per cent), and the students (69
per cent):

Western achievements depend on a free market economy
and on a democratic political system. To reach the same
level of development we should expand the role of the
private sector and encourage the development of democratic political institutions (political parties, parliament,
press, etc.) so as to increase the degree of participation.

Pre-Islamic and technocratic orientations in nationalism, as represented by the dominant ideological tendencies of the monarchical
regime, was significantly less favored. The pre-Islamic orientation of
Pristine Nationalism, found 74 per cent of the students, 72 per cent
of the broadcasters, and 64 per cent of the elite in its favor:

In order to promote the development of Iran we ought
to be inspired by our culture and revive the greatness of
Iran's pre-Islamic past. We ought to keep our culture free
of foreign influences (including Arabic) and rely primarily
on our Aryan heritage.

By contrast, technocratic nationalism registered a lower esteem among
all three groups with a 55 per cent rate of support:

The West's success stems from scientific and technological innovations. In order to achieve the same level of development we should accelerate our scientific and technological progress. Only through science and technology and
not through political ideologies are we going to solve our
problems.

The ideologies of alienation, including nihilism, opportunism, and
cynicism, each registered a low support among all three responding
groups with a 14-20 per cent level of approval. One striking exception,
however, was the students' 46 per cent level of support for the oppor-
tunist position: "A man is wise if he cannot be misled and knows how
to snatch any opportunity that comes his way." Either the youth may
be considered more intellectually honest or their perception of the
adult world was unduly (or appropriately?) pessimistic. Fatalism, also,
scored relatively high among all three groups (57-63 per cent): Individual values are no longer relevant. Today's society imposes its own value
system and we have no alternative but to accept it.

This ideological portrait of an important sector of Iranian society
and opinion leadership, taken at a moment of material triumph, is
revealing. It shows how strong were the religious tendencies combined
with nationalist preferences and how relatively weaker stood the
ideological positions espoused by the government. But the portrait
should not conceal the fact that each respondent had the opportunity
of choosing a number of contradictory ideological positions. Thus,
Islamic as well as secular and pristine (pre-Islamic) nationalist positions both scored relatively high. The combination of these positions
may seem intellectually incompatible, but many respondents appear
to have accepted them as emotionally valid and viable. The mosaic of
cultural and historical forces which have shaped the modern Persian
mind are represented in this portrait, revealing the ideological zones
of national consensus as well as the cultural cleavages and the psychological dualisms and schizophrenia. Since the three groups of respondents also represented three different generations, social strata, and
levels of political access, the differences as well as the similarities were
all the more significant. The underlying reality of this composite

ideological portrait was the fact of an increasing social, economic, and cultural cleavage which cut across age, social class or politics.

The massive demonstrations in the Autumn of 1978 were remarkable, among other things, for being predominantly made up of the younger generation and for the singular absence of any references to Masaddeq, the charismatic liberal nationalist leader of the early fifties. Instead, large portraits of Ayatollah Khomeini and the martyrs of the new urban guerilla struggles were prominently displayed everywhere. The underlying theme of the demonstrations was the expectation of a second coming. For years, the greatest festival spontaneously celebrated by the people was neither *Nowruz* (the Persian New Year, dating to pre-Islamic Zoroastrian times) nor the birthday of the Prophet. It was, as banners throughout the country declared on those blessed occasions, "the sacred birthday of His Majesty Imam Mahdi." Two legitimacies, one spiritual and utopian, the other temporal and ideological, ruled Iran in the name of two competing monarchies.

The emergence of two nations with two belief-systems revealed itself perhaps most dramatically in the two separate but intertwined modes of political communication. The secular view was profoundly Westernized, and couched in Faustian terms: a remorseless search for power by means of the mastery of science and technology. The Shah himself typified such an attitude by his love of gadgets (particularly military gadgets); his fetish of high, capital-intensive, technology (e.g., nuclear energy, in a country endowed with immense resources of oil and natural gas); and his ambition, flaunted with missionary zeal, to transform Iran within 20 years into the world's fifth major industrial power. Symbolic throughout, one of his first acts after returning to power in 1953 was to change the name of the Ministry of Defense to the Ministry of War. But all this show of strength was undermined by a tragic undercurrent of mysticism and martyrdom, a constant appeal to the unseen powers who protected his life in four assassination attempts, a steadfast call to meet his destiny, and in the end a resignation to accept the inevitable instead of engaging in a bloody counter-revolution.[16]

The same themes of power, blood, and martyrdom also ran in the religious opposition's worldview, but as a major note. The emergence of Dr. Masaddeq and Ayatollah Khomeini as the opposition's charismatic leaders in less than a generation reveals a profound continuity of historical archtypes. The historical consciousness of Iranians has been always deeply moved by the memory of those heroic martyrs who achieved positions of spiritual power through acts of defiance against tyrants, by shedding their blood to redeem the weak and the oppressed. The legendary Siyavosh in the "Shahnameh," Imam Hossain in Shi'ite history, and Hallaj in Sufi memory, represent such archtypes. Dr. Masaddeq's combination of (apparent) weakness and determination, and Ayatollah Khomeini's righteous yet (apparently) selfless cause, represented similar drives to power through righteousness and martyrdom.

Khomeini's Doctrines of Political Legitimacy

In this context, the ideological and political significance of Ayatollah Khomeini rested in the innovations he introduced into the Shi'a doctrines of political legitimacy. These transformed Shi'ism from an oppositionist to a revolutionary force.[17] To be fully understood, these innovations should be considered in a historical perspective.[18]

The position of Shi'a political doctrine vis-à-vis the state and established political power has been historically one of grudging tolerance, provided the ruling Shah or Sultan protected the Shari'a. Law and order have been considered by the consensus of the *Ulema* always preferable to conditions of lawlessness and violence. In the early fifties, for instance, the alliance between the liberal nationalists led by Dr. Masaddeq and the radical *Ulema* led by Ayatollah Kashani broke down not only because of personal and ideological incompatibility but also due to increasing political instability and threat of communism. Some elements of the *Ulema*, including Ayatollah Kashani who is considered by Khomeini and his followers as their hero, made an alliance with the monarchy in the coup d'état of 1953 in the hope of greater influence and political stability.[19] With the disaffection of Kashani with the restored monarchy, the tensions arose once again.

Following the death of Ayatollah Boroujerdi (the grand Shi'a Mujtahed) in 1961, the last conservative links between the *Ulema* and the monarchy were ruptured and the tensions came into the open as never before. The monarchical regime tried unsuccessfully to transfer the seat of *marj'a taglid* from Qom to outside the country, by cabling its condolences to Ayatollah Hakim in Najaf, Iraq. In the meantime, the continuing secularist policies of the state, particularly the reforms of the White Revolution, the continuing operation of the Fadaiyan-i Islam guerrillas, the organization of new urban guerrilla movements under the aegis of Islam, and the increasing pauperization and radicalization of the clerical students in Qom—all led to

the emergence of Ayatollah Khomeini as the dominant radical voice
against monarchy.

The bloody riots of June 1963 were the most visible turning point
in the mosque-state relations. Whereas before that date, the institution of monarchy and the Fundamental Laws of 1905 (establishing
a Constitutional Monarchy) had been rarely attacked directly, the
ideological position of the radical *Ulema* changed appreciably subsequent to those events. Khomeini's innovative ideas, reflected in his
lectures in exile delivered in Najef and published subsequently under
a variety of titles including *Willyat-e-Faghih* (The Trusteeship of the
Jurist), met the needs of the hour. In this ideological tract, Khomeini
set forth his departure from traditional Shi'a views with a few polemical syllogisms. First, he argued, that the Quran has commanded
Muslims to "Obey Allah and Obey His Messenger and those of him
who are first in command." Second, Imam Ali and his male descendants up to the twelfth Hidden Imam are the rightful successors of the
Prophet. Third—and here is a quantum leap from traditional Shi'a
doctrines—they and in their absence, the *Fughaha* (the jurists of the
Shari'a) who are the rightful representatives of the Hidden Imam,
must be therefore obeyed in spiritual as well as temporal matters.
Fourth, it follows that from an Islamic point of view, any form of
government other than the direct rule of *Shari'a* and its custodians,
i.e., the Muslim jurists, is unconstitutional. Fifth, this applies especially to monarchy (which is an usurpation) and any form of parliamentary legislation (which is a sacrilege). Because the Islamic Divine
Law is given once and for all, Khomeini proudly declared, there is no
legislation in Islam: "if at all, we should therefore have a Majlis for
planning only."

In one great ideological sweep, Ayatollah Khomeini had thus
obliterated the traditional Shi'a doctrines of legitimacy which subtly
made room for the coexistence of the temporal and spiritual authorities and a system of checks and balances. The assumption by Khomeini of the title of Imam, reserved in Shi'a theology only for Imam
Ali and his eleven direct male descendants, was a symbolic gesture
signifying this radical change. The new doctrine also provided much
needed legitimacy for the new revolutionary leadership's claims of a
new class of young, pauperized, marginal, and alienated clerics educated in the dialectic of Shi'a Islam, Marxism and Ali Shari'ati's syncretic ideas attempting to consummate this uneasy ideological marriage. Furthermore, it corresponded closely to the aspirations of the
radical *Ulema* who felt they had been betrayed twice in this century

by their liberal nationalist allies while corresponding to the belief system of their constituency of the increasingly uprooted and marginal urban population. However, the doctrine contained also the seeds of its own future destruction. By assuming direct political responsibility for the government, the Shi'a utopia could lose much of its mystical appeal while the Shi'a clergy is tainted by the inevitable corruptions of temporal power.[20] With continuing exposure, debate and challenges from competing ideologies, Ayatollah Khomeini's theocratic doctrines could in the end demystify Shi'ism as effectively as the Shah demystified Monarchy. This is not to ignore, however, the interim power and appeal of Khomeini's interpretation of Islam which presents a purist, positivist, and centralist—almost Leninist—political theory.

Khomeinism: The Future of an Illusion

The central thesis of this essay has been that Islam, like any other positivistic religion, can influence (sometimes dramatically) the course of social and political history by its spiritual, moral, and political force, but it cannot construct a modern society, polity, and economy. The reason for this lies in the basic incompatibility of religious epistemology (that claims divine origins and posits everlasting verities) with modern social, economic and political problems which have mundane roots and demand ever-changing, corrective and incremental legislation. While religion is best suited, therefore, to respond to the spiritual longings and ontological insecurities of man, born out of his conditions of finitude, fragility, and immorality, the epistemology of modern science and political ideologies are better suited to deal with problems of accelerating social and political change that seem to be the lot of modern man.

Modern science, religion and ideology provide three symbolic structures, epistemologies, and communication strategies for the resolution and amelioration of the inherent contradictions and sufferings in the processes of social change. However, whenever one of these modes of communication tries to usurp the functions of the other two, we tend to get a depreciation of all three and the failure of each to perform its own unique integrative functions in its own sphere of competence. The language of science is primarily cognitive, its sphere of action primarily objective reality, its method of enquiry trial and error, construction of hypotheses, empirical research or experimentation, its conclusions tentative and subject to the discovery of new evidence.

By contrast, the language of religion is affective, its primary spheres of action are subjective "truth" and the human conditions of death, suffering and evil, its method of inquiry are faith and seeking, discipleship and mastership, its conclusions universal and everlasting. By further contrast, the language of ideology is primarily normative/ behavioral, its primary sphere of action the interplays of the subjective and the objective in the political arena, its method of inquiry both dogmatic and pragmatic, appeals to faith as well as to reason, emotions as well as facts, commitment as well as skepticism, its conclusions tied to class or group interests, lasting yet accommodating to the changing tides of fortune.

The modern world has been peculiarly prone to three types of intellectual and political corruptions out of which a variety of modern totalitarian ideologies and dictatorships have emerged. We may label these three as the corruption of science into scientism, transformation of political ideologies into totalistic dogmas, and the appearance of traditional religions in the form of highly politicized, fundamentalist revivals. Each doctrine is, of course, closely associated with the cultural and political domination of a particular elite in modern society. Scientism is not only what Paul Tillich has aptly called "the tyranny of the cognitive language," but also the ideological expression of the rise of the scientific-technocratic elites in modern industrial society. The claim that positive science is and should be the final arbiter of all truth, including truths in religion, politics and the arts, turns science into a powerful secular religion with little tolerance for alternative epistemologies and claims for leadership.

By contrast, modern totalitarian ideologies in their leftist as well as rightist varieties represent the rise of mass society and mass movements in which the depersonalized and alienated individuals escape from freedom by complete abdication to the collectivity (the nation, the proletariat) and its political party and charismatic leader. Modern totalitarian ideologies (as in Nazism, fascism and Stalinism) usurp the functions of science in their attempts to mold scientific theories (for instance, genetics) to fit their political preferences (Aryan superiority or the dialectics of nature). They also attempt to usurp the functions of traditional religion by establishing a new political eschatology with the nation or the class as the Chosen People, and Aryan domination or dictatorship of the proletariat as the new kingdom of God on earth.

By further contrast, religious fundamentalism in a variety of different historical contexts (including Beginism in Israel, Moral

Majority in the United States, Khomeinism in Iran) seems to represent the backlash of the traditional sectors of the population, led often by politically disenfranchised clerical classes, against the alienating, abstracting, and corrupting pressures of modern mass societies. Fundamentalism's usurpation of the functions of science and ideology is represented by generally anti-intellectual pressures and claims for direct state power. The search for identity, meaning, and chastity in a complicated world characterized by multiplicity of psychic demands, plurality of epistemologies, and seductive pressures is common to most fundamentalist revivals. A return to the "Golden Age" and its positivist certitudes as expressed in the Holy Scriptures and interpreted by fundamentalist religious leaderships is a further common theme.

Khomeinism in Iran, however, has some peculiarly Iranian and Third World qualities as well. It springs out of the long years of Shi'a suffering as a minority sect, its passion for martyrdom and vindication by blood, its deep ambivalence towards power, its xenophobia born of Iran's humiliating experiences of foreign domination in recent centuries, its cult of personality in the tradition of worship of Imams and saints (distinctly different from Sunni Islam), its memory of the traditional power and autonomy of the clerical class usurped by the modern bureaucratic state, its sense of inferiority vis-à-vis the modern scientific-technocratic elites, its populism born out of the rising expectations and frustrations of the religious masses, and finally its utopian longings for the unity of the temporal and spiritual authority in this world.

How far can Khomeinism go before it comes to an ideological and political halt?[21] If we consider the progress of any revolutionary doctrine in three successive stages, namely mobilization, legitimation and consolidation, Khomeinism in Iran has served the first two purposes admirably well but is facing serious difficulties in the third. Khomeini's doctrines were ambiguous enough to mobilize a vast cross-section of Iranian society and a wide spectrum of ideological and political interests (from liberals to nationalists, Marxists and a diversity of Islamic tendencies) against the monarchy. Once in power, however, the radical fundamentalist clerics found themselves in ideological and political conflict with all the other factions. Khomeini's revolutionary charisma and insistence on a purist, positivist, anti-liberal, anti-nationalist and anti-imperialist Islam have so far managed to continue to legitimate, in the eyes of its supporters, the policies of militancy and repression pursued by the government.[22] Khomeinism has in this sense represented a deepening of the class struggle in Iran camouflaged by the rhetorics of a revolutionary Islam.

The consolidation stage of Khomeinism has also begun both in the establishment of an Islamic Constitution, granting full sovereign powers to the chief *Faghih* acting as a theocrat, and in the political struggles that led in 1979-81 to the complete elimination of liberal nationalists (notably Bazargan and Bani-Sadr). However, to use Max Weber's well-known category, the routinization of charisma demands considerable institution-building and orderly procedures for legislation after the death of the charismatic leader. Given the premises of Islamic fundamentalism that confine legislation to the *Shari'a*, a well-developed and explicit body of traditional law, innovations necessitated by the requirements of a modern state will face enormous difficulties. This has been already the experience of the new legislative system; in conflicts between the Majlis, the *Ulema* and the Council of Guardians (*Shoray-e-Negahban*), the radical clerics have bypassed the problem by direct appeals to the charismatic leader. After Khomeini's death, however, the traditional polycentric authority of the Shi'a hierarchy will probably reassert itself and obstruct the processes of routinization. The task of consolidation will have to be, therefore, in all probability taken up by a secular leadership (from the military?) acting in "the spirit" rather than "the letter" of Islam. A Bonaparte or a Nasser, however, will be inescapably counter-revolutionary both socio-politically (in terms of class interests), as well as ideologically (in terms of religious vs. secular legitimations). Or, less probably, the revolution will continue to deepen in the direction of further class struggles with a radical Marxist orientation. In both of these eventualities, Khomeinism will give its place to an ideological *status quo ante*, embodied in the traditional Shi'a doctrines of political legitimacy and expectations of a Second Coming.

Conclusion

The current upheavals in the Muslim world should be viewed in the light of the desperate efforts of ancient societies and cultures to regain their sense of balance and self-respect in the face of great odds, adversaries, and adversities. These efforts will not bear fruit, however, unless this generation of Muslims like all past generations learns how through its own pains and sufferings to recreate its own traditions of civility and to develop its own idioms of political and cultural expression. Muslims, like Christians and Jews before them, cannot enter the modern world unless and until they also learn that when religion is used as a direct instrument of state power, it stands to lose both the majesty of moral law and the relevance of political expediency.

The current fundamentalist tendencies in the Muslim world represent a cult of identity and a passion for certitude that, while soothing temporarily, would not provide lasting answers to the complex problems of social and political change in the modern world. Islamic fundamentalism also represents perhaps, the last dying gasps of a proud medieval tradition and the birth pangs of a modern Islam that will be hopefully more at peace with itself and the rest of the world. The place of Ayatollah Khomeini and Khomeinism in history will be most probably judged on that basis.

APPENDIX I.
BIBLIOGRAPHICAL NOTE ON AYATOLLAH RUHOLLAH KHOMEINI

Antecedents: Maternal grandfather, Imam Mirza Ahmad, a prominent religious figure. Both father, Mostafa Moussavi, and eldest brother, Passandideh, considered ayatollahs.

Birth: Born 9 April 1900 at Khomein, near Isfahan.

Education: Traditional religious studies under brother, Passandideh, then in seminaries at Isfahan, Arak and Qom. Loses mother at age 15.

Career: 1927: Settles in Qom, begins teaching philosophy. Attracts attention for teachings and moral example; shows hostility to Reza Shah's campaign to reduce role of clergy. 1941: Publishes *Discovery of Secrets*—vehement attack on Pahlavi family calling for end to foreign domination of Iran. 1953: Takes distance from Mosadeq, critical of Tudeh (Communist) Party influence. 1953-60: Demonstrates increased opposition to monarchy and Iranian dependence on U.S. 1961: Ayatollah Boujerdi dies. Khomeini becomes main contender for Shiite leadership. 1962: Briefly arrested for attacking plans to enfranchise women and Local Council Election Bill. 1963: (January) Briefly arrested for pamphlet attacking Land Reform. (4 June) Re-arrested, major riots follow. (4 August) Released on understanding not to interfere in politics. (October) In custody again for ordering boycott of parliamentary elections. 1964: (May) Released on new understanding. (October) Attacks bill allowing diplomatic immunity to U. S. military personnel and U. S. $200 million loan. Arrested and exiled to Turkey. Turkish student protests lead to transfer to Najaf, Iraq. 1965-71: Continues to write anti-Shah pamphlets from exile; tape-recorded sermons smuggled into Iran. 1971: (April) Calls for protests against Persepolis ceremonies celebrating 2,500 years of monarchy. Tehran University students and Bazaar observe token fast. 1975: (April) Calls for boycott of newly established single-party system. 1976: Iranian pilgrims visit Majaf after Iran/Iraq treaty; contact with supporters in Iran easier. 1977: Attacks on monarchy more frequent and virulent. (October) Son, Mostafa, killed in mysterious circumstances at Kerbala, Iraq. (December) Tehran students demand his return. 1978: (January) Riots by supporters after *Etelaat* article slandering him. Becomes main focus in religious protest. (9 October) Arrives in France. Begins new campaign for Shah's overthrow. (9 December) Mass Tehran demonstration endorses 17-point resolution declaring him leader of Iranian People and the Revolution. 1979: (1 February) Returns in triumph to Tehran. Establishes alternative government in a school. (5 February) Appoints Mehdi Bazargan as "Prime Minister." (12 February) Collapse of Bakhtiar Government confirms him *de facto* leader of Iran. (31 March) Referendum approves establishment of Islamic republic.

Source: Robert Graham, *Iran: The Illusion of Power*. London: Croom Helm, 1979.

1979

August 3, a Council of Experts was elected nationwide to draft a new constitution.

October 22, the Shah was admitted into U. S. for medical treatment.

November 4, 66 Americans in U. S. embassy in Tehran taken hostage by students to demand the Shah's return to Iran for trial; the takeover condoned by Khomeini.

November 6, Prime Minister Bazargan submitted his resignation to Khomeini.

December 2-3, a new Islamic Constitution overwhelmingly approved by a nationwide plebiscite, giving sweeping power to Khomeini as the Supreme *Faghih*. The referendum widely boycotted in Azarbaijan, Kurdistan, Baluchistan and by moderate leaders such as Ayatollah Shari'atmadari.

1980

January 25, Khomeini's spiritual son, Abol-Hassan Banisadr, was elected the first president of the Islamic Republic.

September 21, Iraq invaded Iran on the Western borders and made initial sweeping advances into Khuzistan province.

1981

January 20, the remaining 52 American hostages released after 444 days of captivity and an unsuccessful U. S. rescue operation.

June 11, Banisadr is dismissed from his post of commander-in-chief by Khomeini and goes into hiding.

June 22, Banisadr is officially deposed from presidency.

June 28, Ayatollah Beheshti along with some 74 other members of the government and the Islamic Republican Party were killed in a bomb explosion in Tehran.

July 24, Ali Akbar Rajai was elected president to replace Banisadr.

July 29, Banisadr and *Mujahedin* leader Massoud Rajavi enter Paris as political refugees. Rajavi is subsequently appointed by Banisadr to be his Prime Minister in government-in-exile.

August 30, President Ali Akbar Rajai and Prime Minister Javad Bahonar killed by a bomb explosion in their offices in Tehran.

September 28, four of Iran's top military leaders were killed in a plane crash.

October 2, Hojjatol-Islam Seyyed Ali Khamenei is elected the third president of the Islamic Republic.

October 12, Amnesty International declares that over 3,350 people have been executed in Iran for political crimes following the Revolution of February 1979.

October 16, moves to expel the liberals from the Majlis gained momentum after Bazargan criticized in a speech the government's policies of terror, mass executions and repression.

November 9, Khomeini's Bureau denies rumors that he intends to transfer all powers to Ayatollah Montazeri, his designated successor as the supreme *Faghih*.

1982
July 13, after recovering lost territories, Iranian forces commanded by Khomeini to move into Iraq towards "liberating Baghdad and Jerusalem."

NOTES

1. Fallaci, O., "Interview with Ayatollah Khomeini," *The New York Times Magazine*, October 7, 1981; "Interview with Oriana Fallaci," *Playboy*, October 1981.

2. Farhang, M. "Interview with McNeil/Lehrer Report," *Public Broadcasting System*, September 1981a; "Iranian Revolution Betrayed My Ideals," *Los Angeles Times*, as reprinted in *Pardis*, November 21, 1981b.

3. Naipaul, V. S., *Among the Believers: An Islamic Journey*, New York: Alfred Knopf, 1981.

4. Gibb, H. A. R., *Modern Trends in Islam*, Chicago: The University of Chicago Press, 1950. Smith, W. C., *Islam in Modern History*, New York: Mentor Books, 1959. Jansen, G. H., *Militant Islam*, London: Pan Books, 1979. Tehranian, M., *Islam and the West: Dependency and Dialogue*, Paper presented at an international conference of media leaders, Rockefeller Foundation's Bellagio Study and Conference Center, Lake Como, Italy, May 4-8, 1981. Said, E., *Orientalism*, New York: Pantheon Books, 1978; *Covering Islam*, New York: Pantheon Books, 1981.

5. Tehranian, M., "Seyyed Jamal Ud-Din Afghani: A Study in Charismatic Leadership," unpublished master's thesis, Harvard University, 1961.

6. Rodinson, M., *Islam and Capitalism*, New York: Penguin Books, 1974; *Islam and Marxism*, New York: Penguin Books, 1974. Mottahari, M., *Khadamat-i Motaghabel-i Islam va Iran* (The Mutual Services of Islam and Iran, in Farsi), Tehran, 1349/1950. Taleghani, S. M., *Islam va Malekkiat dar Mughayessen ba Nezamha-ye Eqtessadi-ye Gharb*, Tehran, 1978. Curtis, M. (ed.), *Religion and Politics in the Middle East*, Boulder, Westview Press, 1981.

7. Tehranian, M., "The Curse of Modernity: The Dialectics of Communication and Modernization," *International Social Science Journal*, June 1980, 32(2).

8. Algar, H., "The Oppositionist Role of the Ulema in Twentieth Century Iran," in N. R. Keddie (ed.), *Scholars, Saints and Sufis*, Berkeley: University of California Press, 1972. Akhavi, S., *Religion and Politics in Contemporary Iran*, Albany: State University of New York Press, 1980. Abrahamian, E., *Iran: Between Two Revolutions*, Princeton: Princeton University Press, 1981. Kazemi, F., *Poverty and Revolution in Iran: The Migrant Poor, Urban Marginality and Politics*, New York: New York University Press, 1980; (ed.), *Perspectives on the Iranian Revolution* (Special Issue), *Iranian Studies*, 1980, 13:1-4. Keddie, N. R., *Roots of Revolution: An Interpretative History of Modern Iran*, New Haven: Yale University Press, 1981; (ed.), *Religion and Politics in Iran*, forthcoming. Katouzian, H., *The Political Economy of Modern Iran: Despotism and Pseudo Modernism*, New York: New York University Press, 1981. Bonine, M. E., & Keddie, N. R., (eds.), *Continuity and Change in Modern Iran*, Albany: State University of New York Press, 1981. Tehranian, M., "Iran: Communication, Alienation, Revolution," *Intermedia*, March 1979b, 7(2); "Communication and Revolution in Iran: The Passing of a Paradigm," *Iranian Studies*, 1980b, 13:1-4. Fischer, M. M. J., *Iran from Religious Dispute to Revolution*, Cambridge: Harvard University Press, 1980.

9. Amir Arjomand, S., "Religion, Political Action and Legitimate Domination in Shi'ite Iran: Fourteenth to Eighteenth Centuries AD," *European Journal of Sociology*, 1979, 20; "Shi'ite Islam and the Revolution in Iran," *Government and Opposition*, 1980, 16(3). Bani Sadr, A., *Iqtesade Towhidi*, Tehran, 1979; *The Fundamental Principles and Precepts of Islamic Government*, translated by M. Ghanoonpour, Lexington, Kentucky: Mazda Publishers, 1981.

10. Al Ahmad, J., *Gharbzadegi* (Westomania, in Farsi), Tehran, 1340/1961.

11. Pahlavi, M. R., *Mission for My Country*, London, 1961.

12. Chelkowski, P. J. (ed.), *Ta'ziyeh: Ritual and Drama in Iran*, New York: New York University Press and Soroush Press, 1979; "Iran: Mourning Becomes Revolution," *Asia*, May/June 1980.

13. Hairi, A. H., *Shi'ism and Constitutionalism in Iran*, Leiden: Brill, 1977.

14. Tehranian, M., *Communication Policy for National Development*, London: Routledge & Kegan Paul, 1977; *Socio-Economic and Communication Indicators in Development Planning: A Case Study in Iran*, Paris: UNESCO, 1981.

15. Assadi A., & Vidale, M., "Survey of Social Attitudes in Iran," in *International Review of Modern Sociology*, 1980, 10:65-85.

16. Jabbari, A., & Olson, R., *Iran: Essays on a Revolution in the Making*, Lexington, Kentucky, Mazda Publishers, 1981.

17. Khomeini, R., *Kashf al-Asrar* (The Discovery of Secrets, in Farsi), Tehran, 1941; *Hokumat-e Islami* (The Islamic Government, in Farsi), Najaf, 1971; *Collection of Speeches, Position Statements by Ayatollah Ruhollah Khomeini*, Arlington, Virginia: U. S. Joint Publications Research Service, JPRS 72717, 1979a; *Islamic Government*, New York: Manor Books, 1979b; *Sayings of the Ayatollah Khomeini: Political, Philosophical, Social and Religious*, New York: Bantam Books, 1980. Nigarandeh, *Barrasi va Tahlili as Nahzat-i Imam Khumayni dar Iran* (Review and Analysis of Imam Khomeini's Movement in Iran, in Farsi), Beirut: Abd al-Hafiz al-Basat, 1978.

18. Millward, W. G., *The Islamic Political Theory and Vocabulary of Ayatollah Khomayni, 1941-63, and Its Relation to the Islamic Revolution in Iran, 1978-79*. Paper presented at 1979 MESA Annual Meeting, Salt Lake City, November, 1979. Amir Arjomand, S., *op. cit.*, 1979 and 1980. Arani, S., "The Theocracy Unravels," *The New Republic*, December 6, 1980; "Iran from the Shah's Dictatorship to Khomeini's Demogogic Theocracy," *Dissent*, Winter 1980, 17; "The Toppling of Bani-Sadr," *The Nation*, July 4, 1981. Alpher, J., "The Khomeini International," *Washington Quarterly*, Autumn, 1980.

19. Roosevelt, K., *Counter Coup: The Struggle for the Control of Iran*, New York: McGraw-Hill Co., 1979. Rubin, B., *Paved with Good Intentions: The American Experience and Iran*, New York: Oxford University Press, 1980.

20. Ramazani, R., "Constitution of the Islamic Republic of Iran," *The Middle East Journal*, Spring 1980, 34(2); "Iran's Revolution: Patterns, Problems and Prospects," *International Affairs*, Summer, 1980.

21. Tehrani, A., *Madina-ye Fazila dar Islam*, Tehran, 1975-76/1354.

22. Dehqani-Tafti, H. B., *The Hard Awakening*, New York: Seabury Press, 1981. Hunt, P., *Inside Iran*, Icknield Way, Tring, Herts, England, 1981. Forbis, W. H., *Fall of the Peacock Throne: The Story of Iran*, New York: Harper & Row, 1980. Tehranian, M., "Communication and International Development: Some Theoretical Considerations," *Cultures*, 1979, 6(3). Tehranian, M., "The Fetish of Identity: Communication Revolution and Fundamentalist Revivals," *Media Asia*, 1981, 8(1).

CHAPTER X

CONCLUSIONS

JOSEPH HELD

Few phenomena are as surprising and even overpowering in the last third of the twentieth century as the proliferation of dictatorships and authoritarian regimes. A future historian will be entirely justified in saying that if the nineteenth century were an era of often triumphant struggle for representative government, then the twentieth illustrated just the opposite. It is likely that the same historian would say that this century represented a phase in the evolution of global political instutions during which mankind groped for answers to problems created by modernization in a confused way, often willingly going along with those whose arguments were based on the almighty gun.

Force and coercion have, of course, been always there as an arbiter of politics within and among nations. But, at least since the Enlightenment, there was rising hope that the necessary force that held societies together could be minimized through principles of legitimacy buttressed by representative institutions. This hope was the strongest in the United States where representative government has been the cornerstone of political life ever since the establishment of the state.

But the general yearning of the peoples of the globe for a better life, for which modernization seemed to offer the best solution, often led to confusion in many societies. Authoritarianism seemed to offer a simple solution; since people were either to get the better things in life or be free, the choice appeared obvious. That this choice, as all other "simple solutions" to complex problems, was a false one was shown by the fact that the exchange of freedom for dictatorship seldom led to the realization of the other side of the bargain. Authoritarianism and dictatorship offered what Majid Tehranian in this volume called ideologies turned into dogmas. They corrupted the societies over which they ruled and failed to create the modern, well-functioning economic systems which they promised. Thus, neither bread nor freedom was provided; this is a major lesson that the majority of mankind has yet to learn in the near future.

Authoritarianism, the heightened expectations of the poor peoples of the globe, encouraged by the examples set by the modernized western nations, have contributed to the emergence of another twentieth-century phenomenon, modern terrorism. To be sure, this problem is not totally new, its roots going back at least to the late Middle Ages when the "hassassins" of the Old Man of the Mountain kept Middle Eastern rulers in fear for their lives. But the aims of modern terrorists, the unprecedented destructive power of their weapons, and the mass terror which they can inspire, represents a new phase in this sordid chapter in history. We have explored the problems of despotism and terrorism in a course offered at Rutgers University, Camden. Entitled "The Despot and the Terrorist through the Ages," the course included a two-day symposium in which this volume originated. The theme of the symposium was somewhat different than that of the volume, but the essays were basically the same as presented at that time. Discussing authoritarianism and dictatorship in our century is, unfortunately, an almost inexhaustible task. Consequently, neither in the symposium nor in this volume were any efforts made to cover every aspect of the problem. The most that we can all hope for is that the book will provide the thoughtful reader with areas of study that would help further research.

Although the two introductory essays by Peter Suedfeld and Ivan Volgyes provided a theoretical basis for the following discussions, the other papers also present dictatorship from the points of view of individual theories.

Professor Suedfeld is a psychologist; his presentation of the cognitive-interactionist theory of authoritarianism and its ramifications, represent some novel ideas that future research will undoubtedly explore. His major point is that authoritarianism and dictatorial leadership need to be looked at not simply through the personality of the dictators, but rather through the pressures and tensions created by their environment. Thus, he argues, authoritarianism could be partly a function of low complexity in the decision-making process, enhanced by difficulties due to the pressure of time in analysing information. Such situations occur in times of stress or emergency. He further argues that the adulation of the dictator is beneficial both to him and to his followers. For the dictator this provides a basis for his legitimacy, since "godlike individuals are legitimate by definition." For the followers it provides self-respect and heightened self-confidence.

Professor Volgyes is a political scientist. In his search for common elements in modern dictatorships he found that these, unlike their predecessors in pre-modern times, want the masses not only to obey their commands, but to participate symbolically in political life. This is a reflection of the fact that, for the first time in man's history, truly mass societies have come into existence. But the dictator would not want the masses to go beyond symbolic participation, since this would mean the limitation of the dictator's power.

From this dichotomy other contradictory phenomena emerged. For instance, in Soviet-type regimes, the elites are genuinely trying to create "decent people acting in decent ways." But their continuous need to adjust ideology to existing realities (or, sometimes, the other way around), the built-in institutional paranoia in their system, defeated their purpose.

Professor Stites is a historian. He explored the phenomenon of what he describes as Stalin's "administrative utopia." The Soviet dictator's suppression of the Russian "utopians" of the 1920s did not lead directly to a straight-laced realism in politics, contrary to the famous dictum of Arthur Koestler's Rubashov. Since the need was there for some sort of belief in the future that was to be better than the present, Stalin produced his own idea of a "utopia." But this was, according to Stites, a nightmarish mixture of militarism and angry class-conflict, including a new Tsar-father figure in the person of the dictator himself. This "utopia" certainly failed to achieve the modernization of Soviet society and Stalin's successors are still struggling with its results.

Professor Gleason is also a historian. His essay deals with the roots of the deification of one terrorist in the case of Lenin. According to Gleason, Lenin tried to establish revolutionary legitimacy (an anachronistic term in itself) for the Russian Social Democrats before the revolution of 1917. By the very logic of his endeavors he was forced to sanction terror as a means of political action. No one can foresee, of course, the ultimate consequences of one's actions but the question is worth pondering whether Stalin's application of mass terrorism would have been possible without Lenin's previous approval of such actions? But Stalin's system had certainly achieved what Volgyes had described as the "symbolic participation" of the masses in politics even if this mostly consisted of a noisy endorsement of Stalin's terror.

Another historian, David Diephouse, approached the sectarian cult of Hitler as a quasi-religious phenomenon attempting to provide legitimacy for the Nazi movement. He finds in the character of the "church militant" of this movement the idea of a "warrior community" offering to replace the "slave morality and ethics" of pre-Nazi Germany with the idea of a ruthless struggle for survival. Once this idea was accepted—even if only passively—by the German masses, war and the concentration camps became unavoidable. We might add that the cognitive-interactionist theory of authoritarianism could probably explain many of Hitler's actions and the fanatical belief of his followers in Hitler's superior nature.

Thomas E. O'Toole delves into the murky world of the Central African dictator, "Napoleon" Bokassa. According to him, Bokassa's power was limited. He remained in control only so long as he fulfilled the needs of a specific elite "clan" to which he belonged. When he tried to create a new legitimacy outside of accepted Central African traditions, he lost his power. The French military intervention that eventually ousted him was only the last act in his saga, and even without it Bokassa could not have remained long in power.

Professor Gran's study is an effort to link specific social conditions in three Arab countries, namely, Egypt, Libya and Iraq and the dictatorships of Nasir, Qadhafi and Qasim on the one hand, to what he calls the analytical tool of political economy on the other. He believes that the system that enabled these three dictators to function was state-capitalism. According to Gran, the system represented a markedly great step towards establishing certain levels of political participation and freedom for the masses in these countries. However, as Volgyes had pointed out, this did not mean more than "symbolic participation." In any case, Gran maintains that these dictatorships were not representatives of vulgar or traditional authoritarian systems. One must add, however, that evidence indicates that even such "benevolent dictators" (and the editor finds this designation somewhat less than realistic) were unable to create an efficiently working economic system or a harmonious society for their respective nations. Although blame for this failure is usually placed on "outside factors" (such as, for instance, "imperialistic pressures") dictatorship in these instances, as in most others, failed to achieve the measure of modernization that they promised their peoples.

Vlad Georgescu raises the question of why personality cults flourished almost exclusively in societies claiming to be socialist? His answer is that their elites rule over a classless society (editor's note: at least in name) and, therefore, are not subject to moderating pressures from competing social interests. An additional condition seems to be in the last third of the twentieth century that such a society have a certain measure of independence from the Soviet Union, as is currently the case with Romania. At the same time, the economic policies of such regimes are usually a throwback to the Stalinist model. Thus, the personality cult is, in most instances, an attempt to hasten modernization and answer its problems. What is surprising is that, despite the overwhelming evidence that such a system does not work, there are still serious politicians willing to try it.

In the last essay Majid Tehranian evaluated the theocracy of Ayatollah Khomeini in Iran. According to him, the underlying factors that brought Khomeini into power included fears and anxieties of a traditional society split by too rapid changes under the Shah. The apparent atomization of the social fabric, the introduction of Western values alien to most of the masses, and the general shame felt for backwardness propelled into power a fanatical religious group masquerading as a revivalist movement.

Islam is a positivist religion, professing infallibility for its values, trusting in the "eternal truths" of what it claims to have been divine revelation. Such a movement, according to Tehranian, cannot compromise with modernity.

What seems to emerge from these studies is the fact that the choice of dictatorship and other authoritarian systems has not answered the desires of the broad masses of the globe in creating better conditions of life. The paradox in our times has always been the belief that the cumbersome system created by representative institutions is too slow in responding to the call of the poor people for a better life. Dictators were often believed to be able, by their very authority, to work more efficiently, and be able to take short cuts on the road to modernization. We have learned, however, that short cuts do not really exist, and that authoritarian systems can be even more cumbersome and slow in responding to changing circumstances. It is a matter of great urgency that this lesson be universalized and learned by the great majority of mankind.

EAST EUROPEAN MONOGRAPHS

The *East European Monographs* comprise scholarly books on the history and civilization of Eastern Europe. They are published under the editorship of Stephen Fischer-Galati, in the belief that these studies contribute substantially to the knowledge of the area and serve to stimulate scholarship and research.

1. *Political Ideas and the Enlightenment in the Romanian Principalities, 1750–1831.* By Vlad Georgescu. 1971.
2. *America, Italy and the Birth of Yugoslavia, 1917-1919.* By Dragan R. Zivjinovic. 1972.
3. *Jewish Nobles and Geniuses in Modern Hungary.* By William O. McCagg, Jr. 1972.
4. *Mixail Soloxov in Yugoslavia: Reception and Literary Impact.* By Robert F. Price. 1973.
5. *The Historical and Nationalist Thought of Nicolae Iorga.* By William O. Oldson. 1973.
6. *Guide to Polish Libraries and Archives.* By Richard C. Lewanski. 1974.
7. *Vienna Broadcasts to Slovakia, 1938-1939: A Case Study in Subversion.* By Henry Delfiner. 1974.
8. *The 1917 Revolution in Latvia.* By Andrew Ezergailis. 1974.
9. *The Ukraine in the United Nations Organization: A Study in Soviet Foreign Policy. 1944-1950.* By Konstantin Sawczuk. 1975.
10. *The Bosnian Church: A New Interpretation.* By John V. A. Fine, Jr., 1975.
11. *Intellectual and Social Developments in the Habsburg Empire from Maria Theresa to World War I.* Edited by Stanley B. Winters and Joseph Held. 1975.
12. *Ljudevit Gaj and the Illyrian Movement.* By Elinor Murray Despalatovic. 1975.
13. *Tolerance and Movements of Religious Dissent in Eastern Europe,* Edited by Bela K. Kiraly. 1975.
14. *The Parish Republic: Hlinka's Slovak People's Party, 1939-1945.* By Yeshayahu Jelinek. 1976.
15. *The Russian Annexation of Bessarabia, 1774-1828.* By George F. Jewsbury. 1976.
16. *Modern Hungarian Historiography.* By Steven Bela Vardy. 1976.
17. *Values and Community in Multi-National Yugoslavia.* By Gary K. Bertsch. 1976.
18. *The Greek Socialist Movement and the First World War: the Road to Unity.* By George B. Leon. 1976.
19. *The Radical Left in the Hungarian Revolution of 1848.* By Laszlo Deme. 1976.
20. *Hungary between Wilson and Lenin: The Hungarian Revolution of 1918-1919 and the Big Three.* By Peter Pastor. 1976.

21. *The Crises of France's East-Central European Diplomacy, 1933-1938.* By Anthony J. Komjathy. 1976.
22. *Polish Politics and National Reform, 1775-1788.* By Daniel Stone. 1976.
23. *The Habsburg Empire in World War I.* Edited by Robert A. Kann, Bela K. Kiraly, and Paula S. Fichtner. 1977.
24. *The Slovenes and Yugoslavism, 1890-1914.* By Carole Rogel. 1977.
25. *German-Hungarian Relations and the Swabian Problem.* By Thomas Spira. 1977.
26. *The Metamorphosis of a Social Class in Hungary During the Reign of Young Franz Joseph.* By Peter I. Hidas. 1977.
27. *Tax Reform in Eighteenth Century Lombardy.* By Daniel M. Klang. 1977.
28. *Tradition versus Revolution: Russia and the Balkans in 1917.* By Robert H. Johnston. 1977.
29. *Winter into Spring: The Czechoslovak Press and the Reform Movement 1963-1968.* By Frank L. Kaplan. 1977.
30. *The Catholic Church and the Soviet Government, 1939-1949.* By Dennis J. Dunn. 1977.
31. *The Hungarian Labor Service System, 1939-1945.* By Randolph L. Braham. 1977.
32. *Consciousness and History: Nationalist Critics of Greek Society 1897-1914.* By Gerasimos Augustinos. 1977.
33. *Emigration in Polish Social and Political Thought, 1870-1914.* By Benjamin P. Murdzek. 1977.
34. *Serbian Poetry and Milutin Bojic.* By Mihailo Dordevic. 1977.
35. *The Baranya Dispute: Diplomacy in the Vortex of Ideologies, 1918-1921.* By Leslie C. Tihany. 1978.
36. *The United States in Prague, 1945-1948.* By Walter Ullmann. 1978.
37. *Rush to the Alps: The Evolution of Vacationing in Switzerland.* By Paul P. Bernard. 1978.
38. *Transportation in Eastern Europe: Empirical Findings.* By Bogdan Mieczkowski. 1978.
39. *The Polish Underground State: A Guide to the Underground, 1939-1945.* By Stefan Korbonski. 1978.
40. *The Hungarian Revolution of 1956 in Retrospect.* Edited by Bela K. Kiraly and Paul Jonas. 1978.
41. *Boleslaw Limanowski (1935-1935): A Study in Socialism and Nationalism.* By Kazimiera Janina Cottam. 1978.
42. *The Lingering Shadow of Nazism: The Austrian Independent Party Movement Since 1945.* By Max E. Riedlsperger. 1978.
43. *The Catholic Church, Dissent and Nationality in Soviet Lithuania.* By V. Stanley Vardys. 1978.
44. *The Development of Parliamentary Government in Serbia.* By Alex N. Dragnich. 1978.
45. *Divide and Conquer: German Efforts to Conclude a Separate Peace, 1914-1918.* By L. L. Farrar, Jr. 1978.
46. *The Prague Slav Congress of 1848.* By Lawrence D. Orton. 1978.
47. *The Nobility and the Making of the Hussite Revolution.* By John M. Klassen. 1978.
48. *The Cultural Limits of Revolutionary Politics: Change and Continuity in Socialist Czechoslovakia.* By David W. Paul. 1979.
49. *On the Border of War and Peace: Polish Intelligence and Diplomacy in 1937-1939 and the Origins of the Ultra Secret.* By Richard A. Woytak. 1979.
50. *Bear and Foxes: The International Relations of the East European States 1965-1969.* By Ronald Haly Linden. 1979.

51. *Czechoslovakia: The Heritage of Ages Past.* Edited by Ivan Volgyes and Hans Brisch. 1979.

52. *Prime Minister Gyula Andrassy's Influence on Habsburg Foreign Policy.* By Janos Decsy. 1979.

53. *Citizens for the Fatherland: Education, Educators, and Pedagogical Ideals in Eighteenth Century Russia.* By J. L. Black. 1979.

54. *A History of the "Proletariat": The Emergence of Marxism in the Kingdom of Poland, 1870–1887.* By Norman M. Naimark. 1979.

55. *The Slovak Autonomy Movement, 1935–1939: A Study in Unrelenting Nationalism.* By Dorothea H. El Mallakh. 1979.

56. *Diplomat in Exile: Francis Pulszky's Political Activities in England, 1849–1860.* By Thomas Kabdebo. 1979.

57. *The German Struggle Against the Yugoslav Guerrillas in World War II: German Counter-Insurgency in Yugoslavia, 1941–1943.* By Paul N. Hehn. 1979.

58. *The Emergence of the Romanian National State.* By Gerald J. Bobango. 1979.

59. *Stewards of the Land: The American Farm School and Modern Greece.* By Brenda L. Marder. 1979.

60. *Roman Dmowski: Party, Tactics, Ideology, 1895–1907.* By Alvin M. Fountain, II. 1980.

61. *International and Domestic Politics in Greece During the Crimean War.* By Jon V. Kofas. 1980.

62. *Fires on the Mountain: The Macedonian Revolutionary Movement and the Kidnapping of Ellen Stone.* By Laura Beth Sherman. 1980.

63. *The Modernization of Agriculture: Rural Transformation in Hungary, 1848–1975.* Edited by Joseph Held. 1980.

64. *Britain and the War for Yugoslavia, 1940–1943.* By Mark C. Wheeler. 1980.

65. *The Turn to the Right: The Ideological Origins and Development of Ukrainian Nationalism, 1919–1929.* By Alexander J. Motyl. 1980.

66. *The Maple Leaf and the White Eagle: Canadian-Polish Relations, 1918–1978.* By Aloysius Balawyder. 1980.

67. *Antecedents of Revolution: Alexander I and the Polish Congress Kingdom, 1815–1825.* By Frank W. Thackeray. 1980.

68. *Blood Libel at Tiszaeszlar.* By Andrew Handler. 1980.

69. *Democratic Centralism in Romania: A Study of Local Communist Politics.* By Daniel N. Nelson. 1980.

70. *The Challenge of Communist Education: A Look at the German Democratic Republic.* By Margrete Siebert Klein. 1980.

71. *The Fortifications and Defense of Constantinople.* By Byron C. P. Tsangadas. 1980.

72. *Balkan Cultural Studies.* By Stavro Skendi. 1980.

73. *Studies in Ethnicity: The East European Experience in America.* Edited by Charles A. Ward, Philip Shashko, and Donald E. Pienkos. 1980.

74. *The Logic of "Normalization:" The Soviet Intervention in Czechoslovakia and the Czechoslovak Response.* By Fred Eidlin. 1980.

75. *Red Cross, Black Eagle: A Biography of Albania's American Schol.* By Joan Fultz Kontos. 1981.

76. *Nationalism in Contemporary Europe.* By Franjo Tudjman. 1981.

77. *Great Power Rivalry at the Turkish Straits: The Montreux Conference and Convention of 1936.* By Anthony R. DeLuca. 1981.

78. *Islam Under the Double Eagle: The Muslims of Bosnia and Hercegovina, 1878–1914.* By Robert J. Donia. 1981.

108. *Propaganda and Nationalism in Wartime Russia: The Jewish Anti-Fascist Committee in the USSR, 1941–1948.* By Shimon Redich. 1982.

109. *One Step Back, Two Steps Forward: On the Language Policy of the Communist Party of Soviet Union in the National Republics.* By Michael Bruchis. 1982.

110. *Bessarabia and Bukovina: The Soviet-Romanian Territorial Dispute.* by Nicholas Dima. 1982

111. *Greek-Soviet Relations, 1917–1941.* By Andrew L. Zapantis. 1982.

112. *National Minorities in Romania: Change in Transylvania.* By Elemer Illyes. 1982.

113. *Dunarea Noastra: Romania, the Great Powers, and the Danube Question, 1914–1921.* by Richard C. Frucht. 1982.

114. *Continuity and Change in Austrian Socialism: The Eternal Quest for the Third Way.* By Melanie A. Sully. 1982

115. *Catherine II's Greek Prelate: Eugenios Voulgaris in Russia, 1771–1806.* By Stephen K. Batalden. 1982.

116. *The Union of Lublin: Polish Federalism in the Golden Age.* By Harry E. Dembkowski. 1982.

117. *Heritage and Continuity in Eastern Europe: The Transylvanian Legacy in the History of the Romanians.* By Cornelia Bodea and Virgil Candea. 1982.

118. *Contemporary Czech Cinematography: Jiri Menzel and the History of The "Closely Watched Trains".* By Josef Skvorecky. 1982.

119. *East Central Europe in World War I: From Foreign Domination to National Freedom.* By Wiktor Sukiennicki. 1982.

120. *City, Town, and Countryside in the Early Byzantine Era.* Edited by Robert L. Hohlfelder. 1982.

121. *The Byzantine State Finances in the Eighth and Ninth Centuries.* By Warren T. Treadgold. 1982.

122. *East Central European Society and War in Pre-Revolutionary Eighteenth Century.* Edited by Gunther E. Rothenberg, Bela K. Kiraly and Peter F. Sugar. 1982.

123. *Czechoslovak Policy and the Hungarian Minority, 1945–1948.* By Kalman Janics. 1982.

124. *At the Brink of War and Peace: The Tito-Stalin Split in a Historic Perspective.* Edited by Wayne S. Vucinich. 1982.

125. *The Road to Bellapais: The Turkish Cypriot Exodus to Northern Cyprus.* By Pierre Oberling. 1982.

126. *Essays on World War I: Origins and Prisoners of War.* Edited by Peter Pastor and Samuel R. Williamson, Jr. 1983.

127. *Panteleimon Kulish: A Sketch of His Life and Times.* By George S. N. Luckyj. 1983.

128. *Economic Development in the Habsburg Monarchy in the Nineteenth Century: Essays.* Edited by John Komlos. 1983.

129. *Warsaw Between the World Wars: Profile of the Capital City in a Developing Land, 1918–1939.* By Edward D. Wynot, Jr. 1983.

130. *The Lust for Power: Nationalism, Slovakia, and The Communists, 1918–1948.* By Yeshayahu Jelinek. 1983.

131. *The Tsar's Loyal Germans: The Riga German Community: Social Change and the Nationality Question, 1855–1905.* By Anders Henriksson. 1983.

132. *Society in Change: Studies in Honor of Bela K. Kiraly.* Edited by Steven Bela Vardy. 1983.

133. *Authoritariansim in Greece: The Metaxas Regime.* By Jon V. Kofas. 1983.

134. *New Hungarian Peasants: An East Central European Experience with Collectivization.* Edited by Marida Hollos and Bela C. Maday. 1983.

135. *War, Revolution, and Society in Romania: The Road to Independence.* Edited by Ilie Ceausescu. 1983.
136. *The Beginning of Cyrillic Printing, Cracow, 1491: From the Orthodox Past in Poland.* By Szczepan K. Zimmer. 1983.
137. *Effects of World War I. The Class War After the Great War: The Rise of Communist Parties in East Central Europe, 1918–1921.* Edited by Ivo Banac. 1983.
138. *Bulgaria 1878–1918. A History.* By Richard J. Crampton. 1983.
139. *T. G. Masaryk Revisited: A Cirtical Assessment.* By Hanus J. Hajek. 1983.
140. *The Cult of Power: Dictators in the Twentieth Century.* Edited by Joseph Held. 1983.
141. *Economy and Foreign Policy: The Struggle of the Great Powers for Economic Hegemony in the Danube Valley, 1919–1939.* By György Ránki. 1983.
142. *Germany, Russia, and the Balkans: Prelude to the Nazi-Soviet Non-Aggression Pact.* By Marilynn Giroux Hitchens. 1983.
143. *Guestworkers in the German Reich: The Poles in Wilhelmian Germany.* By Richard Charles Murphy. 1983.
144. *The Latvian Impact on the Bolshevik Revolution.* By Andrew Ezergailis. 1983.
145. *The Rise of Moscow's Power.* By Henryk Paszkiewicz. 1983.
146. *A Question of Empire: Leopold I and the War of the Spanish Succession, 1701–1705.* By Linda and Marsha Frey. 1983.
147. *Effects of World War I. The Uprooted: Hungarian Refugees and Their Impact on Hungarian Domestic Policies, 1918–1921.* By Istvan I. Mocsy. 1983.
148. *Nationalist Integration Through Socialist Planning: An Anthropological Study of a Romanian New Town.* By Steven L. Sampson. 1983.